Supporting Students for Success in Online and Distance Education

Supporting Students for Success in Online and Distance Learning, 3rd Edition, provides a comprehensive overview of student support both on and off campus. While online and distance learning are the world's fastest growing areas of educational development, they have a fundamental weakness—their graduation rates, which can be lower than 20%. In this powerful new edition, Ormond Simpson builds on a rich history of research in distance and e-learning to show how retention rates can be improved through tested support methods, often at a net financial profit to the institutions involved.

By comparing the evidence as well as the cost-effectiveness of various support tactics, this book describes how to promote student success and encourage skill-development from a number of different perspectives: definitions and purpose, theory and psychology, ethics, costs and benefits, activities, sources, media, proactive and reactive, assessment and feedback, staff development, writing support into course materials, research, quality assurance and institutional structures. This concise, practical guide is informal and jargon-free, yet its approach to evidence is rigorous, making it invaluable reading for all those interested in recruiting and teaching diverse students for successful online and distance learning.

Ormond Simpson is currently a Fellow of the University of London Centre for Distance Education, UK. His most recent post was at the Open Polytechnic of New Zealand where he was Visiting Professor. Prior to that he was Senior Lecturer in Institutional Research at the UK Open University and worked in student support. He has run workshops and seminars in South Africa, Ghana, China, the West Indies, Colombia, South Korea, The Gambia, Papua New Guinea, Canada, Brazil, and throughout Europe.

Open and Flexible Learning Series

Series Editors: *Fred Lockwood, A.W. (Tony) Bates and Som Naidu*

Supporting Students for Success in Online and Distance Education

Third Edition

ORMOND SIMPSON

Routledge
Taylor & Francis Group

NEW YORK AND LONDON

Third edition published 2012
by Routledge
711 Third Avenue, New York, NY 10017

Simultaneously published in the UK
by Routledge
2 Park Square, Milton Park, Abingdon, Oxon OX14 4RN

Routledge is an imprint of the Taylor & Francis Group, an informa business

© 2012 Taylor & Francis

The right of the editor to be identified as the author of the editorial material, and of the authors for their individual chapters, has been asserted in accordance with sections 77 and 78 of the Copyright, Designs and Patents Act 1988.

First edition published by Routledge 2000

Library of Congress Cataloging in Publication Data
Simpson, Ormond.
   Supporting students for success in online and distance education/
   by Ormond Simpson.—3rd ed.
   p. cm.—(Open and flexible learning series)
   Rev. ed. of: Supporting students in online, open, and distance learning, c2002.
   Includes bibliographical references and index.
   1. Distance education. 2. Open learning. I. Simpson, Ormond. Supporting students in online, open, and distance learning. II. Title.
   LC5800.S55 2012
   378.1'75—dc23   2012024647

ISBN: 978-0-415-50909-1 (hbk)
ISBN: 978-0-415-50910-7 (pbk)
ISBN: 978-0-203-09573-7 (ebk)

Typeset in Bembo and Gill Sans by
Florence Production Ltd, Stoodleigh, Devon, UK

Certified Sourcing
www.sfiprogram.org
SFI-00453

Printed and bound in the United States of America
by Edwards Brothers, Inc.

To my wife, Vicki Goodwin,
with grateful thanks for her many motivational
messages, often in liquid form

Contents

Illustrations

Figures

Tables

Series Editor's Foreword

Much has happened in the world of distance education since the publication of *Supporting Students in Online, Open and Distance Learning*. This third edition, not only updating and developing previous content, incorporates the arguments from the book *Student Retention in Online, Open and Distance Learning*. Over this period we have seen new Mega Distance Learning Universities established, other Open Universities grow, and distance learning techniques permeate all levels of education and training around the world. Indeed, we have seen countries that were former consumers of distance education courses become international providers.

What we haven't seen over the period since the original publication of this book is a steady reduction in student dropout and failure in these institutions. It's true, of course, that simple comparisons of dropout and failure rates between institutions are fraught with danger. Often the figures are based on different assumptions, calculated from different base figures and affected by a range of different factors—even when such data can be obtained! However, the snapshot provided by Ormond in Figure 1.3—"Final graduation rates (%) in a variety of higher education institutions"—is sobering to staff and potentially devastating to students. In Figure 1.3, Ormond notes that the famed U.K. Open University (UKOU) has a graduation rate of approximately 22%, about a quarter of that achieved by students studying full time in other U.K. universities. I found the figure sobering, since I worked within the U.K. Open University for 25 years and can attest to the dedication of staff striving to create quality distance teaching materials and students who study around work, home and other commitments. I found the implications of Figure 1.3 potentially devastating when I recall a recent working visit to the University of South Africa, where I talked to students who had paid their fees, who were studying under difficult conditions, who described their hopes and aspirations—yet where approximately 95% would fail to graduate. What's the dropout rate on your course? What is the graduation rate within your institution? Is there room for improvement, and could proactive student support contribute to an improvement? In this context the author's comment, "You are far more likely to get support for student support by showing that it makes sense financially than through any ethical argument," is worth noting.

In this book, *Supporting Students for Success in Online and Distance Education*, Ormond does not offer a simple "silver bullet" to solve the problem, nor does he pontificate. Rather, based on his considerable experience, and supported by case studies, he argues that success amongst learners is a complex problem—but one where progress can be made, be this in exploring different models of motivation, illustrating how Proactive Motivational Support (PaMS) can make a significant difference or by building support into the learning material. I suspect you will find all sections of the book valuable. However, I also suspect that its main success will be in sensitizing you to the needs of your learners and what we can do to support them, and that you, like me, will gain much from this book that will benefit your learners.

Fred Lockwood
Yelvertoft
June 2012

Preface

This book is an amalgamation, a rewrite and development of two previous books by the same author: *Supporting Students in Online, Open and Distance Learning* (second edition, 2002) and *Student Retention in Online, Open and Distance Learning* (2003). Both books appear to have been popular with readers, having combined sales of nearly 5,000 to date and with a Chinese edition published (2007).

Reviews of these previous books have also been very positive. For example, "[T]his is the best book I have seen on this subject"—Professor Phil Race (Emeritus Professor, Leeds Metropolitan University, U.K.); "a very unusual combination of humane wisdom from years of practice and hard-headed data about what works"—Professor Graham Gibbs (recently Director of the Institute for the Advancement of Learning at Oxford University, U.K.) and many others.

The purpose of the new book is similar to that of previous books: to provide an overview of student support in online and distance higher education with particular reference to the promotion of student success. While aimed specifically at higher, further or tertiary distance education, there will be much in it that will be pertinent to distance education at other levels as well as to on-campus full- and part-time higher education.

The book will look at the evidence for how support promotes student success and the cost-effectiveness of different approaches. The contents of the book include such topics as the advantages and disadvantages of online and distance education in costs and sustainability; levels of dropout in distance learning and why it is important—the effects of dropout on students, institutions and society; descriptions and definitions of student support; theories of support and learning motivation; costs and benefits of support and making a "profit" out of support; ethical issues in student support; writing support for success into distance courses; researching student support; staff development and appraisal; institutional structures for student support; and barriers to success in student support.

The book is designed to be concise but informal, accessible to readers who have English as a second language, largely jargon-free and practical—things which obviously appealed to readers of the previous editions. The book makes extensive use of case-studies and accounts drawn largely from the author's experience. At the same time the approach to evidence is rigorous, particularly important in an area where there can be inadequate data, un-evidenced assertions and hype.

There is an associated website, "Supporting Students at a Distance": www.ormondsimpson.com, which contains journal articles referred to in the text, as well as presentations, podcasts, videos and support advice for distance tutors and students. This website will be available for at least three years after the book's publication. There is also a blog where readers can post comments and questions to the author.

This book is aimed at a wide audience of staff and students in distance learning. It will be essential reading for senior managers, administrators, finance officers, advisers and tutors, as well as course writers, instructional designers, editors, e-learning specialists and anyone concerned with student success. It will be important as a set book for postgraduate courses in distance education. The book will also be of interest to staff in on-campus education settings who are increasingly faced with the need to support students more efficiently, which often means at a distance, as student numbers increase and resources dwindle. Equally, as students find themselves paying more for their education, issues of retention will become increasingly important, as they are likely to demand better support for their investment. The book's focus on cost-effective student support for success will thus make it very pertinent to the full-time setting.

The author is currently a Fellow of the University of London Centre for Distance Education and has worked in distance education for nearly 40 years in various roles, in practical everyday support as well as in institutional research. His most recent post was at the Open Polytechnic of New Zealand, where he was Visiting Professor. Prior to that he was Senior Lecturer in Institutional Research at the U.K. Open University and worked in student support. He has given keynote lectures and has run workshops and seminars in the United States, South Africa, Brazil, Ghana, New Zealand, China, the West Indies, Colombia, South Korea, The Gambia, Papua New Guinea and Canada. He has published three books, more than 30 journal articles, 11 book chapters and staff training materials for the Indira Gandhi National Open University and the U.K. Open University. His experience means that the book will be as relevant to education in developing countries as in more technically advanced economies.

How to Read this Book

Student support is a wide, detailed and sometimes confusing area of study. The chapters within the book are designed to be self-contained as far as possible and are cross-referenced to where the same topics appear elsewhere in the book. This book therefore need not necessarily be read sequentially, and hopefully it can be sampled anywhere for areas of particular interest to the reader.

Acknowledgments

I am particularly grateful to Professor Fred Lockwood, previously of the U.K. Open University, without whose gentle but persistent encouragement this book and its predecessors would never have made it into publication.

I am also grateful to many colleagues and students in the open, online and distance education world whose discussions have contributed towards the book. In no particular order I would like to thank Professor Mary Thorpe, Alan Woodley and the late Peter Knight of the U.K. Open University Institute of Educational Technology, Dr. Paul Prinsloo of the University of South Africa, the late Peter Rutland of the Open Polytechnic of New Zealand, Dr. Jinhee Kwon previously of the Korean National Open University and now of Penn State University USA, Professor Li Yawan and Guo Quinchun of the China Open University, Dr. Ilona Boniwell of the University of East London, Jason Pennels of Cambridge Education, Anne Gaskell, editor of Open Learning, Liz Marr and John Rose-Adams of the U.K. Open University's Centre for Inclusion and Curriculum, Professor Jonathan Brown, Professor Greville Rumble, and the many other staff of the several distance institutions with whom I have had the privilege of working.

My especial thanks are due to the many students of my own over the years who have allowed me to experiment on them. I hope that the failure of some of those experiments won't have affected their overall success . . .

Chapter 1

Introduction

Distance Education—Successes and Failures

Civilization is in a race between education and catastrophe.

(H. G. Wells)

Online and distance education is very likely the fastest growing area of education in the world today, in both the developed and developing worlds. And, while the origins of this growth are fairly recent, the roots of distance education go back a long way. Some authors date its beginnings to the invention of the "Penny Post" (the ability to send a letter anywhere in the U.K. for one old penny) and Isaac Pitman's resulting correspondence course in shorthand.

But there are counterclaims from other countries, notably Australia and the United States, and other authors suggest that St. Paul's epistles represent a very early form of open and distance education, with distance text in the form of letters and face-to-face support in the form of sermons. My own belief is that there is a case to be made for the Ten Commandments as the first distance learning text, delivered, as it happened, by tablets—of stone, rather than the later electronic form . . .

Whatever the arguments about its origins, there can be little doubt that there are now large numbers of distance institutions at every level worldwide, many of them very large—the Open University of China, with around 2.7 million students; the Indira Gandhi National Open University in India, with more than 3 million students; Anadolu University in Turkey, with 1.7 million students; the University of South Africa, with 300,000 students; the Open University in the U.K., with 250,000 students; and so on.

Some of these institutions now have a global reach, with students in many places apart from their home countries—for example, one of the oldest distance education providers, the University of London International Programme, founded in 1858, has 50,000 students studying in 190 countries and has five Nobel Laureates amongst its alumni, including Nelson Mandela. And the arrival of e-learning means that international competition between institutions will only go on increasing. Private institutions are being set up—corporate universities such as the "Coca-Cola University" are the fastest growing sector of higher education in the United States, for example, and countries that were previously net importers of education, such as Malaysia and—very significantly—China, are now moving towards becoming exporters of education.

There are many reasons for the success of distance education, three of the most important being costs, sustainability and access.

Costs and Benefits of Distance Education

The subject of costs and benefits of distance education will be examined in more detail in Chapter 11. But there can be little doubt that distance education is considerably cheaper for governments, institutions and students.

For Governments

Those governments that subsidize higher education in some way, either through grants to institutions or through grants and loans to students, not only benefit from the intrinsically lower costs of distance education, but also from the fact that distance students are also often economically active while studying—in other words, they are contributing to society through their contribution to Gross National Product and most directly through their taxes.

For Students

The main cost of a university degree to full-time, face-to-face students is not the tuition fees they pay, but the loss of earnings they experience while studying. Since in many cases distance students pay lower fees and can continue to earn, the cost of their degree is much less (see Chapter 11).

For Institutions

The cost of providing distance education to the institutions themselves will depend on whether they are "single-mode," only offering distance education, or "dual-mode," offering both face-to-face and distance education. Costs in a single-mode institution will be somewhat arbitrary depending on their financial structures, but Rumble (1992) has shown that a dual-mode institution will always be able to provide its distance education provision at a lower cost than is likely to be achieved by a single-mode institution, partly through synergy with its full-time provision. This suggests that distance education is generally less expensive to institutions than conventional education and partly explains the immense growth in distance education programs in recent years as institutions reach out for new customers.

Sustainability of Distance Education

In a time of global austerity and global warming, issues of sustainability become increasingly important. Roy, Potter and Yarrow (2007) have suggested that distance education is far more sustainable than conventional education, both in energy (13% of conventional education use) and in carbon dioxide (CO_2) production (18% of conventional educational use)—see Figure 1.1.

These sustainability advantages arise from savings on things like estate maintenance, which is obviously much smaller for a distance university without any students present on campus. (It is interesting to note that, in a later paper, Roy concludes that e-learning is not more sustainable than standard correspondence education despite the apparent savings on paper and postage. Rumble [2004] and Hulsmann [2000] come to similar conclusions about the comparative costs of e-learning versus conventional distance education. I shall return to this issue in Chapters 8 and 11.)

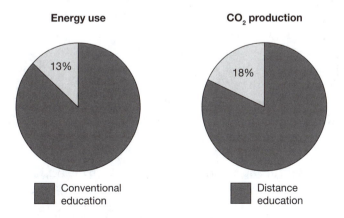

Figure 1.1 Sustainability of conventional education and distance education compared (Roy, Potter and Yarrow 2007)

Such an advantage in sustainability can only be an advantage to distance education over conventional education, as the costs of energy and pressure to reduce CO_2 production inexorably rise.

Access to Distance Education

Perhaps the overwhelmingly important characteristic of distance education for many people is its accessibility. With the advent of distance learning, a student no longer had to travel to a fixed location several times a week. No longer did they have to be at a specific place at a specific time. They could study largely at their own time and wherever they happened to be, only needing a home address for the delivery of their correspondence texts. Indeed, even that was not essential—an early student I met was of "no fixed abode" and used a local laundromat as his delivery point for his course materials. And of course there are many students with disabilities for whom distance education is the only possible way of learning—see Chapter 14.

This accessibility is not only in physical terms, but in social and psychological terms as well. Distance students can try study completely privately, secure that no one but their family need know about their studies and any potential failure unless they choose to share that knowledge. Some students experience social anxiety—up to a third of students in face-to-face education can experience acute social anxiety in public learning situations such as taking part in discussions or giving presentations (Russell, 2008). For such students the isolation of distance learning can paradoxically be a blessing—at least, when they first start learning.

The development of e-learning now even obviates the need for materials to be delivered by snail mail—conventional portal delivery services—as course materials and support can be delivered over the internet to a student's computer, with assignments returned the same way.

The more recent growth of Open Educational Resources (OERs), where institutions make their course materials (texts, video clips, podcasts and so on —now often referred to as "learning objects") freely available on the web, may also contribute to access. One of the first initiatives was started by the Massachusetts Institute of Technology (MIT) in 2001, with its MIT OpenCourseWare project: http://ocw.mit.edu/index.htm, followed by several others, for example, the U.K. Open University's OpenLearn Project: http://www.open.edu/openlearn in conjunction with the British Broadcasting Corporation (BBC). Following on from OERs are "MOOCs"—Massive Open Online Courses—such as the recent Stanford course in Artificial Intelligence, which had 160,000 students, some 23,000 of whom were given a non-accredited certificate as a downloadable pdf at the end of the course (a "pass" rate of approximately 14%, which as we will see is roughly average for distance education courses).

However, it is not yet clear just how e-learning and OERs will contribute to making education more accessible. Indeed, there are serious issues about exclusion—in the United States at the time of writing (2012), some 23% of the population have no internet access at home (and of the remainder some still only have dial-up); in the U.K. the figure is 30%. While some of these households in both countries will have access through work internet cafes and so on, this may be insufficient for study. And such households will be very heavily concentrated in the already educationally disadvantaged parts of both populations. I will return to this issue in Chapter 8.

The levels of internet access in the developing world are considerably less than the above, so distance education institutions that focus on e-learning and OERs, while facilitating access to some, are also excluding many others from their resources. Since e-learning is no less expensive than conventional distance education (Rumble 2004) and yet, as we shall see, apparently so far no more effective in producing student success, it means that resources are then directed away from people who are often in most need of them. It is unlikely that the rush to e-learning will slow in the lifetime of this book, but this caveat about access and success will occur again in the text and the book will take a skeptical, evidence-based attitude to e-learning, while not agreeing with Professor David Noble (1998) that "e-learning is a technological tape-worm in the guts of higher education" (p. 5). The book's approach will be more in line with Professor Martin Trow's assertion (2000) on the subject of e-learning, that "the future of learning will see a combination of traditional and distance learning rather than a replacement of traditional forms. But the short history of the computer has provided us with many surprises, some of them even welcome."

Quality of Distance Education

For many years one of the weaknesses of distance education was thought to be its quality—that it was inferior in every respect to conventional higher education. This may well have been true during the era of the correspondence colleges, but I think it would be hard these days to maintain that a distance degree is inherently inferior to a degree from a conventional university—as long as the distance degree was awarded from an accredited institution. (One of the problems of distance education is certainly the growth in "degree mills"—spurious online distance education institutions that can look very convincing.)

It may be true that until the advent of the internet distance education was in the grip of an "iron triangle" whose sides were respectively cost, access and quality (Daniel 2011)—see Figure 1.2. Daniel's iron triangle suggests that in pre-internet distance education, altering any one of the sides would change the other two. So, for example, trying to increase quality would either increase cost or lower access, or both. Correspondingly, increasing access would either lower quality or increase cost, or both. Daniel's thesis was that the technology revolution would break this iron triangle and allow for increasing quality and access while lowering cost.

However, this triangle really needs the metaphysical impossibility of a fourth side—a side representing "output"—the ability of distance education to produce graduates. Because, apart from issues of access, cost and quality, there is a very serious elephant in the distance education room—the elephant of student dropout.

Figure 1.2 Daniel's (2011) "iron triangle" of quality, access and cost

Student Dropout in Distance Education

While there has been a huge growth in distance learning in the last 30 or so years, this growth often disguises a fundamental weakness at its root. That fundamental weakness is its dropout rate.

Dropout rates are notoriously difficult to discover (institutions are hardly likely to publicize them to any extent) or to estimate (What constitutes a fully registered student? What are they studying for? How long are they likely to take?). But it is vital to have such figures, and the simplest comparison is probably to take final graduation rates. Figure 1.3 shows the final graduation rates in a variety of higher education distance institutions compared with those in conventional U.K. institutions of higher education, taken over periods of

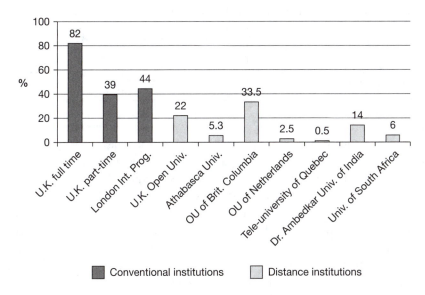

Figure 1.3 Final graduation rates (%) in a variety of higher education institutions (the London International Programmes are a mix of distance and face-to-face modes)

up to 11 years and collated from various sources (Higher Education Funding Council for England, Powell 2009; Venkaiah and Salawu 2009).

It can be seen that even a well-resourced distance education institution like the U.K. Open University has a graduation rate of only just over a quarter of its full-time equivalents in the U.K. Of equal concern is that the rate is only just over half that of part-time students at conventional institutions in the U.K. with whom it might be most accurately compared. And since half of U.K. Open University students graduate with ordinary degrees and the other institutional rates given are for honors degrees, the U.K. Open University's graduation rates should be quoted as around 11% on a strict like-for-like basis.

Other distance institutions fare worse: some have graduation rates in single figures. There are also institutions where figures are not widely published, such as the aggressively marketed University of Phoenix, where Haigh (2007) suggests that only 4% of their students graduate within six years.

It might be argued that this situation is a temporary one: as distance institutions develop their understanding of distance learning provision, their graduation rates will increase. Historical data on graduation rates is even harder to find than current graduation rates, but data from the U.K. Open University suggests that, in its case, rates are not increasing—see Table 1.1.

It can be seen that the graduation rate has been dropping since the U.K. Open University opened in 1971. While special circumstances will have

Table 1.1 Percentage graduation rates of U.K. Open University students by year of entry

Year of entry	1971	1976	1981	1994
% of students who have graduated 11 years after entry	59%	51%	48%	22%

applied to entry in the early 1970s due to a waiting list of entrants with a high level of previous qualifications, such an explanation does not apply to later entry. And later data from graduation numbers suggests that U.K. Open University graduation rates continue to fall—see Figure 1.4.

I have used U.K. Open University figures in this example as the university has been something of a cynosure of distance education internationally and maintains a high-quality database, from which the figures are easier to access than many institutions. Of course, it would be unjustified to extrapolate from the U.K. Open University to all distance education institutions and suggest that their graduation rates are falling as well. But in the absence of other evidence it seems unlikely that graduation rates are generally increasing anywhere on any large scale.

Figure 1.5 shows the cumulative rates of graduation for the U.K. Open University—that is, the percentage of students who have graduated in the years after their entry.

The Figure demonstrates another characteristic of the U.K. Open University, which probably applies to most distance institutions—the length of time it takes students to graduate. It can be up to 11 years before a particular U.K. Open

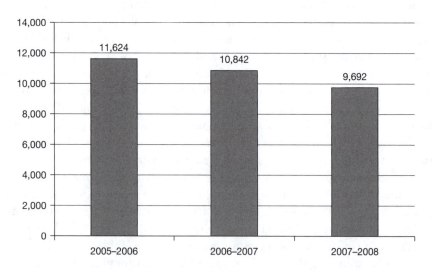

Figure 1.4 Annual graduation numbers at the U.K. Open University, 2005–2008

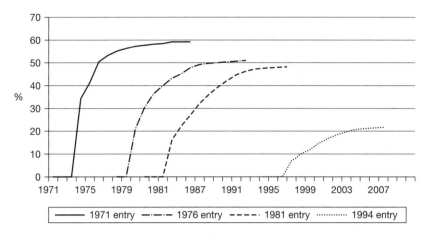

Figure 1.5 Cumulative percentage of U.K. Open University students who have graduated in the years after their initial entry

University entry cohort have all graduated (the record for the longest time taken for a U.K. Open University student to graduate is 27 years currently, but there are still some in a race between graduation and death). This is obviously in part due to the part-time nature of distance study, but it nevertheless has implications for the eventual financial returns to the student from the qualification—see Chapter 11.

The Implications of Dropout from Distance Education

What, then, happens to students who drop out from distance education (apparently the large majority)? Some clearly switch to other institutions, some may be happy with some kind of intermediate qualification, others drop out because their situation has changed—physically or economically—and so on. However, few institutions appear to have any accurate idea of the numbers involved in these various categories or what happens to those students who do not fall into these groups, who are possibly still the majority.

There is some evidence for the effects of student dropout from full-time higher education, at least in the U.K. Figure 1.6 is derived from a survey conducted by Bynner (2001) and shows the relative probability of experiencing depression, unemployment and—for women—violence from their partners for various educational qualification levels, including non-completion—that is, dropout.

It is possible to plot similar graphs for indebtedness and physical ill-health. It can be seen that non-completing students appear to have up to one third higher probability of subsequent depression, unemployment and violence than either graduates or people who never went to university in the first place.

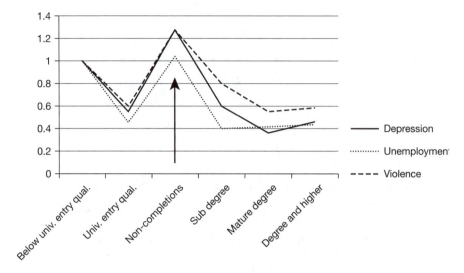

Figure 1.6 Probability of experiencing depression, unemployment and—for women—partner violence for various educational qualification levels—adapted from Bynner (2001)

It is possible, of course, that those students dropped out because they became depressed rather than becoming depressed because they had dropped out. But it seems intrinsically more likely that an act—dropping out—caused the depression rather than that students became spontaneously depressed and then dropped out. And, after all, such students were not so depressed as to not get into university in the first place.

Given a nearly 20% dropout amongst the approximately 45% of the 18-year-old cohort in the U.K. who start in full-time university each year, this may mean that nearly 10% of the cohort may suffer the effects of dropping out, including an increased probability of experiencing depression. Depression is, in fact, a very substantial problem, at least in Western societies. Sir Richard Layard of the London School of Economics (LSE) maintains, for example, that depression is the most significant mental health issue in the UK and costs the country hundreds of millions of pounds in lost production and treatment each year (Layard et al. 2007). Adding in the costs of unemployment and ill-health, it may be that full-time student dropout costs the UK several billions pounds each year. There seems little data available on whether this might be the case in other nations. It may be possible that students in other environments, such as the United States (where dropout rates are higher), are more resilient than British students, but we simply don't know.

Since dropout from distance higher education is much higher than full-time higher education, what are its effects? Dropping out of a part-time distance course can usually be achieved almost anonymously and with little fuss, so we may hope that it has less dire effects than dropping out of a full-time course. But there is almost no research into what happens to distance education dropouts. Admittedly such research would be difficult to carry out, but it seems extraordinary that, since dropout students constitute distance education's main output, its effects are so little examined.

There are a number of theories that attempt to explain the much higher dropout rates in distance education. Most depend on the inherent fact of distance between students, their tutors and institutions, such as Moore's "Transactional Distance" Theory (Moore, 1990, pp. 10–15), about the psychological and communication space between student and institution.

But, whatever the possible theories about the reasons for dropout in distance education, the argument in this book is that it is ultimately unsustainable, for reputational, financial and ultimately ethical reasons. The book will also argue that there is a way of overcoming this state of affairs—through supporting distance students for success, the subject of the rest of the book.

Chapter 2

Student Support in Online and Distance Education
Definitions and Practices

> In retrospect, distance education's long-term legacy will inextricably be tied to its capacity to empower and leverage educational access and opportunities for underserved populations who have been denied access due to diverse economic, social, political and/or cultural barriers.
>
> (*Dr. Don Olcott, Jr., Past President, United States Distance Learning Association and presently CEO, the Observatory on Borderless Higher Education [OBHE]*)

Definitions of Student Support

Defining "student support" in online and distance education is complicated, as a number of expressions and models have been used over the years to describe it. The expressions "counseling," "guidance," "advice," "teaching," and "tuition" have all been used to describe the process, and the models have included the "industrial model," which describes course writing as "production" and student support as "delivery" or "after-sales service."

In fact, the range of activities that comes under the heading of "student support" is enormously varied. I have kept track of student support actions that I have taken recently. Without trying to categorize them, I have done the following:

- worked with colleagues at an American community college to try to write support into an Open Educational Resource (OER) math course;
- sent a set of "motivational emails" to students on the London University International Programmes Law degree;
- given a presentation to tutors at a South African distance education university about retention in distance education;
- talked with a student on the phone who was demoralized by a poor exam result, trying to help him put it into perspective;
- texted a student to remind them that their assignment was due;
- arranged for an elderly student in a remote village to get a small grant for fares to take a taxi to her face-to-face tutorials in the nearest town;
- emailed some part-time tutors to see if they would be willing to record some video clips to put on YouTube for a math course;
- organized a small graduation ceremony in a local prison;
- written a bid to fund a student mentoring project;
- placed some staff development materials on a computer conferencing site;
- arranged payment and thanks for a part-time tutor who had just undertaken some extra work with a student on numeracy;
- written to the widow of a student who has died;
- helped a colleague edit a taster pack of materials designed to give new students a taste of a course;
- emailed a student who has been taking courses for three years without passing any of them;
- explained by phone the concept of kinetic energy to a student on an introductory science course.

If you have any experience of online and distance learning, then I have little doubt that you will have a similar, probably even more varied, list—and it is very difficult to classify this cavalcade of activities in any way that makes sense.

So it is important to try to keep the terms and models as clear as possible. In this book, I will define student support in the broadest terms, as all activities beyond the production and delivery of course materials that assist in the progress of students to success in their studies. The book will look at support from the perspectives of definitions and practices, sources, media, costs and benefits, support for different students, designing support into course materials and support structures for success.

Practices in Student Support—What Do Your Students Need?

The obvious way to start thinking about student support is to think about your students and potential students. Who are they and what do they need? You could ask yourself the question, "What skills, personal qualities and values does anyone need to become a successful student in open and distance learning?" I have asked this question as an exercise with groups of distance educators in a number of different countries and there is surprising unanimity about the resulting list. To succeed as a student in distance learning a person needs the following qualities and skills:

Intelligence	Can deal with job pressures
Numeracy	Can handle demands of family
Literacy	Can manage the paperwork
Motivation to learn	Can organize own online environment
Ability to ask for help	Can prioritize
Self-confidence	Can accept constructive criticism
Sense of humor	Can handle assessment stress

You may well have other items on your list, and you would be entitled to say that these qualities are what anyone needs to succeed at almost anything and I'm sure you would be right. But what is most interesting about this list is the following:

- The relative importance of items on the list—for example, is motivation more important than self-confidence? Can there be such a thing as too much self-confidence?
- The difference between a quality and a skill—for example, how far is motivation an innate quality or can it be enhanced? If so, how far can tutors or advisers develop a student's motivation and by what means?

We can attempt to classify items on the list in some way that might give us some ideas about how student support could be structured. One such way is to group items and label them as shown in Figure 2.1.

This gives me a way of thinking about students and the support they need in the form of a picture—see Figure 2.2.

Obviously this is a light-hearted illustration of a complex concept. Nevertheless I often carry this image in my head as it reminds me of the critical need to support students holistically—as people with more than just cognitive needs—and that, indeed, quite often it is organizational and emotional support that is most effective in helping them to success, rather than focusing on their intellectual characteristics. So, for example, often when I am working with a student who is in difficulties, my question is often not, "What problems is this student having with this course?" but, "Why has this student lost their learning motivation?"

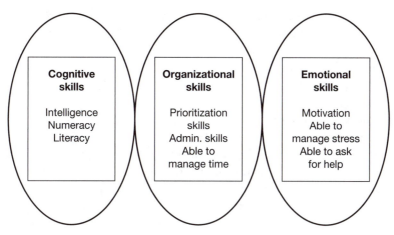

Figure 2.1 Skills that students need to succeed in distance learning

Categorizing Student Support—Academic and Non-Academic

The holistic model also suggests a way of classifying student support into two main modes. The first is *academic (or tutorial) support*, which deals with supporting students with the cognitive, intellectual and knowledge issues of specific courses or sets of courses—in other words, teaching. This will include, for example, developing general learning skills, numeracy and literacy as well as explaining concepts and assessing students' work. The second is *non-academic or counseling support*—the support of students in the emotional and organizational aspects of their studies.

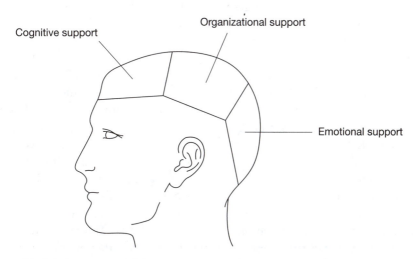

Figure 2.2 A holistic picture of the support needs of a distance student

There are further sub-divisions within these two divisions. Academic support consists of:

- defining the course territory;
- explaining concepts;
- exploring the course;
- feedback—both informal and formal assessment;
- developing learning skills—such as numeracy and literacy;
- chasing progress—following up students' progress through the course;
- enrichment—extending the boundaries of the course and sharing the excitement of learning;
- motivating students to learn.

The first two items in the list above may well be the responsibility of the course material rather than the tutor in a distance education environment. The challenge there, as we shall see later, may be to move tutors away from traditional explicative modes of working in order to emphasize the other facilitative modes.

Non-academic support consists of:

- advising—giving information, exploring problems and suggesting directions;
- assessment—giving feedback to the individual on non-academic aptitudes and skills;
- action—practical help to promote study;
- advocacy—making out a case for funding, writing a reference;
- agitation—promoting changes within the institution to benefit students;
- administration—organizing student support;
- motivating students to learn.

You will notice that "motivating students to learn" appears in both lists. This is because, of all of the activities in online and distance learning, motivating students is the most important and it can be done in both academic and non-academic modes—see Chapter 6.

You'll also notice in the second list that three of the items—advocacy, agitation, and administration—do not involve working directly with students. In fact, much important student support activity may not necessarily occur directly at the student–institution interface. Sometimes the best way you can support a student is by changing the institution, for example. And as we shall see, the direction, sources and media of support are all important as well.

The structure of distance support adopted by this book then appears as shown in Figure 2.3.

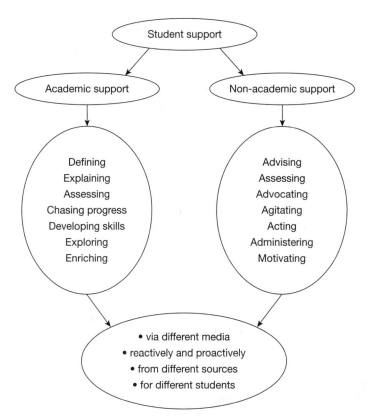

Figure 2.3 The structure of student support in online and distance education

There is clearly much overlap between these divisions as we shall see later and to some extent the divisions are artificial and arbitrary, but such is the complexity of student support as a subject that I think you will find them useful in defining the terms we shall be using throughout the book. I am also not happy with the terms "academic" and "non-academic" support, but such phrases seem preferable to using terms that may be used differently elsewhere or may have unhelpful connotations. If you like this distinction but can think of better terms in which to describe it then you should use them!

These two areas are not entirely distinct of course; tutors working with students may move effortlessly and unconsciously from one mode (academic) to another (non-academic), as they move from a discussion of (say) aspects of child psychology, into how the students will manage to submit the following week's assignment. Nevertheless, it is a distinction that remains useful in many student support activities. For example, as tutors move from one mode to another they will be using a slightly different set of qualities and skills as they do so. Many of the skills will be similar but the emphasis will be different, as shown in Figure 2.4.

You may want to argue over what skills should appear precisely where. Chapter 3 will look at them in more detail. For the moment, consider this set of queries that have crossed my desk recently. Are these academic or non-academic issues? How relevant is the distinction?

- A student phones to say that he is getting behind in the course because he is finding it hard to concentrate. "Is there some way of increasing powers of concentration?" he asks.
- A student emails you—"Hello—it's me again! I can't get this essay in on time either. Can I have my usual extension? About three weeks, OK?"
- A student phones—"I broke my wrist last week and I'm finding it hard to write. What can I do?"
- A student just cannot handle algebra.
- A student asks if it is OK to discuss the next assignment in a self-help forum with other students.
- You email a student who has not submitted his very first assignment and he replies that he finds the course very demanding. This is his first distance education course and he has not done any introductory study.
- A student whose grades have been average phones you and says that he is getting very behind and asks whether he could put in the next assignment late. He sounds rather depressed.

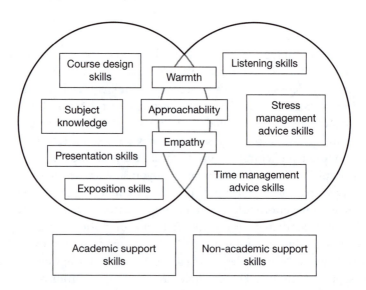

Figure 2.4 Skills and qualities used in academic and non-academic support

- You receive a letter from the husband of one of your students to say that his wife has had to go into hospital for an operation. He writes that she is OK but is likely to be unable to work for several months.
- A student emails you and says, "I'm sorry—I just can't face sitting the exam. I'm terrified of exams and just go to pieces."
- At a face-to-face meeting a student says she wants to talk about some problems at home. She tells you her husband is being difficult about her studies. Suddenly she bursts into tears.
- As an adviser you receive an email from a student that says, "I'm really not happy with the grade the tutor gave me on the last assignment. I just can't see why he's given me a D. Would you have a look and see what you think?"
- A very anxious student phones you for the second time this week for a reason that strikes you as really rather trivial.
- A student has been putting in poor assignments. They show some knowledge but are rather jumbled, with many irrelevancies, and do not really answer the question.
- You phone a student who has failed to submit an assignment. He tells you, "I'm going to have to drop out. Frankly I just don't seem to be able to find enough time."
- One student in the online forum for your course module makes a lot of comments and others do not contribute.
- A student emails to say she is pregnant and the baby is due in about six months.
- A student phones you and says that he just can't get the computer conferencing software to work properly.

These are all genuine issues that I've come across in the last year and there are few that would fall into a clear distinction between academic and non-academic matters. Even the query about algebra, which looks as though it is entirely an academic issue, turned out to have more to it than seemed at first sight (it was a severe case of "math anxiety"—now a well-recognized syndrome). But unless we try to categorize to some modest extent, we may be either overwhelmed by the complexity of the problems students raise or, worse, we may tend to be just tutors *or* advisers and forget the need to be both. So, this arbitrary distinction is maintained when the activities of academic and non-academic support are looked at in more detail in Chapters 3 and 4.

Chapter 3

Non-Academic Student Support

The important thing is not so much that every child should be taught, as that every child should be given the wish to learn.

(John Lubbock, biologist and politician, 1834–1913)

This chapter looks more closely at the first of the two categories of student support defined previously—non-academic support—from various perspectives:

- categories within non-academic support;
- activities that occur in non-academic student support;
- the skills needed for non-academic support.

Much of what will be said in this chapter will also apply to academic support.

Categories of Non-Academic Support: Developmental and Problem-Solving Support

One possible way of categorizing non-academic support further is to divide it up into developmental support (concerned with helping the students develop goals, motivation and skills) and problem-solving support (designed to help students overcome problems as they arise during their studies). See Figure 3.1.

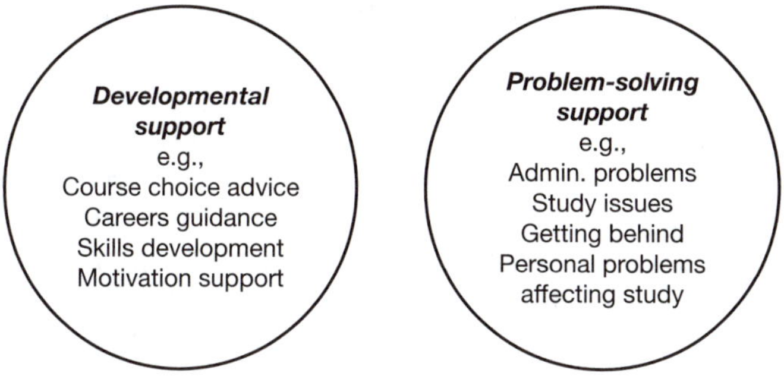

Figure 3.1 Developmental and problem-solving categories in student support

Developmental Support

This support helps students towards particular goals. Examples are:

- vocational advising—helping a student towards a particular career or career change;
- course choice advising—helping a student choose a particular course or study program;
- learning skills advising—helping students develop appropriate skills for their studies;
- general motivational counseling.

I shall be returning to aspects of these, but perhaps it is worth just explaining the inclusion of the last item now. Motivation is the essential of student progress. It seems very probable to me that some of the issues raised by students are to do with their losing touch with what has been driving them up to that point. So it seems useful to explore a student's motivation in the hope that it will both clarify and restore that driving force. I will return to this in Chapter 6.

Problem-solving Support

This is support to help students overcome barriers and hazards that are affecting their progress. Examples are:

- institution-related problems—falling foul of rules and regulations, fee problems;
- study problems—learning skills generally such as study concentration, assignments and exams;
- time problems—getting behind or being disorganized;

● personal problems—domestic and other problems that have impinged on study.

Again, the distinctions are somewhat arbitrary. For example, the distinction between study and time problems is made because it reflects to some extent the distinction that was made previously between emotional issues and organizational issues. Nevertheless, it often seems that there is a link between students who profess that problems of concentration affect their study where stress seems to be a factor, and those admitting to organizational difficulties where time management is important.

Personal factors are much more difficult and are strictly outside the scope of this book. However, it would be a poor student support system that did not make some effort to try to support students through the many events that can disrupt their lives. There are three points worth considering:

— *"Holding."* For some students their studies are a lifeline, something that sustains them when the rest of their lives are in dreadful shape. There are examples of students who have continued to study despite apparently quite appalling personal problems, such as divorce, bereavement and severe physical and mental disability. There is a concept from counseling theory that seems to be of use here—"holding." This is specifically about not attempting to solve people's probably longstanding, complex and difficult problems, but providing a background of support for them which enables them to continue their lives or their studies. Such support may be no more than a slightly increased level of contact or expressions of encouragement and support. However, it may also be rather more—in which case, support for the support staff may need to be considered.

— *Staff who get involved.* Managers of student support staff may find themselves in a position where they become concerned that students are making too great demands on their staff. The demands may not be specific; their staff may become involved of their own volition and want to do more for someone whose situation is particularly harrowing. It will be important to help support staff set reasonable boundaries to their responsibilities.

— *Dealing with distress.* Occasionally there is a chance, at some point, of being contacted by a student who is in considerable distress. In the end there is one resource that should be available to anyone in student support and it is just common humanity—trusting your own feelings and doing what feels right, without the white coat.

In all these cases it is the support management's responsibility to ensure that there is good support for advisers and a good referral system.

Activities in Student Support

I suggested in Chapter 2 that non-academic support covered the following activities:

- advising—giving information, exploring problems and suggesting directions;
- assessment—giving feedback to the individual on non-academic aptitudes and skills;
- action—practical help to promote study;
- advocacy—making out a case for funding, writing a reference;
- agitation—promoting changes within the institution to benefit students;
- administration—organizing student support;
- motivating students to learn.

I will take these in turn, devoting most space to advising, as it illustrates several basic principles in student support.

Advising

I think of advising as encompassing three basic activities—informing, commending and exploring.

— *Informing* is the process of giving accurate, timely and appropriate information to students about any aspects of their studies—"That course starts in September and you still have time to enroll."
— *Commending* may seem a slightly curious word to use, but it means the process of outlining a range of options to a student while suggesting that one or more may be the most appropriate—"There are three introductory Math modules you could take, but with your background I'd suggest that 'Success with math' is the most appropriate."
— *Exploring* is the process of helping students clarify the options open to them in such a way as (ideally) to enable them to come to a decision for themselves—"I'm so sorry to hear of your daughter's illness: let's talk it through and see whether it's best to drop out now or carry on."

These activities can form a "spectrum" of student advice, as can be seen in Figure 3.2:

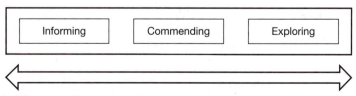

Figure 3.2 A "spectrum" of student advice giving

These activities are not clearly differentiated from one another—you may well be selective in the information you offer so that you are effectively commending a course of action, or you may commend some action as part of an exploring process. In addition you may well move from one part of the spectrum to another and back again in one interaction. You may start by exploring an issue with a student, and then offer a piece of information relevant to that exploration, which in turn will allow you to commend a particular way forward. Or perhaps a query that is presented as a straight information request may need exploring before the correct piece of information can be given. And perhaps beyond the "exploring" end of this spectrum there are the areas of counseling and psychotherapy that are beyond the scope of this book.

Manipulation

Before looking at each of these areas in turn, it will be useful to look at Figure 3.3, which shows a different presentation of the same advice spectrum, in which the axes are as follows:

— *Horizontal.* The student is included in the solution to the issue (the solution is very much dependent on the student's particular characteristics and needs) versus the student is excluded from the solution to the issue (the solution may be an item of information that is completely independent of the student).

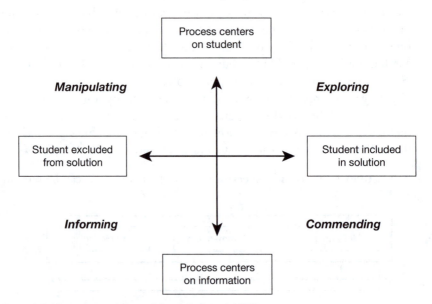

Figure 3.3 Manipulation (adapted from de Board 1983)

— *Vertical*. The process concentrates on information versus the process concentrates on the student.

This leads us to the same three activities as in the spectrum—for example, giving an item of information is independent of the student (in the sense that the item will be the same regardless of who the student is) and the process does not involve the student apart from the posing of the initial question. However, interestingly this presentation indicates the existence of a fourth mode of student advising where the process ostensibly centers on students but the solution actually excludes them. This is "manipulation," where advisers attempt to get students to accept their solutions by apparently including them in the discussion of the problem.

There could be some debate about whether manipulation ever has a part to play in student support. I concede that on occasions in the past I have tried to get students to accept solutions to their problems that suit me rather than them. However, I suspect that I have seldom achieved my aims and that manipulation as a process is not only unethical but also ineffectual. But it is a continuous temptation to guard against.

Selecting

Another concept that may be helpful is "selecting." If a question is a non-academic issue, is it an informing, commending or exploring issue? Or might you have to operate in two or three different modes in order to try to help this student? It should be remembered that it may be as frustrating for a student who is only requesting a straightforward piece of information to be subjected to the exploring mode as it is for a student whose issue needs exploring to be fobbed off with just a piece of information.

Informing

In many ways, giving information is the Cinderella activity of non-academic student support. It is not glamorous, it is taken for granted and it is often seen as a clerical level task. Yet it is a vital activity in student support and needs much more careful attention.

The challenges are considerable: institutions are becoming steadily more complex as different programs develop and require their own information resources. Information becomes spread out and lurks in numerous different places. Many institutions are now far too complex for one individual to comprehend and there is an increasing tendency to refer students on to different sections of the organization. Yet students are increasingly used to "one-stop shopping" of the kind provided by insurance companies and banks.

Of course, the development of the internet has come to our rescue. In theory, students are able to surf the internet to find the information they need. But anyone who has tried to recover a specific item of information from the internet will know that this is not always easy and can be very time-consuming. Often it seems that students find it hard to see where they are going on the internet and are easily confused by it.

There are institutional problems, too. Where information is seen to be important to recruit new students, then considerable resource is put into it. Where information is only for current students, it often has a much lower profile. The contrast in many institutions between their introductory brochures (often hard copy, color, pictures, designer layout) and the administrative information needed to navigate through the institution on the internet (dense and text-based) is often marked.

In addition, there will be institutional differences as to what information should be in the student domain. I remember an argument with my own organization's exams office over the level of information that should be available to students on its assessment policies. I preferred greater openness; they argued that if students knew more precisely what they need to do to pass, they would lower their sights to do just that. They preferred to simply tell students "to do their best." I saw that as a misunderstanding of the nature of distance student life, where time is the most precious resource, and circumstances often mean that there is a need to target studies in order to survive at all.

Thus, how information is supplied to students and what information is supplied are difficult areas that need research and negotiation.

Commending

Commending a particular course of action to a student often usually follows informing and/or exploring. It is a truism that people often only take the suggestions that it suits them to take. Indeed, it is an everyday experience that students generally only take particular recommendations on board when they arise from a process in which they persuade themselves that those recommendations are right.

So one of the great temptations of student support is the tendency to commend particular courses of action to students without understanding the student's own point of view. It is not surprising that recommendations given like that are subsequently ignored. In my own institution, this became particularly obvious in the area of guidance when advising new students what course to take. New students often appeared to persist in taking courses that appear superficially attractive despite advice that those courses are in fact out of their reach because of their academic or time demands.

Clearly there are attractions in giving early recommendations and there has to be some element of *caveat emptor* ("let the buyer beware") when working with adults. However, it is very tempting to make a recommendation quickly so the institution can move on to the next query without taking the time to help the student think through the implications of the recommendation. If a recommendation is to be effective, there will often need to be some exploration.

Exploring

Exploring is actually a less frequent activity in distance education support. I estimate that, of the student support I undertake directly with students, some 50% is giving information, 30% is commending and only 20% (if that) is exploring in any sense. Yet, because it is a more challenging activity, there is much more to say about the processes, the skills and qualities involved.

Advising Qualities and Skills

Student support advisers will express a range of personal qualities and use a variety of skills in their work. The suggestions made by Rogers (1961) about psychotherapeutic counseling may still provide an appropriate framework for the study support context (see Chapter 5).

Personal Qualities in Student Support

Rogers suggested a list of personal qualities that should be expressed by a counselor. The qualities he suggested were:

1. *Warmth* (or "non-possessive warmth" in Rogers' terms)—the ability to be appropriately friendly and approachable. Interestingly, in a small-scale survey of U.K. Open University tutors of what qualities students most valued in a tutor, being friendly and approachable was second in a hierarchy of skills and qualities—see Table 3.1 (Gaskell and Simpson 2001).

(This survey was of tutors operating by phone and face-to-face. This hierarchy of skills and qualities may be different for tutors online, and in any case may not be the criteria by which tutors are selected by an institution.)

2. *Empathy*—the skill of understanding other people's feelings without "taking them over" in any way. This is not always easy; for example, most of the people working on student support in an institution have been successful students in the past. It may be difficult for them to understand the feelings of a student who is experiencing failure or exam stress.

Table 3.1 Qualities and skills most valued in tutors by distance students

Priority	Quality most valued
I	Knows subject
2	Is approachable
3	Gives good feedback in face-to-face tutorials
4	Gives good feedback on assignments
5	Can help develop study skills
6	Is easy to get hold of
7	Marks promptly
8	Understands students' problems
9	Can help with time management
10	Can explain grades clearly

I took a call recently from a student. He started by asking, "Can you help me?" and continued to explain his rather complex query. However, he seemed confused and aggressive as I tried to clarify his query. He kept saying, "I don't know if you can help me." Suddenly I realized that I had to respond to the anxiety in his voice and I dropped the rather bureaucratic mode into which I had slipped. "Look, I can feel that you're really quite worried about this and actually I don't know if I can help you," I said, "but I will have a very good try if you can tell me your problem." I must have hit a note of empathy, because he seemed to relax and our interview immediately continued more easily.

3. *Acceptance*—the quality of non-prejudice, of accepting other people's values and background and of not expressing criticism of them. This looks simple, but again is not always easy. For a start, there is a sense in which criticism is the lifeblood of the educational process. Of course, this is (or should be) criticism of students' work rather than of them personally. It means being able to say, "I'm sorry, John—I get the feeling that you don't seem to have been able to give this assignment as much time as it needed," rather than "John—I'm sorry but you're just being too lazy on this assignment."

The problem is that expressing criticism directly or indirectly that can be interpreted personally will usually shut down any useful dialogue, especially where students already lack confidence. Students' diffidence in contacting tutors may be due partly to feelings that they will be the subject of criticism, expressed or unexpressed, as a result.

The issue of values is also important—for example, Cohen et al. (2006) used students' values to help motivate them to learn (see Chapter 6). In addition, educators probably hold a raft of values that are not always held to the same extent by their students—for example, values about working to a schedule and studying systematically, but which may not have to be held by students in order for them to progress in their studies.

I remember trying to work with a tutor who had very strong ideas about the values of punctuality, precision and order. She was increasingly unable to deal with the disordered work lives of her students and particularly the difficulty they had in getting work in exactly on time. She finally found the job intolerable and resigned.

Another of the most frustrating cases I had was of a student with very tightly held perfectionist values. He would only submit work which he believed was of the highest standard and if he was not convinced of its worth he would refuse to submit it. I was quite unable to persuade him that it was necessary to cut corners sometimes and put in work that was slightly less than perfect just to progress on his course. Eventually the stress of holding such values was too great for him and he withdrew.

Another aspect of acceptance (or rather non-acceptance) is prejudice in various forms, such as:

- sexism—assumptions about a student based on their sex;
- elitism—an "-ism" to which educators are particularly prone perhaps, it is not uncommon to come across cases where a tutor has unconsciously dismissed a student's chances because of that student's socio-economic or educational background;
- ageism—for example, assuming, probably unconsciously, that older students will be too slow or younger students insufficiently committed to study;
- racism—unexamined assumptions about the influence of ethnic background on learning can be difficult to eradicate from even the best-intentioned staff.

I sometimes remind myself of the mnemonic "SEAR" ("sexism, elitism, ageism, racism") when working with students just to remind myself to watch out for these common assumptions.

However, this concept of acceptance may seem altogether too fuzzy and soft. What do we do when we find someone's views or behavior quite intolerable—for example, someone who is behaving in a racist way in a tutorial? Rogers (1961) suggests that it should be possible to draw a distinction between accepting people but not accepting their behavior, although the difference may be hard to draw in practice.

> I recently oversaw a computer conference where a student made a comment that the tutor thought was sexist. The tutor immediately deleted the comment from the conference and sent a sharp email to the student telling him what he had done. The tutor had been irritated previously by the student's apparent lack of engagement with the course and his response was a reflection of that. However, his response was not just to the student's behavior but also to the student himself and that was not helpful. Had the tutor reflected a little longer, he might have found a way of making it clear that it was the student's comment that was unacceptable without putting down the student as well. As it was, the student made a formal complaint about the episode that took a good deal of work to resolve.

It will be important that any distance institution has clear Equal Opportunities guidelines in place. Such guidelines will need to address all aspects of student support as well as the course materials.

4. *Openness*—the quality of honesty, of not being seduced into authority roles or the "white coat" syndrome. It also means not making promises that cannot be kept but sharing one's inadequacies where appropriate and admitting one's limitations.

> Several years ago, a student approached me for advice. She addressed me as Professor Simpson and was clearly and quite unduly overawed by what she perceived to be my authority and expertise. Sadly, I got off on this fantasy myself and delivered some well-meant but wholly inappropriate advice that she took away and afterward very sensibly ignored.

Skills in Student Support

The function of bringing these qualities to bear on the student–supporter interaction is to develop and maintain a high level of dialogue between the student and supporter. Someone who is warm, accepting, open and empathic will have set the groundwork for dialogue, but it will still be necessary to use both listening and interview structuring skills to carry the dialogue forward.

1. *Listening skills*. Effective listening skills can seem very simple, especially when they are laid out, as here, as a set of techniques. Yet analysis of the breakdown of student support—students losing faith in their tutors, students becoming alienated from their studies—often shows that the reasons are not to do with systems faults or inadequate theoretical stances, but because students were not listened to adequately. Perhaps these simple listening skills are not as obvious as they might be. The skills include:

(i) *Reflection or mirroring*—reflecting to students what they have said but in such a way as to reassure them that they have been heard, to clarify their statements and to carry the dialogue forward. Consider three possible responses to a student's statement:

> *Student*: "I'm dropping out because I'm bored by this course."
> *Adviser*: (a) "But you've only been on the course a month," (b) "Some parts of the course are rather boring," (c) "You feel the course doesn't interest you any more."

(a) is non-accepting and faintly critical; (b) is better but does not really take the dialogue forward. Response (c) is a simple reflection. It tells students that they have been heard and will encourage them to continue and clarify their feelings.

(ii) *Open-ended questions*—using questions that do not have a simple "yes" or "no" answer where possible. Such questions encourage further exploration of the issues rather than bring discussion to a full stop. For example:

> *Student*: "I was thinking of switching to that music course."
> *Adviser*: (a) "You like music, then?" (b) "What is it about studying music that attracts you?"

(a) just invites a "yes/no" answer but (b) is an open-ended question that invites a more considered response.

(iii) *Acknowledgments*—simply acknowledging students' statements without responding with a further question. This encourages students to continue with their train of thought. For example:

> *Student*: "I don't know—I just want to get out of sales."
> *Adviser*: "Mmm?"
> *Student*: "I'd like a job that was really worthwhile."

Acknowledgments are particularly important on the phone where there are no visual clues to reassure callers that they are being heard.

(iv) Silences—being able to endure silence in a dialogue. This can be quite difficult—advisers may feel that they have to fill gaps in the conversation. However, if it is clear that someone is struggling to articulate a difficult concept, then an interruption, no matter how well meant, can be disruptive of that process.

2. Selecting skills. Of course, no amount of reflecting, acknowledging and other kinds of response will help develop the dialogue unless the responses are appropriate. I suggested earlier in this chapter that there were three activities in advising—informing, commending and exploring. I also suggested that one of the important skills for an adviser would be to select which response is appropriate to a particular statement. This also applies to the responses in the process skills below—choosing a challenging response inappropriately may well close a dialogue down rather quickly, for instance.

3. Process skills. There is a process of moving through various stages in any dialogue and different activities at different stages. Those stages that seem the most important are:

(i) Clarifying—helping a student clarify a need or feeling, probably through a process of repeated reflection: "Ah, so what you're saying is that you've lost your motivation?"

(ii) Checking—going back occasionally to check that you are getting a reasonably accurate overall picture of the problem or issue: "So there are really two issues here—you've lost your motivation, but there's also a problem to do with finding the time because of your new job responsibilities?"

(iii) Contextualizing—placing students' concerns in a wider context or pattern: "Actually, in my experience a lot of students run into this same kind of problem at this time of year." This can be reassuring to students, who may need to know that their particular position is not unique and may indeed be quite common. Perhaps there is a sense in which contextualizing legitimizes a problem as an appropriate one to have and for which there are time-tested responses.

(iv) Conceptualizing—offering theories or explanations or pointing out patterns in a problem: "Might you be finding it hard to concentrate on your essay because you're worried about what the tutor might say when she reads it?" Conceptualizing appeals to both advisers and students because it sometimes offers a kind of intellectual insight into problems rather in the way that Rational-Emotive Therapy purports to do (see Chapter 5). At the same time there is a danger of an adviser using conceptualizing to take over a student's problem, to become a white-coated dispenser of

prescriptions which may be inappropriate: "Yes, I've come across this problem before—it happens a lot. What you need to do now is . . ." Conceptualizing must therefore be used sparingly and carefully.

(v) *Challenging*—pointing out hidden issues or inconsistencies: "I understand that you feel you have run out of time to do the course. However, I also note that you've taken on a lot of extra voluntary work. Could it be that actually the course is less important to you?" Alternatively, perhaps more obviously, "You tell me that you're very keen on the course but I see you've not actually been able to complete any assignments on it. Can you tell me why you've not been able to do that?" Challenging is obviously a difficult technique to use; if used inappropriately (over-challenging or under-challenging), it is likely to feel like non-acceptance by the student and the dialogue will close. Clearly, challenging is an important part of a tutor's skills, but there is a danger that it can leak inappropriately into an advisory environment. There are substantial differences between challenging statements in a student's essay and challenging a student's personal thoughts.

I'd been trying to get a student to submit an assignment on the course I teach. I knew he was not particularly motivated—his father had paid for the course and this is not always a good sign in my experience. At any rate, despite several promises the assignment failed to arrive, so just before the last possible date it could be submitted I phoned the student. Once again he promised he'd do it, but I was sure he wouldn't. At that point, I realized I should have challenged him. For one desperate moment I thought of saying, "Can I speak to your father?" but that seemed like an over-challenge. Maybe I could have said something like, "You're not going to do it, are you?" At least we would have known where we stood, he might have been better off and I would have felt better about our interaction. As it was, my well-known tendency to under-challenge asserted itself and I copped out by just wishing him good luck and putting the phone down.

(vi) *Consequent Action*—agreeing jointly at the end of the dialogue the action to be taken by the student, the adviser or both: "OK, then, you'll look into the resources at your local careers office and I'll see what information we've got in our library." Sometimes such consequent action agreements are like a contract that binds both sides, thus involving students intimately in the resolution of the issues they have raised.

Not all of these activities will be present in every session, of course—a simple informing or commending activity may only involve a brief clarification,

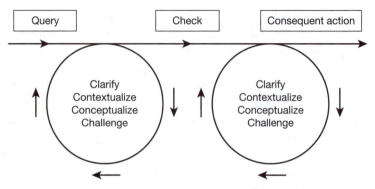

Figure 3.4 Advising cycles

followed by a consequent action, or not even that. On the other hand, you may need to go through two or more cycles of the activities—see Figure 3.4.

It is easy to talk about such qualities and skills in the abstract, but less easy to illustrate them. The following is an exercise that was originally designed to help new advisory staff reflect on the issues involved in this section. You might like to try it! The scoring system is designed to give some very approximate feedback.

Non-Academic Student Support—Values and Responses Exercise

This exercise is designed to gauge your values and responses in a student support environment. At the end of the exercise, which takes about 10 minutes, you can score it and get some feedback on your perceptions and skills.

Section I—Values Exercise

Below are a number of statements about the educational advising of students. Please ring the number that most clearly corresponds to your natural reaction to each statement.

Agree strongly   *Agree*   *Disagree*   *Disagree strongly*

1. The main job of an adviser is to get students through their courses.

    1   2   3   4

2. Students with problems just need clear advice on what to do.

    1   2   3   4

3. It is all right for advisers to show their feelings.

    1   2   3   4

4. The trick to advising is to get people to think they found your solutions for themselves.

    1   2   3   4

5. Advisers can only help students if they have experienced the problems themselves.

    1   2   3   4

6. Advising is mainly about helping students clarify their needs.

    1   2   3   4

7. An adviser needs to be able to probe and analyze people.

    1   2   3   4

8. An adviser never gets impatient.

    1   2   3   4

9. Students who fail can be helped by advising.

    1   2   3   4

10. Advising is just listening.

    1   2   3   4

Section I—Comment

Score yourself as shown.

Statement 1: Disagree 2, Strongly disagree 1.

The main job of an adviser is to help students make the right decision for themselves; that may not always be to continue study. Obviously an adviser will explore what help might be appropriate in overcoming obstacles but not to the extent of manipulating a student to continue on a course whatever the cost or even if it will exacerbate a student's feelings of failure.

Statement 2: Strongly disagree 2, Disagree 1.

Students with problems need help in clarifying and understanding those problems. Sometimes because of that clarification it will be appropriate to give information or advice. However, advice is generally only effective when it is mutually agreed and arises naturally out of the exploration.

Statement 3: **Agree 2, Strongly agree 1.**

Advisers are not distant white-coated authorities; they have feelings and should share them as they feel appropriate.

Statement 4: **Strongly disagree 2.**

Advising is not about manipulation in any form.

Statement 5: **Disagree 2, Strongly disagree 1.**

People's problems may be similar, but the solutions are unique to them. An adviser working only from his or her experience may well attempt to impose his or her solutions on the student.

Statement 6: **Strongly agree 2, Agree 1.**

Probably the best definition of advising of any kind.

Statement 7: **Strongly disagree 2, Disagree 1.**

While insight and empathy are important skills for an adviser, the image of an adviser as detective, interrogator or psychoanalyst is unhelpful. It implies an unequal relationship between counselor and client (and is likely to put any client on the defensive).

Statement 8: **Disagree 2, Strongly disagree 1.**

An adviser is just a human being and every human being feels impatient with others occasionally. An adviser should find a non-aggressive and non-critical way of expressing that feeling if appropriate.

Statement 9: **Strongly agree 2, Agree 1.**

Students fail for many reasons, many of them non-academic, such as problems with time management and motivation and assessment anxiety. Advising may well help such students. Even those students who cannot handle the academic demands of a course may be helped by counseling on referral and coming to terms with their position.

Statement 10: **Disagree 2, Agree 1.**

The essence and main activity of advising is indeed active, perceptive listening. However, a good counselor will also use his or her experience and skill to help the student clarify and conceptualize the issue or problem as well as challenging the student's perceptions when appropriate.

Section 2—Dialogue Analysis

Below are a series of statements from a student, each with a range of responses from an adviser. Ring the letter of the response that is closest to the response you would make as an adviser. Don't take too long— just the top of your head response is good.

Mary is a new student and has been studying for a couple of months.

1. *Mary*: I have to be honest with you, Jean/Jim. I just don't think the course is for me.
   Adviser:
   a) Oh, goodness, Mary, it's a bit early to be deciding that! Give it another week or two at least.
   b) I'm sorry to hear that, Mary. But that's how it goes sometimes.
   c) Why, what's wrong with the course?
   d) You feel the course isn't what you wanted?

2. *Mary*: I just can't get started on it.
   Adviser:
   a) I have that problem sometimes!
   b) Tell me what happens when you try to study.
   c) It's a question of willpower, Mary. You've just got to force yourself to get down to it.
   d) So you're stuck?

3. *Mary*: It's my concentration really. I study quite well for a while but then my mind starts to wander.
   Adviser:
   a) Some bits of the course are rather boring.
   b) Well, it's like I just said. You can't get away from the need to exercise simple willpower.
   c) You're distracted by something?
   d) Mmm?

4. Mary is silent for a while and then sighs heavily.
   Adviser:
   a) You seem to be easily discouraged.
   b) Sorry, I don't seem to be helping you much.
   c) Would you like to tell me how you're feeling?
   d) What are you thinking?

5. *Mary*: The fact is that my family never really wanted me to do the course.
   Adviser:
   a) You're under a lot of pressure from them?
   b) That sounds pretty tough.
   c) Families are often like that.
   d) You know, it's your life—you should tell them exactly what's what.

6. *Mary*: I just can't talk to them about it.
   Adviser:
   a) They don't want to listen to you?
   b) What do you think will happen if you do?
   c) Yes, I know it's difficult, but you're going to have to sometime, aren't you?
   d) It might be easier than you think.

7. *Mary*: They just don't understand why I'm doing this.
   Adviser:
   a) I do know how you feel. But I'm sure if you tried to tell them again they'd understand.
   b) You know, there are times when you just have to stand up for yourself.
   c) It's difficult getting your feelings across, isn't it?
   d) You've not been able to make them understand?

8. *Mary*: So, tell me what I do?
   Adviser:
   a) What do you think you ought to do?
   b) Well, you know what I think.
   c) I can't tell you, but I'd be happy to discuss it with you further if you like.
   d) That's a tough one. You're in a very difficult position, but there's no hurry—we can talk some more.

9. *Mary*: Look, I know you're busy and I really don't want to take up more of your time.
   Adviser:
   a) No, that's all right. That's what I'm paid for.
   b) I'm glad you've been able to tell me this.
   c) It is getting late—let's discuss this again.
   d) Do stay—I've plenty of time.

10. *Mary*: I just don't feel able to decide anything at the moment, anyway.
Adviser:
a) OK. But I'd like to have another chat if that would be all right with you. Would next Tuesday do?
b) It's a difficult decision. Let's have another chat sometime.
c) I'm sure it will all be for the best.
d) Well, don't let it go for too long. You need to get it sorted out soon.

Section 2—Comment

Most responses to statements can be categorized as:

Directive or non-directive
Closed or open
Non-reflective or reflective

Directive responses tend to push the student into a particular course of action—for example, Statement 1, Response (a): "Oh goodness, Mary, it's a bit early to be deciding that! Give it another week or two at least!" Directive responses can often sound faintly critical and are seldom effective, as they rarely deal with the real issues. *Non-directive* responses leave the student to decide on direction—for example, Statement 1, Response (b): "I'm sorry to hear that, Mary. But that's how it goes sometimes."

Closed questions just invite "yes/no" or similar specific responses—for example, Statement 2, Response (d): "So you're stuck?" *Open* questions invite the student to expand and explore the issue—for example, Statement 2, Response (b): "Tell me what happens when you try to study."

Reflective responses mirror back the student's statement to students in such a way as to clarify the statement, reassure them that they have been heard and encourage them to explore further—for example, Statement 1, Response (d): "You feel the course isn't what you wanted?"

Non-reflective responses do not attempt to mirror the student's feelings or statements—for example, Statement 1, Response (c): "Why, what's wrong with the course?"

Advisers generally use non-directive, open, reflecting responses as far as they can to encourage students to explore, clarify and move towards a resolution of an issue for themselves.

Statement 1
Response (a)   Score 0—directive and unhelpful.
Response (b)   Score 1—non-directive and non-critical, but not particularly helpful in exploring the issue.
Response (c)   Score 0—faintly defensive and unlikely to encourage the dialogue.
Response (d)   Score 2—a clear, open reflection.

Statement 2
Response (a)   Score 1—friendly and non-directive, but the adviser is "taking over" the problem with his or her own experience, which is not always helpful.
Response (b)   Score 2—not a reflection, but an appropriate non-directive and open response.
Response (c)   Score 0—directive and faintly critical.
Response (d)   Score 0—closed.

Statement 3
Response (a)   Score 0—sympathetic but not helpful in clarifying the problem.
Response (b)   Score 0—directive and possibly unhelpful.
Response (c)   Score 1—reflective and helpful, but possibly a little closed.
Response (d)   Score 2—all that is needed at this point, really.

Statement 4
Response (a)   Score 0—something of a put-down, even if sympathetically said.
Response (b)   Score 0—not likely to encourage confidence.
Response (c)   Score 2—gives student permission to go on in a non-directive way.
Response (d)   Score 1—as above, but not so well put.

Statement 5
Response (a)   Score 2—a reflection.
Response (b)   Score 1—all right, but putting words into the student's mouth.
Response (c)   Score 0—OK, but not very helpful—the adviser is taking over the problem again.
Response (d)   Score 0—directive and rather censorious.

Statement 6
Response (a)   Score 1—a good try at a reflection, but not what she said.
Response (b)   Score 2—a little better than above, as it moves forward more.
Response (c)   Score 0—rather critical.
Response (d)   Score 0—irrelevant to the student's feelings.

Statement 7

Response (a)   Score 0—well meaning, but probably of no use.

Response (b)   Score 0—considerably worse.

Response (c)   Score 1—helpful.

Response (d)   Score 2—is slightly better.

Statement 8

Response (a)   Score 0—the adviser feels he or she is on the spot and bounces the question straight back.

Response (b)   Score 0—directive.

Response (c)   Score 2—open and honest, but leaving the door open.

Response (d)   Score 1—not as honest as (c): it implies the adviser may be able to offer a solution at some future point.

Statement 9

Response (a)   Score 0—it sounds as though the counselor is under some rather tedious obligation.

Response (b)   Score 2—a small validation for the student's courage in getting so far.

Response (c)   Score 1—honest but also slightly dismissive.

Response (d)   Score 0—could sound insincere.

Statement 10

Response (a)   Score 2—a clear commitment to give more help if the student wants it.

Response (b)   Score 1—rather vague and no clear commitment to follow up.

Response (c)   Score 0—woolly and pathetic?

Response (d)   Score 0—directive.

Your Scores

30–40 You clearly have excellent qualities of empathy and openness. It may be that you will want to be just a little more directive in your work sometimes!

20–29 You have a good feel for the skills and qualities of an adviser—you may occasionally be judgmental, so watch out for that.

10–19 You would still make a good educational adviser, but you should be careful not to be too directive—allow your students a little more space to find their own solutions sometimes.

0–9 You probably have many fine qualities and skills, but being an educational adviser may not be amongst them!

Note: I hope you found that dialogue interesting. I can't claim that it is absolutely realistic, although I don't think it is a complete work of imagination—I have had conversations with students along such lines. I hope that my responses might have got me a score into the 20s . . . But there is another point to this dialogue and the others that appear in this book. It is relatively easy to talk about student support in general terms, but without some examples, however fictional, it is impossible to get a feel for what support is like in practice. I hope you will read the dialogue in those terms.

Non-Academic Support—Assessment, Action, Advocacy, Agitation and Administration

To some extent, there is less to say about the remaining activities in non-academic student support, since they are very institution-dependent. The kind of actions that can be taken, the cases that can be advocated and the causes that can be agitated about will be very dependent on the institution in which a student supporter works. However, there are some general issues that will be worth looking at.

Assessing

Assessing can be defined as the gathering, processing (and usually feeding back) of information about students' skills, knowledge and interests in order to support them in making appropriate choices.

This book maintains the distinction between academic and non-academic assessment. Academic assessment encompasses not only assessment of a student's academic progress on a course but also pre-course assessment that might involve, for example, numeracy and literacy diagnostic tests. That still leaves the issue of assessing a student's non-academic development in a course—for example, their progress in developing learning skills, as well as a broad field that takes in vocational and other diagnostic activities. There are a number of points at which assessment can be used.

(i) *Course and program choice.* Assessing the student's interests, aptitudes and motivation in order to commend particular courses and programs should be a very important part of any pre-course advice aimed at enhancing student success. I'll return to this in Chapter 9.
(ii) *Learning styles.* At one point in the recent past there was a great deal of interest in using learning styles to assess students. However these have not been found to be useful in helping students—see Chapter 5.
(iii) *Statistical analyses.* It is now possible to develop statistical programs that will predict a student's chances of success with a fair degree of accuracy.

There have been some interesting experiments with sharing such information with students—see Chapter 7.

(iv) *Learning skills and learning outcomes.* Many distance institutions have emphasized the development of distance learning skills as a particular subset of learning skills. There is the expectation that there is value in undertaking assessment of learning skills development during a course in the expectation that a student who sees his or her skills increasing may develop self-confidence as a learner much faster than in the absence of such feedback. This assessment of learning skills is sometimes carried out by using "learning outcomes" in assessing a student's work. This is a typical set of learning outcomes I am required to use in marking student assignments for one institution:

Learning Outcomes on your Assignment

First Group: The Subject of the Course

Learning Outcome 1
You have included relevant specialist words and phrases from the course

Learning Outcome 2
You have applied relevant ideas from the course

Learning Outcome 3
You have selected relevant evidence, examples and/or information from the course

Learning Outcome 4
You have produced a relevant, reasoned answer

Second Group: Learning Skills/Study Skills

Learning Outcome 5
You have communicated effectively in writing

Learning Outcome 6
You have used an appropriate structure or format

Learning Outcome 7
You have followed relevant academic conventions

Learning Outcome 8
You have thought about your own learning

However, I have been unable to find any evidence that students find learning outcomes more useful than being given a grade and conventional feedback, nor that using them increases student success. As I will suggest in Chapter 5, the evidence for the importance of learning skills development is not clear.

(v)   *Vocational assessment.* Assessing students' interests, abilities and skills has been a part of the careers adviser's armory for a long time. Relatively sophisticated computer-assisted careers guidance systems (CACGS) have been developed that can be used at a distance. Such programs mostly work by comparing students' responses with previously calibrated responses from workers in particular careers, producing suggested matches for the students to particular careers. Students can then refine their responses if the suggestions do not seem appropriate (Copeland et al. 2011).

(vi) *Self-assessment.* Self-assessment or self-diagnosis has been used in distance institutions, often as an inexpensive tool. See Chapter 9 for a more detailed view.

(vii) *Learning Plans and Personal Development Plans (PDPs).* Some institutions have introduced Personal Development or Learning Plans designed to encourage students to reflect on their learning. A simple learning plan is shown below—in this case, the student is asked to complete it and send it to their tutor before the course starts. This is an actual example of a Learning Plan returned to me by a new student on a math course.

Your Learning Plan

Please complete this plan and send the top copy to your tutor and keep the other copy for reference.

1.   What would you like to learn from this course?

   I want to be able to refresh my basic mathematical skills to enable me to continue on into other scientific modules. I also use mathematics in my day-to-day job and this module would enhance my speed and understanding of the subject in my professional life. My particular weaknesses are negative numbers, working with fractions and I sometimes get stuck with understanding data when trying to work out percentages.

2.   What skills are you hoping to improve during this course?

   I am keen to improve my learning skills and to strengthen my ability to focus on studying texts and activities. Most of my mistakes are from rushing, so

I would like to use this module to see if I am capable of sitting down and working through a structured academic deadline in a more calm and focused fashion. Also, I would like to be able to become better at communicating my answers more clearly to others as I sometimes confuse even myself trying to answer a question.

3. What else are you hoping to get from the course?

   The feeling of completing this course would seriously be a great confidence boost. Not only would I have a stronger grasp on math but I would feel that I would be able to move on to the next step towards my longer term goal of a degree.

4. How do you think your previous experiences of life, work, and education have given you skills and knowledge to help with this course?

   As a Lighting Designer I frequently use math in unit conversion, geometry and calculations. I also work as a Production Manager working on foreign currency rates and many types of spreadsheets and formulas. Also working across the globe I spend a lot of time working out different time zones, schedules, etc. All of these things will help aid my progress on this course.

The intention behind getting students to send such plans to their tutor is threefold—to get the student interacting on the course with something non-threatening; to get students to initiate contact with the tutor; and finally to give the tutor some helpful background on the student. Perhaps their most use is in encouraging early contact between students and tutor or institution.

Clearly these are desirable end products, although, in my experience of receiving them over a number of years, there is no connection between receiving one from a student and that student's subsequent success. I have been unable to find any evidence elsewhere as to their value in promoting student success. But there may be some value in encouraging students to think about their potential strengths more clearly—see Chapter 6.

Linked with learning plans is the use of Learning Portfolios, or Personal Development Plans (PDPs), where students are required to keep records of their learning progress and the skills they believe they have acquired throughout their course, as well as the goals they hope to achieve. While this may be some help to them in career terms, I've been unable to find any clear evidence that they increase student retention and success. Perhaps, as often seems to be the case with such schemes, only those students who are very likely to succeed anyway are likely to use them.

Action

Sometimes the simplest possible student support is the most effective. Arranging a lift home, putting two people with similar needs in touch, phoning up a dilatory section of the institution and asking for some outstanding item to be sent, setting up a special face-to-face meeting with a tutor—these are all simple actions that can have disproportionate success.

Although the different sorts of action that can be taken in any institution will depend on that institution, there are certain requirements that must be in place:

(i)   *Closeness and immediacy*. Action often arises out of a student's immediate needs, so there must be support as close to the student as possible and response as speedily as possible.

(ii) *Empowerment of staff*. This means that the staff nearest the student must have some power to undertake action (within certain guidelines) without having to refer. For example, if the student support nearest the student is a part-time tutor, then that person must have some power to take action (such as offer some extra one-to-one time) and know that he or she will be supported, in receiving compensation for that time.

(iii) *Guidelines*. In such a situation, there must of course be clear guidelines as to the extent to which empowerment applies. There will need to be clear staff development about the boundaries of empowerment and the reasons for empowerment.

Recently a tutor I know had a student who was sent to Saudi Arabia on business. The airline lost his luggage including his study text. She located a pdf of the text online and emailed the url to him. She could have simply referred him to the correspondence delivery department of the institution and he would have received a set of replacement materials at his home but that would have been little help to him. So this is a very modest example of a tutor taking responsibility for a simple action and yet without that small action that student would have dropped out.

Advocacy

Advocacy has always been a very distinct part of student support in distance education, with several aspects:

(i) *References* for jobs, further courses and funding. A characteristic of distance education is that the institution may know very little about its students, so it will be necessary to set up systems for overcoming these difficulties. These might be forms for requesting information from students for particular purposes as well as a format for references that does not disadvantage distance students against their colleagues from conventional institutions.

(ii) *Appeals* against the institution's rulings. This can be a very difficult area. Perhaps because its students are more remote from the institution than in a face-to-face organization, it may be easier for conflicts and misunderstandings to arise. In addition, in any conflict between institution and student there is heavy weighting towards the institution, with its resources, stamina and ability to be the final judge in many cases.

But this picture is changing. With increases in student fees there seems to be an increasing assertiveness on the part of students and an increasing tendency to resort to litigation. In addition, the anomaly of institutions acting as judge and jury in their own cases has been noticed—in the U.K., the Dearing Report recommended that internal complaints procedures should reflect "natural justice" and there is now an Office of the Independent Adjudicator for Higher Education (OIA).

This can leave a student support adviser in a very difficult position. How far can, or should, he or she act as a mediator between the institution and a particular student who appears to have had a bad deal? There is no easy answer to this, especially in the light of increasing employment insecurity and the use of short-term contracts for staff.

This is an extreme example of the problem. A student who had failed to get an answer to her query from one of the offices in my own institution contacted me. Her request for a response seemed reasonable and, indeed, on my first contact with the office on her behalf, they indicated that they would indeed write to her. Some six months later, despite at least four reminders from me by email and phone, they had still failed to respond to the student. At that point, I wrote to the office saying I would have to take the final recourse of any citizen in a democracy faced with an unresponsive bureaucracy. This was to hold a peaceful demonstration outside the office concerned and that I would appear on a certain date with a placard and leaflets. I got my response (at the cost of continuing frosty relations with the office concerned—a consequence that is not unimportant). However, it is extremely unlikely that I would have taken that risk if I had not been tenured staff.

I like to think that such a situation would be unlikely to arise now with prescriptive complaints procedures in place, which requires answers within certain time scales, together with a charter of student rights.

Agitation

Agitation and advocacy are ultimately linked—a rather arbitrary distinction is that, whereas advocacy has sometimes to do with changing the institution's procedures for a single student, usually as a one-off, agitation is changing the institution's procedures for all students, permanently.

The term "agitation" is being used slightly tongue-in-cheek, of course, yet sometimes when I see how institutions in which I have worked have changed, it often seems more as a result of underground movements and individual insistence than as a result of rational debate and due committee processes. As Cornford (1908) noted in his definitive work on how universities resist change, *Microcosmographica Academica*:

> You have found a change in your practice which you believe is useful. You think it would be even more useful for the institution as a whole to change its practice. You think (do you not?) that you only have to state a reasonable case and people must listen to reason and act upon it at once. But . . . if you want to move people you must address your arguments to prejudice and the political motive.

While Cornford's work is now more than 100 years old, much of what he said then still seems to apply to universities today. That being said, there have to be such processes through which student support staff can represent their experiences and work for changes in institutional policies. Again, there seem to be a number of issues:

- distance education institutions tend of necessity to be heavily managed— the administration tends to play a larger role than in conventional organizations, and tends to have more power and can be resistant to change;

- institutions that cater for very large numbers—the "mega-versities"— prefer to treat their customers as in the mass where possible in order to keep costs minimized. Customizing the institution to meet students' various needs—"post-Fordism"—is expensive;

- academic standards. Uniquely in the service industries, educational institutions have to maintain standards that quite deliberately set hurdles that their customers have to overcome. If too many exceptions are made, if regulations become too student-friendly, there is an argument that academic standards may be compromised. Indeed, that argument is already made in respect of both universities and schools where improved pass rates are sometimes interpreted not as the result of improved standards of support but as the result of decreasing academic standards;

- short-term non-tenured contracts. There has been a substantial increase in the last few years in the use of short-term contracts in some institutions. While such contracts provide flexibility for the institution in rapidly changing environments, staff who are on such contracts are less likely to want to take on entrenched interests within the institution. If they are hoping for a renewal of their contract, then a low profile and an aversion to trouble may be their natural policy.

In the light of these opposing forces, it sometimes seems extraordinary that institutions do actually adapt to students at all. Nevertheless, there are a number of positive trends, several of them already mentioned:

- the increasing assertiveness of students as previously mentioned and their use of litigation;

- pressure on institutions to develop their appeals and complaints procedures;

- and, in particular, competition between institutions.

The Role of Student Support Advisers in Agitation

So where does this leave the role of student support advisers? They need to be sure:

1. that their institution has clear processes for taking on board student demands;
2. that there are clear complaints and appeals procedures. If those procedures have some independent involvement, so much the better;
3. that the representation of the student-facing support workers must be prioritized by the institution's senior management. The world is littered with examples of commercial enterprises that failed to stay in touch with

their customer base despite their customer service workers actually knowing where the service had failed. They simply lacked the representation to say so;

4. that student support advisers should be able to take modest risks. There will be circumstances when it will be useful to remember one of the "Intrapreneur's Ten Commandments" (Pinchot 1990)—"It is easier to ask for forgiveness than for permission." See Chapter 15 for my own 10 principles for attempting change in distance education institutions;

5. that they are prepared to refer and use the institution's student charter. They should also clarify the perceptions of their role by the rest of the institution. Are they to be trench war defenders of the institution, mediators between the institution and its students or knights on chargers on behalf of students? If it is to be the second, then there will need to be clear and well-defined skills development in mediation.

> Some years ago I started collecting the opinions of students who had just completed courses, to pass them on to students contemplating taking those courses. The obvious thing to do was to place the collected opinions on the web, but when I asked for permission to do so this I was refused. I went ahead anyway on a private basis and after a few years the site "Student reviews" was taken over by the institution and it can now be found on http://www3.open.ac.uk/coursereviews/course.aspx. See Chapter 9 for a fuller description.

The downside of proceeding with stealth is that you are unlikely to get the credit for the innovation—as I didn't, in this case . . .

Administration

The administration of student support will depend on the structure of the institution. But an adviser clearly needs to be a good administrator, particularly in things like record keeping, progress monitoring and chasing up. Some underlying principles may be true of any institution and are covered in Chapter 7.

Conclusion

This chapter has been about the categories and activities in distance student "non-academic support." It has looked at developmental and problem-solving support, advising (which covers informing, commending and exploring), and assessing, action, advocacy, agitation and administration.

As a practical exercise you might like to look at the following list of student queries. What kind of response would you make to each one—Informing, Advising, Exploring, Action, Advocacy or Agitation? Compare your answer with mine, but bear in mind that these activity categories are quite subjective!

"Which courses do I need for a math degree?"
- *Informing.* This looks like a straightforward request for information, at least at this stage.

"I can do either course A or course B—which should I do?"
- Advising. This needs a little unpacking before any advice can be given.

"My daughter is seriously ill. Should I drop out?"
- *Exploring.* You cannot decide for the student—much will depend on his or her circumstances and feelings, which need clarifying.

"I cannot go to the tutorial because I cannot afford the bus fare."
- *Action.* Hopefully you can find some way of funding this student's bus fare.

"I missed the due date of this assignment because I was ill. Can I submit it now?"
- *Advocacy.* If submitting late is against the institution's regulations you may need to be an advocate for the student to be allowed to do so— if you think their case is strong enough.

"I have got behind because there is far too much material in this course."
- *Agitation.* You may find that you agree with the student, in which case you may want to try to get the institution to change the course.

Finally there is a 15-minute video "Counseling in Distance Education" that demonstrates some of the points in this chapter, which can be accessed by the website www.ormondsimpson.com or directly on http://tinyurl.com/distance-counseling.

Chapter 4

Academic Support—Tuition

Distance education is different from conventional education in one very important aspect: the teaching in distance education is mainly carried out by the course text, whether that text is in print form or online via podcasts, video and audio material, discussion forums and so on. This means that the role of the teacher in distance education is usually markedly different from the similarly named roles in conventional education. And, although "academic support" is the more accurate description for the activities described in this chapter, the terms "tutor" and "tuition" are so widespread that I will use them. However, you should bear in mind that the terms imply certain activities that are more relevant to conventional education than to distance learning. So the transition for tutors from a conventional face-to-face tuition system to distance tuition is not always easy.

Tuition Activities

The principles underlying academic support are very similar to those underlying non-academic support, although of course tuition also depends on the subject being taught.

Like non-academic support, tuition covers a wide range of activities. Perhaps again they fall into a spectrum, as shown in Figure 4.1, running from those that are strictly course-material-related to those that depend much more on the tutor.

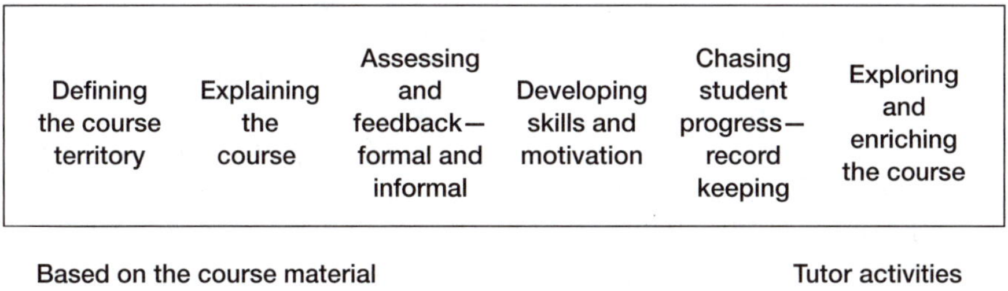

Defining the course territory	Explaining the course	Assessing and feedback— formal and informal	Developing skills and motivation	Chasing student progress— record keeping	Exploring and enriching the course

Based on the course material   Tutor activities

Figure 4.1 A "spectrum" of tutor activities

Defining the Territory

In most distance education systems, the course content—the syllabus—is defined by the course material. There are exceptions to this—institutions where the territory is negotiated between the student and institution such as the Empire State College of New York—and it could be argued that courses with projects leave some of the territory up to the student.

Nevertheless the definition of territory in distance education is usually set by the written course material and is generally much more specific than in conventional educational settings, where even a set syllabus still allows the conventional tutor some control over the detailed content. This is both a weakness and a strength in distance education: a weakness because a distance tutor may be teaching to someone else's material and may not be as committed to it as the authors; and a strength as, for the same reason, a distance tutor will not be committed to the defense of that material at all costs. Thus a distance tutor may be able to encourage students to criticize course material more freely, perhaps partly answering the occasional objections that distance education can be an unduly authoritarian form of instruction—see Chapter 5.

Explaining the Course

Again, in most distance education courses, the essential explication of the course is carried out by course material. This material may be in print, online, on a DVD, or in the form of video, audio or other media, so that the explanations come from different sources and may be from different perspectives, but the principle remains.

Obviously there is still a substantial role for the tutor in providing alternative explanations of particularly difficult points, but there are also dangers, particularly for tutors from conventional institutions new to distance education. Familiar with situations where they are entirely responsible for the explication of a course, they may try to replicate that, forgetting that that is the business of the course material. Such misunderstandings may become apparent when they complain that they have insufficient time to cover the course.

There is also a role for distance tutors in anticipating specific difficulties in a course and attempting to pre-empt them, perhaps by supplying extra explanatory material, although the danger of replicating the course remains. As importantly will be the "agitation" role of the distance tutor in feeding back those points of difficulty to the course writers if they themselves did not write the course.

Assessment—Formative and Summative

A very important part of the distance tutor's role—as important as progress-chasing and closely related to it—is assessment. Assessment can be "summative," counting towards the student's course grade; or "formative," feedback that does not count towards a final grade.

Summative Assessment

It's often said that assessment drives learning. That may well be true, but it is important to note that there is evidence that assessment—at any rate, summative assessment—also drives student dropout, at least in distance education. Figure 4.2 is a "rivergram" showing progress through a U.K. Open University science foundation module, where the width of the river at any point is proportional to the percentage of students who are still active at that point. The lines labeled "Assignment 1," Assignment 2" and so on are where summative tutor-marked assignments occur (there are six assignments in the module, with a final exam).

The rivergram can be seen as a stream flowing left to right with students as the "salmon" traveling upstream left to right and leaping up waterfalls at each assignment. There is substantial dropout before each waterfall or assignment—of the 100 students starting the course, some 38 drop out before the first one, with only two bypassing it and returning to take the second assignment. There is similar dropout before subsequent assignments and, after only three assignments, 48 of the students have entered the exit stream and dropped out of the course.

Of course, this is only indirect proof that assignments can cause dropout. There may have been events between assignments which may have caused dropout, which was then only picked up by the non-appearance of the subsequent assignment. However, other data from Open University withdrawal surveys generally supports this picture of dropout driven by assessment.

If assessment does drive dropout, what can a distance tutor do to overcome the problem? There is some evidence from the use of formative assessment.

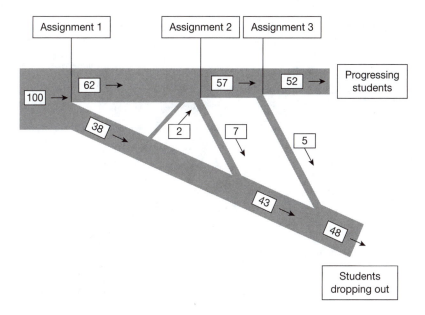

Figure 4.2 A rivergram of the number of students dropping out before each assignment on the science foundation course at the U.K. Open University

Formative Assessment

As noted earlier, formative assessment is feedback to students on work that is not graded or used for assessment except sometimes in a qualifying sense— i.e., it must be completed to allow summative assessments to be submitted, or it carries a very small weighting (say 10% or less) towards the final grade. In *Retention and Student Success in Higher Education*, Yorke and Longden (2004) argue strongly for the retention value of formative assessment in conventional education. There is also evidence of the retention effect in conventional education from studies in the United States such as those of Black and Wiliam (1998) and Kluger and De Nisi (1996). Perhaps the phrase "Assessment drives learning" might be more accurately stated as "Feedback drives learning." Indeed, as Hattie and Timperley (2007) note, feedback can improve learning, both at school and university level, more than any other factor.

In distance education there is also evidence of the value of formative assessment in enhancing student success from the U.K. Open University in the form of another "rivergram." The science foundation module whose assignment rivergram was illustrated in Figure 4.2 was subsequently rewritten, and a formative assignment introduced as Assignment 1. The revised rivergram is shown in Figure 4.3.

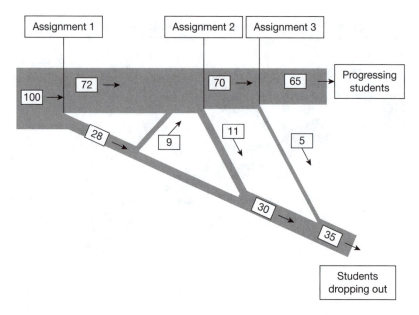

Figure 4.3 A rivergram of the number of students dropping out before each assignment on the rewritten science foundation module at the U.K. Open University, with a formative first assignment

It can be seen that fewer students drop out before the first (now formative) assignment—28 versus 38—and that more students return to the second assignment having skipped the first—9 versus 2. Thus, there are more students on the "progress channel" at every stage than in the pre-formative assessment module—72 versus 62, 70 versus 57 and so on. It is not possible to compare the overall retention rates of the two modules, as their contents and exam strategies were different, but nevertheless the overall pattern of more students carrying on at every stage is clear.

Thus, a distance tutor's role in assessment may well be to introduce formative assessment into their support activities where possible. Note that giving formative assignments formal grades may reduce their value. Black and Wiliam (1998) found that assignments with feedback and marks, or marks only, led to less learning than assignments with just feedback. Similarly, Kluger and De Nisi (1998) found that graded feedback actually depressed future performance in one third of all the feedback research they studied. In a further one third, the graded feedback had no effect and only in one final third did performance increase. They suggest that feedback must be focused on building learners' self-efficacy, and closing the gap between their goals and current performance. Feedback pointing out poor performance, suggesting the performance is "wrong" or that the goals are unclear, often led to deterioration in performance.

How a tutor introduces formative assessment into his or her course will depend on the structure of the course. Most distance courses will have some kind of "self-assessment questions" (SAQs) built into the text that a tutor might be able to use in some way. Students have a tendency to skip SAQs, but a tutor actually requesting answers to them may get students to take them more seriously. And a tutor can interact with an answer, clarify it and phrase the next question in appropriate relationship with it without damaging a student's self-confidence.

Technology may help in online courses—for example, in the use of "polling software." This is the online or texting equivalent of asking for a show of hands. A multiple-choice or free-text quiz can be designed using the software, which can then be inserted (for example) as a slide in a synchronous podcast or PowerPoint presentation. Students are invited to respond to the quiz either on the internet or by texting their answers to a phone number. Either way their answers can then be shown graphically in the same presentation, the histograms for (say) "yes," "no" or "I don't know" building up as students answer. A number of systems exist such as *Poll Everywhere* (http://www.polleverywhere.com).

However the use of multiple-choice quizzes has been criticized by Gibbs (2010), who suggests that they lead to "shallow learning" (focused on the memorization and replication of information) rather than the desired "deep learning" (focused on understanding and synthesizing knowledge—Marton and Säljö 1976). But I would argue that for potential dropout students, any kind of successful initial learning may increase their confidence and motivation, thereby reducing their likelihood of dropping out. After all, to take the metaphor literally, throwing non-swimmers in at the deep end is unlikely to produce successful swimming. Starting at the shallow end is rather more likely to produce eventual success at the deep end. And most distance students are working under such time pressures that they seem to me to resort to a compromise which I think of as "strategic learning"—doing the best they can in the time they've got.

Giving Feedback

However well tutors use formative assessment, summative assessments carried out by tutors are very important in distance education; for many students, such feedback is the most substantial teaching contact they have with their tutor. For some it may be the only contact. Giving such feedback is a difficult task— too kind or elliptic, and students will not understand where they are and what they need to do to improve; too direct and unvarnished, and they may be so discouraged that they will drop out inappropriately. There are a couple of suggestions from psychological theory—Dweck's (1999) suggestion of validating or praising effort rather than achievement and "metacognitive awareness."

1. *Validating effort rather than achievement.* Dweck (1999) found that it is more effective to praise students' efforts rather than their achievements. Indeed she found that praising achievement could actually be counterproductive, as, when students thus praised ran into subsequent difficulties, they tended to give up more easily, believing that they had reached the ultimate level of what their intelligence could achieve. She suggested that students need to be persuaded that final success can be achieved through resilience and persistence, overcoming setbacks by learning from them and going on. Of course, many good tutors in open and distance learning already unconsciously take this approach with students, for instance when marking assignments. However, they may be not always be as rigorous in praising effort at the expense of achievement as Dweck suggests they should.

2. *"Metacognitive awareness"* (Sadler 1989, pp. 119–144) is the idea that students need to be able to make the same judgments of assignments that tutors make. That means students being able to see exemplars of different grades, getting some idea of what grade they might get for a particular assignment and—where possible—being able to enter a dialogue with tutors and other students about those grades. Both Hattie (2009) and Gibbs (2010) believe that metacognitive awareness of assessment is an important factor in learning and consequent retention. Hattie, in his meta-survey of several hundred studies, rated "self-reporting of grades" (i.e., students have a reasonably accurate understanding of their levels of achievement and chances of success) as the most important factor in student success out of the 130 factors. He also suggested that tutors should use "enhanced worked examples" (see below) in their teaching. Gibbs (2010) quoted findings from the Scottish "Re-engineering Assessment Practices in Scottish Higher Education" (REAP) study, which found worthwhile improvements in first-year performance and retention on a whole range of courses through simple mechanisms such as marking exercises.

These findings are from conventional education fields. But it seems likely that they also apply to distance education, where assignments play an even more critical role, so it may be worthwhile to introduce both marking exercises and enhanced worked examples into distance assessment.

- *marking exercises*—are where students are given specimen student assignment answers and asked to mark and discuss them. This way, Gibbs argues, they will gain insights into what makes a good assignment. Practical examples of how to do this either face-to-face or online can be found on the website www.ormondsimpson.com/page4.htm under "All Together" and "All Together Online."

- *enhanced worked examples*—examples where the thought processes behind the example are explained as well as the answer itself. Marking exercises may not work quite so well for numerate subjects like math and science, so enhanced worked examples may be more useful for these examples. A math example can be seen on www.ormondsimpson.com/page3.htm in the presentation "Assessment in Tutoring; Enhancing Student Success."

For instance in (say) a math worked example it will be best to explain why certain lines of working are pursued at various points as well as the final working. Similar examples could be developed even in more discursive subjects, such as sociology, although such examples might be more about the line and strength of the argument.

Assignment Feedback

It may be easier to see these ideas in action from an example of an assignment feedback. This is not meant to be a perfect example, but I hope it gives a feel for the general approach.

Joan was a new student on a physics course. She had very little background in the subject and found math difficult. Her main aim in taking it was as grounding for some earth science courses in which she was interested.

Her first assignment on the course was a borderline pass, but she put a lot of work into it. The tutor wrote to her as follows:

"Well done Joan, you obviously worked very hard on this difficult assignment and made a very good effort at something that I appreciate was very new to you.

"Q1—A clear account. You lost some marks because you misunderstood how to measure the length—see my comments on the script.

"Q2—Well laid out and clearly calculated. Again, you lost some marks because of one particular slip—confusing the difference between average and final speed.

"Overall—a very sound beginning. You have some problems with math but they can be overcome—we'll talk about them in the next tutorial. I've attached a worked example of the answer with my own notes on how to tackle the question. Keep this level of effort up and you'll do fine!"

3. *"Feedback sandwich."* This is an example of a "feedback sandwich"—the bad news is sandwiched between positive opening and closing comments. Comments on the script itself are too detailed to put here, but they were friendly (using the student's first name), encouraging, used humor where possible, and tried to balance any criticism with some positive comment. For example, "Joan—there's an arithmetic slip here which gives you the wrong answer which was bad luck as your working was quite correct up to here!"

4. *Giving feedback on a low grade or failed assignment.* If a student's work is clearly a fail, then the task must be approached even more carefully. For example, when working as a tutor I insert a simple leaflet along with my comments on a low-grade assignment. It's called "Not done as well as you hoped?" and has headings like:

"Not done as well as you hoped on your assignment?"

"Put it into perspective and keep going"

"What went wrong? Did you answer the question? Can you see why you lost marks? Did you run out of time?"

"Getting it better next time"

"Do you think I got it wrong? Appealing against an assignment grade"

"Good luck for your next assignment!"

The full text can be seen on the website www.ormondsimpson.com in the "StudyAid Pack."

Media for Feedback

Finally it may be worth experimenting with other media for feedback. At the Open Polytechnic of New Zealand some tutors in graphic subjects record their marking using a video camera focused on the script as they assess it. The resulting video recording is then sent to students on a DVD. With online assignments it is easy to insert audio clips in returned assignments—Ice et al. (2007) found an extremely high student satisfaction with embedded asynchronous audio feedback as compared to asynchronous text-only feedback. Screen recording software such as Jing (www.techsmith.com/index.html) can be used in a similar way. But there is no evidence as to the effects of such media on retention as yet.

Designing Assignments

If you are in the position of designing assignments, then it is useful to bear in mind that learning motivation is the key to student success (see Chapter 6) and to make them as motivational as possible. There is not a lot of evidence as yet, but there are two possibilities for designing motivational assessments:

1. *Wigfield's theory.* Wigfield and Eccles (2002, pp. 92–120) suggest that learning motivation is a product:

   (assumed possibility of accomplishing a task)
   multiplied by
   (the perceived value of that accomplishment).

   If either of those quantities are zero, then the multiple (the learning motivation) is also zero. This suggests that assessment tasks need to be carefully graded, particularly at the start of a module, so that students believe their chances of success are high.

2. *Ipsative assessment* is assessment or feedback that compares a student's achievement, not with an absolute standard, but with their previous performance (Hughes 2012). The suggestion is that this is more congruent with Dweck's (1999) findings that students praised for effort are more likely to increase their efforts than students praised for their achievement.

   One example of ipsative assessment is from U.K. Dyslexia Action in their postgraduate course for specialist teachers. Students are required to read a set text and then have several weeks to complete an online assessment consisting of a computer-marked multiple-choice test. They can have as many attempts at the test as they wish, and at each try are told whether their answers are right or wrong, but nothing else. Course tutors can offer help at any point before the deadline at which a threshold has to be reached. Results so far suggest that most students achieve the threshold and find the process motivational, often improving their scores beyond the threshold (Goodwin 2012). However, further research is needed into how ipsative assessment can be applied and what the effect, if any, on retention might be.

Developing Learning Skills and Motivation

For a long time in distance education, one of a tutor's roles was deemed to be to help develop students' learning skills. For the reasons outlined in Chapter 5, I shall suggest that this is less important than developing a student's motivation to learn. This is because there does not seem to be a specific set of distance learning skills that every student should use; it is more important that a student should be well motivated to learn and have reasonable confidence in their study methods, whatever they are. A student who is well motivated to learn will probably find the study methods that suit them best and will develop confidence in those methods with only minimal help. There is a case study in Chapter 5 of a student who studies while watching television that may illustrate this.

Developing a student's motivation to learn is dealt with in Chapter 6. Nevertheless there still is a role for a tutor in helping his or her students clarify their study methods, to eliminate obviously poor methods, to overcome study anxiety and to develop confidence in their methods. Some students will already be effective learners when they begin their studies, but it is the nature of distance education—particularly open learning, where there are no entry qualifications—that there will be many students who come from educationally disadvantaged backgrounds and who do not have effective or appropriate study methods for the courses they are about to take. For example, a study in the U.K. Open University (Datta and Macdonald Ross 2002) revealed that up to a third of the new students embarking on an introductory course had reading skills and comprehension below the readability levels of parts of the course—see Chapter 12. Clearly, in a situation like this, the course materials themselves—apparently already too difficult for many students—are unlikely to be very successful in developing confidence amongst those students.

Therefore, the burden of helping those students develop "study survival skills" at the beginning of courses will fall very particularly on their tutor. In the absence of clear evidence, my experience is that a tutor should give simple study advice, but probably not fall into the trap of making study appear complex and challenging. When I look at some of the many "How to Study" books available in my local bookshop I find myself wondering if a student doesn't have to be already pretty good at study in order to make sense of them.

But I do try to get my students to experiment with various ways of studying to see what works for them best. So I give my students the simplest possible advice, using the "SQ3R" model as an email or handout at the beginning of a module. "SQ3R" stands for "Study, Question, Read, Recall, Review," and is just one of a number of simple study models that may be helpful in giving new students a starting point for their way of working. The full text (it's only one page long) can be found on www.ormondsimpson.com in the "Support for Students and Tutors" page.

Then I follow up with a set of "motivational emails" to try to keep students' learning motivation switched on—see Chapter 8.

Progress Chasing and Record Keeping

These may seem odd activities to have under tutoring, with their connotations of industrial production processes. Perhaps "Student progress monitoring and follow-up" would be more accurate. Whatever it is called, it is one of the key activities of a tutor in distance education—far more so, perhaps, than in conventional education. At its simplest, progress chasing means a tutor checking on the progress of his or her students at appropriate intervals (possibly around assignment submission dates) in order to see where they have got to and to take proactive action if they appear to be falling behind. It also means keeping good records (perhaps a simple chart of contacts), so that it is clear when a student may have slipped through the net. This is an excerpt of the chart I keep for my own students—see Table 4.1.

If the chart is reasonably well designed, it should be possible fairly rapidly to pick up students who are becoming inactive. In this case, from the absence of recent "x"s in her row, it looks as though Diane needs some particular effort at contact. On a web-based course, it will be necessary to have some kind of mechanism—preferably an automatic one—for checking how often students are logging on to the course website.

Progress monitoring is particularly important, as it is one of the student support activities that directly addresses the vital area of student learning motivation.

Table 4.1 Example of a tutor's student records

Student	Intro letter sent	Intro email sent	Intro phone call	Student on Virtual Learning Environment (VLE)	Learning Plan received	Second phone call	Assign-ment 01 in	Email 2 sent	. . . and so on
Alex	✓	✓ x	✓ x	✓	x	x	✓ x	x	✓
Ben	✓	✓ x	✓ m	x		✓ n/a		✓	
Chris	✓	✓	✓ x		x	✓ x	x	✓	
Diane	✓	✓ x	✓				✓ m		✓
Ed	✓	✓ x	✓ x	x		✓ m		✓	

Key
Letter or email: ✓ = sent, x = received
Phone call: ✓ = made, x = answered, n/a = no answer, m = message left
Assignment: x = received

For a number of years I supervised a group of tutors teaching the same course. There were two in particular who seemed to be in vivid contrast. Peter was quite elderly, and was a rather dry, punctilious man with an occasionally acerbic touch. His face-to-face teaching was competent but uninspiring, and his main characteristic was that nothing seemed to worry him; no organizational catastrophe (and I generated quite a number) seemed to throw him. He eventually told me that he had landed with the first wave of troops in Normandy on D-Day and that—as he put it—"Nothing has ever really worried me much since."

Jeff was Peter's opposite: young, dynamic and charismatic, he was a gifted face-to-face teacher who could make his subject come alive and could enrich his students' studies.

I kept track of their students' results and noticed that they were in contrast, too. Consistently, year after year, one of them got better results than the other.

There'd be no point to this anecdote if the answer was obvious. It was old Peter who outperformed young Jeff every time. And the answer was simple: if I phoned Peter up and asked him, "How's that pregnant student of yours getting on?" he'd immediately answer, "I spoke to her last week— everything's fine." Jeff would have scratched his head and said, "I've not heard from her for a while, so I can't really tell you."

This case study illustrates a particular idea I will return to when we look at e-learning. It is the notion that all that is needed for student success is "good teaching." That notion is fine if by what is meant by "good teaching" is engaging with students' learning motivation. But sometimes what people mean by "good teaching" is putting a lot of effort into making excellent face-to-face tutorials, presentations, podcasts, video clips and so on. Emphasizing this kind of good teaching at the expense of developing learning motivation and progress chasing will not necessarily contribute to student success. The world's best face-to-face tutorial will not enhance the success of students who have lost motivation and don't turn up.

Exploring, Enthusing and Enriching

Having said that, there is a role that only a tutor can play and which is enormously important for developing and maintaining motivation amongst students. This role is where a tutor can encourage students to study in depth, to push beyond the boundaries of the course and to develop a sense of excitement about their learning and progress. Most tutors can easily think of examples of exploration and enrichment from their own experience—visits to galleries and concerts, suggestions for outside reading, discussions on current newsworthy topics, examples, demonstrations, experiments, presentations on the tutor's specialist topic and many others.

There are no fixed recipes for these activities; one can remember teachers who fired one's imagination in different ways through their own enthusiasm, commitment and encouragement. The excerpt below, from a student's letter I received a few years ago, captures a little of the sense of inspiration that tutors can sometimes inspire in students.

> *"I'm very grateful to all the tutors on all my courses. But it was S— on my first course who really made it all work for me. She was very supportive and always helpful but she had a particular enthusiasm for the psychology side of the course—I didn't know what it was but she really caught my interest because she was so encouraging—I wrote a lot of crap sometimes which she couldn't let me get away with but she also made me feel that I got things right on the button sometimes too. Therefore, I'm now studying to work in Psychology full time!" (Student)*

Balance Between Tuition Activities

It is impossible to lay down where the priorities in these activities will lie. Clearly, the implications are that, in a distance education system, the tutor will spend little time defining the course. Priorities in the other activities will be set by students' needs and expectations, the institution's organization and policies and above all by the time and resources available to the tutor.

Students' needs will depend on both their current knowledge and skills base and on the stage they have reached in their studies. Perhaps explaining and learning motivation development will be particularly important in the start and pre-start stages. In the mid-course stage a tutor's assessment and progress-chasing skills will be particularly needed and towards the end of the course perhaps there will be space for exploring and enrichment.

Of course, the tutor's institution may have needs to do with academic credibility and quality assessment. These are not necessarily entirely compatible with enhancing student success—for example, academic credibility may involve emphasis on (say) face-to-face tuition, which could be at the expense of progress-chasing activities carried out at a distance. However, I would like to think that there will be an increasing emphasis on student access and success as the competitive environment in distance education grows. This may mean a move towards learning motivation development and progress-chasing activities—I can only hope.

Tuition Styles

There are different styles of approach in all the various activities that a tutor undertakes. It is possible to distinguish between two extremes—the didactic and facilitative (Wright 1987).

● *Didactic*—the tutor is very much in the formal lecturer role, explaining and presenting.
● *Facilitative*—the tutor facilitates the student's own exploration of the course.

Again, this is not a clear distinction, but a spectrum, as shown in Figure 4.4.

Clearly, the extremes are fairly theoretical and even in conventional education most tutors operate somewhere in between and vary their style. However, given the points previously made about the tutor not necessarily having responsibility for course content, it is not surprising that there is an emphasis in distance education on using facilitative modes of tuition. So, tutors are often expected to have many of the elements of discussion or group work in their face-to-face and online activities. Thus, a typical facilitative online tutorial might have:

● a computer forum discussion on specific issues, the tutor facilitating the discussion, but involving students as much as possible;
● emails between the tutor and individual students working on specific problems;

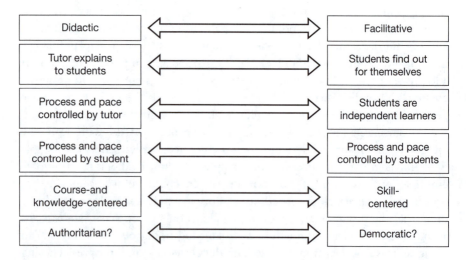

Figure 4.4 Tutorial styles in distance education

- students discussing together in a forum without a tutor for general discussion.

In each case, the intention is to involve the students in the activity of learning rather than make them passive participants. In a face-to-face tutorial, a similar approach can be taken even more easily—see Chapter 8 for further discussion, including a video example on YouTube.

There will be other activities in a tutorial from time to time—a short presentation on some topic of particular interest, or an explanation to the whole group of something that has confused many of them. And of course the balance will also depend on the subject matter of the module. While students might clarify their understanding of a topic in (say) sociology through discussion, they are unlikely to discover the Second Law of Thermodynamics in an online debate.

What Do Students Want?—Expectations of Tuition

At this point tutors—particularly those from conventional educational systems—sometimes raise the issue of "What do students really want?' Sometimes the answer suggested is that what students like are purely didactic teaching methods, lectures and formal presentations, and that they are happiest sitting in rows, the passive recipients of the tutor's knowledge and skill.

It is easy to see how this perception can arise. Certainly in the first face-to-face tutorial for a course, it is hard for students to take an active role for reasons of embarrassment, lack of knowledge and general uncertainty. As mentioned in Chapter 1, there is evidence that many students experience social anxiety that affects their ability to take part in discussions, give presentations or even ask questions (Russell 2008). It is therefore not surprising that a tutor will want to take the initiative and start by delivering a talk or podcast. General questions directed to the students will not always elicit much in the way of answers for similar reasons and so the tutor is reinforced in his or her perceptions.

In fact, what research there is suggests that students want structure; they need to feel some confidence that the tutor knows what he or she is doing in terms of both their course knowledge base and the teaching skills they bring to their work. After that, the students want to feel a sense of progress and interaction with the tutor and with other students (Thorpe 1988). It looks as though most students prefer a style that is predominantly facilitative, that allows them interaction with the tutor and other students and some influence over direction and content, too. Within that framework, didactic elements are clearly acceptable. Being authoritative is fine; being authoritarian is not.

Finally, this chapter has merely outlined some of the principles underlying academic support in distance education. These ideas are developed in subsequent chapters by examining how they apply in different media.

Chapter 5

Theories of Student Support

Theory without practice is sterile; practice without theory is blind.

(attributed to Friedrich Engels)

I embark on this chapter with some tentativeness. Like many practitioners of student support—perhaps yourself?—I have spent too long working at the coalface of support and too little time stepped back from it, trying to understand what basic patterns, values and theories underlie my work. But without some kind of theoretical framework, no matter how simplistic, there is nothing to judge our policy and organizational developments, our structural innovations or even our changes in day-to-day working practice. The quote from Engels is apposite in that respect. And as the psychologist Kurt Lewin (1951) said, "There is nothing so practical as a good theory."

Of course, there are many theories about learning, such as behaviorism, cognitivism, constructivism (currently the most favored, apparently) and, perhaps the newest theoretical kid on the learning block, "connectivism" (Siemens 2011). However, I'm not clear how helpful these learning theories are for designing distance student support in practice. I believe we need a theory that deals with the very particular issues in learning at a distance. So is there a theory unique to distance education?

Theories of Distance Education

There is debate as to whether distance education constitutes a discipline in its own right and consequently whether there can be such things as theories of distance education. There is certainly a great deal of research into different aspects of distance education and it is now taught to higher degree level in several universities.

There have been attempts to apply accepted educational theories dating back, for example, to Baath (1979), who wrote about how contemporary teaching methods applied to correspondence education. Such theories have often concentrated on the production of course material rather than student support, and the questions raised have been around such issues as:

- Is distance education an inferior substitute for conventional education or a unique mode of education in its own right? Are there things that cannot be taught by distance education (the "brain surgery by post" criticism)? Is the quality of the educational discourse inherently poorer in distance education than other modes?
- Is distance education actually rather closed? Rumble (1989, p. 28) argued that distance education systems may be open or closed but that many so-called "open learning systems" are remarkably closed. For example, e-learning actually excludes large numbers of people who don't have access to the internet.
- Is distance education an inherently authoritarian form of education? After all, the content is usually almost entirely defined by one version of the printed word—the correspondence or online material that is sent to students. Students rarely have time to study outside this material. Alternatively, does it allow for student autonomy to a much greater extent than conventional education? After all, if an institution has a course production model where tutors teach the material but do not write it, there is no particular onus on them to defend it.
- Is distance education an antisocial form of education? Does it isolate its students and again does that mean that it is in some sense a poor relation of more conventional methods? Peters (1989, p. 3) interpreted distance study as an "industrialized" form of teaching and learning and stressed the structural incompatibility of that with a locally organized educational system. He warned of the possibility of a process of alienation or isolation that can occur when students are confronted with technical artefacts instead of live human beings.

Other arguments look at specific issues in distance education, such as:

- the target groups for distance education—for example, whether women have perceptibly different approaches to support networks;
- the media that distance education uses;
- the environment both economically and politically in which distance education operates;

- the equal opportunities issues specific to distance education;
- and many of the other numerous facets of this rapidly developing field.

There have also been attempts to develop overarching theories specific to distance education; for example, Holmberg's (1995, p. 47) theory of "guided didactic conversation," which attempted to involve students affectively in study by conversational manners of writing that tried to address individual students and involve their reactions, views and experiences. Another example is Perraton (1987), who maintained that attempts to define a single theory of distance education were naive and that it was necessary to see distance education as a system of three interrelated elements: teaching, administration and assessment. Each element will require a slightly different approach to the development of theory—teaching from existing theory, administration in generalizations drawn from practice and assessment from value judgments about quality.

Perraton may well be right, but I would maintain that teaching is actually a sub-section of student support, which may need an overarching theory of its own.

Theories Underlying Student Support

As student support has developed as study, there have been a number of specific approaches to possible theories. The three models that may have been most important are:

- counseling models—humanistic and behavioral;
- learning style models;
- motivation models.

Counseling Models

There are many different schools of counseling, but it may be helpful to distinguish two very broad categories—humanistic or person-centered (Rogerian) counseling, and behavioral therapy models.

Humanistic Counseling

Humanistic or person-centered counseling revolves around a basic judgment about the "self-directedness" of individuals and how they deal with issues in their lives by being helped to clarify their feelings in such a way as to enable them to make decisions for themselves. It is drawn very much from the works of the American Carl Rogers (hence the alternative name "Rogerian" to describe this school). The central principle of Rogerian counseling is derived from the practices of "active listening" and "unconditional positive regard," and the skills and qualities needed for Rogerian counseling were outlined in Chapter 3. As Rogers (1961) wrote:

> Very early in my work as a therapist I discovered that simply listening to my client very attentively was an important way of being helpful. So when I was in doubt as to what I should do, in some active way I listened. It seemed surprising to me that such a passive kind of inter-action could be so useful.

The theory has been much developed by later writers and practitioners, notably in *The Skilled Helper* (Egan 1975), into a more proactive and initiative-taking mode, moving a little towards the more directive modes of behavioral therapy.

Other schools of humanistic counseling include Fritz Perl's Gestalt therapy, with its emphasis on non-verbal expression and acting out of feelings. Typically, a Gestalt counselor will invite clients to act out a dialogue between them by moving from one chair to another or by using a cushion as an object of address. The philosophy is avowedly existential. Gestalt techniques are essentially psychotherapeutic and have not found many practical expressions in educational contexts as far as I know.

Behavioral Therapies

Behavioral therapies tend to be much more to do with modifying people's behavior and rather less to do with their feelings. The appeal is to people's intellect and less to their emotions.

An example is cognitive behavioral therapy (CBT), which focuses on a person's cognitive processes—thoughts, images, beliefs and attitudes—and how these can be challenged and changed in order to change how that person feels (Rachman 1997). It has had some success in treating depression. Another example is Rational Emotive Therapy (RET), where it is held that "Activating events" in a person's life lead to "Beliefs," both rational and irrational, and these beliefs lead to "Consequences" (the "ABC" approach—Ellis 1962). It is the counselor's task to show clients how this process has worked in their own life and—in effect—argue them into changing those beliefs and hence alter the consequences.

Another example might be Berne's (1964) Transactional Analysis (TA), with its division of the psyche into three states—"person, adult and child"—and its emphasis on the "games" that can be played between the various states in various people.

The reason I have illustrated some of these theories is that any of them may offer insights in particular situations. I can remember one student I had been trying to help but with little success. I had offered him the opportunity to submit an assignment late, to have an extra tutorial from his tutor and to make representations to the exam board on his behalf. Each of these offers was rejected by the student for some excellent reason, and each time I would try something different.

Finally, in an insight from TA, I realized I had perhaps been drawn into a game of "Why don't you . . . ?—Yes, but . . . ," where every suggestion I made—"Why don't you . . . ?"—was met with a perfectly valid, "Yes, but . . ." The "pay-off" for the student was presumably showing how hard he had tried and how useless my attempts to help were.

It even seemed worthwhile naming this particular variant, so I called it "The Success-Resistant Student"—the person for whom success was more threatening than failure, because at least failure didn't involve uncomfortable and difficult changes in his life.

Whether I was right in my diagnosis, I cannot be sure. However, when I gave up on my attempts to help this student I certainly felt a lot better and it seemed to make no difference to him.

Using Counseling Ideas in Student Support

Clearly both humanistic and behavioral stances have their attractions to someone working in student support. The student-centeredness, non-directional and apparently non-expert nature of Rogerian counseling is certainly very attractive to staff talking to students with difficult and inexplicable problems, and "When in doubt, listen," is not bad advice for anyone not sure what to do. Rogerian counseling formed the basis of the skills I suggested as being the most helpful in the "Commending" and "Exploring" activities in student advising in Chapter 3.

But equally, the more directive theories can be attractive, particularly those like CBT or TA that appear to have some logical rationale. After all, in education we are supposedly firmly in the realm of the intellectual, so what better theory than one that appeals to the intelligence of the student, such as CBT? Thus, in practice people working in student support often appear to apply an eclectic mix of theories to their work.

For example, people working with students experiencing severe exam stress may well use a mixture of humanistic and behavioral approaches. They may start by listening to students talk about their experiences and feelings about assessment. They would try to clarify those feelings and establish how they arose, in the hope that students would find talking about them and understanding them a help in itself. But they would probably also work more directively. They might suggest ways of tackling stress physically, such as breathing exercises or meditation or (in a behavioral manner) through exam rehearsal.

Such an eclectic approach still requires a range of personal qualities and skills on the part of the student support worker, as suggested in Chapter 3. Underlying all the skills and qualities are the essential concepts of facilitation and reflection that seem philosophically and practically appropriate to study support in distance education.

Learning Style Models

Learning style models achieved a great deal of popularity a few years ago. The idea was that all students have preferred learning styles that can be identified through various tests and which can then be exploited by their teachers and students themselves in order to learn more effectively. There are more than 20 such learning style inventories, and one of the most popular was the Honey and Mumford Learning Inventory (1986), which claimed to identify "activist," "theorist," "reflector" and "pragmatist" styles by means of a questionnaire.

Learning styles were particularly popular in distance education circles, as it looked as though students could be assessed for their favored learning style at a distance and then be advised to study by that style. It is possible that for some students being told that they possessed a (say) "theorist" style of learning might perhaps have increased their confidence if they had hitherto not seen themselves as a learner at all. However, Price and Richardson (2003), found in a survey that, while the various different inventories were at least consistent, there was no evidence that any teacher had used such styles to teach more effectively, nor had any students learned better through knowing their style. Weimer (2012) went further, quoting Riener and Willingham (2010, p. 35), who stated, "There is no credible evidence that learning styles exist."

Learning Skills Development Models

Linked with the idea of learning styles was the concept of learning skills development. This suggested that the important thing in student support was to first identify areas of weakness in students' educational background and previous learning abilities, offer them remedial support where it seemed appropriate and teach them a set of "distance learning skills," which they could then apply to their studies. This seemed entirely logical, but where remedial teaching was actually assessed, it sometimes didn't seem to work very well— for example, in a follow-up of math remedial support to postgraduates at the London School of Economics, it was found that it gave them little or no help

(*Times Higher Education* 2006). As Anderson (2006) noted, "Remediation may work in the short term but will disable students for higher achievement. The best that remediation can help anyone to become is mediocre."

In addition, attempts to teach learning skills separately from the courses being studied did not appear to be very successful, and it seemed to be difficult to assess how effective it was to insert such materials into the courses themselves. A kind of circular argument appeared to emerge—someone who was a good learner must have good learning skills, but the only way you could tell if someone had good learning skills was that they were a good learner.

Finally, it appeared that students themselves often found ways of studying that would not have been recommended in any model of distance learning skills.

I once interviewed a series of students about how they learned (there is a poor-quality video clip of a short part of the interview on http://tinyurl.com/talk-about-learning). One student in the clip, asked how she used the "learning objectives" in the teaching materials, said she never looked at them and added (paraphrased): "I don't study in ways that are very orthodox. Quite often when I'm working I spread my books out on the kitchen table in front of the television. Then if what's on the television is more interesting than what's in my books I tend to watch it and the other way round if my books are more interesting."

This is not a study method that any distance educator is likely to recommend! Yet this student was very successful, gaining a first class honors degree in record time through her distance study.

Some studies found that learning skills were not as important as other skills—for example, students getting self-efficacy and stress management training got higher retention than students getting learning skills training (Zajacova, Lynch and Espenshade 2005). Gibbs (1981) suggested that there may be no clear, fixed set of learning skills appropriate to all circumstances and all learners, and that the important thing to do is to help learners experiment and develop study methods that work for them. Morgan, Taylor and Gibbs concluded that "Learning skills training that does not consider motivation . . . [and] may result in little skill improvement" (Morgan, Taylor and Gibbs, 1982, p. 107). This latter comment suggests that the key to success in distance education may lie not so much in learning skills as in learning motivation—see Chapter 6.

Theories of Student Retention

Finally there are theories that apply particularly to student retention. The most commonly quoted theory is that of Tinto (1993), quoted in Yorke (1999).

Tinto argued that student dropout is a longitudinal process of interactions between the individual and institutional systems during which the individual's experiences—as measured by their integration with those systems—modify his or her goals and commitments in ways that lead to persistence or dropout. In this model, therefore, the key concept in determining an individual's dropout is their level of "integration" with the institution. For example, he found that those students who were involved in more "socially integrated learning communities" earned more credits and got higher grades than traditional students. In fact, the differences were relatively small—the persistence rates of such students were 77.5%, as against 75% for his control group, although they were more likely to express an intention to continue (88.8% versus 77.9%).

This model has been examined a number of times, most recently by Yorke (1999), who concluded that the theory appeared to provide a better fit with data from part-time students than full-time ones. Thus the theory might be particularly helpful in dealing with online open and distance learning students who are likely to be part-time.

The concept of integration was examined by Kember (1995), who focused on adult learners studying at a distance. He suggested that successful students were those who were able to integrate both socially (that is, with family, employment and so on) and academically (encompassing all contact with the educating institution). Kember's model was subsequently criticized by Woodley, De Lange and Tanewski (2001), who argued that, although the model's recommendations were eminently sensible and fitted with qualitative data, they did not arise directly from the model itself.

Bajtelsmit (1998) also questioned whether Tinto's theoretical model was appropriate for non-traditional students such as part-time distance students. He proposed a model that put more emphasis on the influence of the external environment, particularly the student's family and job, while de-emphasizing the social integration in the institution. Bajtelsmit's model emphasizes the individual's background, distance learning skills and academic support systems as the most important variables.

McGivney (1996) carried out a very substantial survey of literature and findings in U.K. further and higher education. Although hers was a very pragmatic approach that made little reference to theory, it was nevertheless clear from her findings that the areas of pre-course contact and transition to study were critically important in retention. These, of course, are the stages at which it might be expected that integration would take place.

But, given the various criticisms of Tinto's social integration model and the fact that most of these theories may explain student retention but do not seem to give clear practical guidance on enhancing it, my preference is for the practical theory of learning motivation. That concept deserves a chapter to itself—Chapter 6.

Chapter 6

Learning Motivation for Distance Education Student Support

> The best predictor of student retention is motivation. Retention services need to clarify and build on motivation and address motivation-reducing issues. Most students drop out because of reduced motivation.
>
> (Anderson 2006)

Learning motivation is such an important aspect of distance student support that it warrants a whole chapter to itself. When distance students who have dropped out of distance education are asked why, they give a wide range of answers—usually time problems, frequently job and family issues, sometimes illness, bereavement and so on—and undoubtedly many of these reasons must be right. But there are students who have experienced the most severe problems but have kept going, and practically all the same reasons must apply to part-time students, whose dropout rates are far less.

So, like Anderson, I suspect that in the end what drives most students out of distance education is loss of the motivation to learn, whatever the activating event that finally tipped the balance. Students who can maintain that motivation can succeed under the most extraordinary difficulties. Almost anyone who has worked in distance education has stories of students who have overcome the most horrendous personal, family and other problems because they were determined to complete their studies.

Indeed, I would argue that motivation is not only a necessary condition for success but is often also a sufficient one. A learner who is fully motivated will overcome barriers of situation and time, find ways of developing appropriate skills and be able to deal with the stress of study with very little extra external support, and will become that most desirable of distance students—the "independent learner."

I would further argue that distance learners are particularly vulnerable to loss of motivation. Studying usually in isolation from their institution, tutors and other students, with concerns about family and work anxieties, almost always trying to squeeze study time in amongst other demands, and often feeling that they're getting behind, it is no wonder that they may lose the motivation to learn.

So the question of what motivates students to learn is a particularly important one for distance education. But an equally important question is, "Can that motivation to learn be enhanced by the efforts of distance educators—in particular, distance student supporters?" To answer that question, we need to look at the psychology of learning motivation more closely—not *how* students learn (which has too often been the single focus of research), but *why* they learn. This is the subject of this chapter.

Theories of Learning Motivation—I

Psychologists have researched human motivation for many years and the literature is extensive. However, there has been less work on what motivates human beings to study and learn. This is now changing with relatively recent research.

When it comes to theories specifically about learning motivation, there are a quite a number—for example, "Self-Determination Theory," "Achievement Goal Theory," "Self-Efficacy Theory," "Interest Development Model," "Expectancy Value Theory," "Epistemological Identity Theory," "Self–Concordance Model," "Belief in a Just World Theory" and others. Some of these seem to offer useful insights about different aspects of distance learning.

(i) Self-Determination Theory (Vansteenkiste 2004), for example, emphasizes the role of "Autonomous Study Motivation," which might apply to distance learners. Autonomy implies that learners' motivation depends on them having some freedom about their study behavior. This freedom is promoted by choice, participation in the processes of learning and recognition of the learner's feelings, both positive and negative. Autonomous Study Motivation is

contradicted by deadlines, surveillance, guilt-invoking diktats and ignoring the learners' negative emotions.

Clearly there are difficulties here, given the emphasis in much distance learning on rigid progress markers such as fixed assignment submission dates. However, there is some evidence from the U.K. Open University that modules that allow students the most freedom in terms of choice of material to study, options and general participation in the course structure, tend to have the maximum student retention (Crooks 2005).

But, while distance educators often pay lip service to choice and participation, there seems to be little recognition of the learner's feelings—especially negative feelings. There seems to be little appreciation in the literature that distance learners may sometimes experience anxiety, hopelessness, boredom, disappointment and anger, and that strategies may be needed to help learners overcome such feelings. For example, few distance institutions seem to have anything on their websites that admit that learning can be a painful and disappointing process. It is almost as though educators believe that admitting that such feelings can exist will, in itself, cause learners to experience those emotions. It sometimes feels as though much distance learning support material is written with a "perfect student" in mind, one who is already independent, fully up to speed with IT, and ready to explore the use of blogs, wikis, podcasts and so on—and, of course, fully motivated to learn.

(ii) Epistemological Identity Theory. It has been suggested (Mansell, Greene and De Backer 2004) that the most effective model of motivation for learning is the "Epistemological Identity" motivation theory, which is essentially about learners being able to say, "I'm convinced this particular learning is exactly right for me." Thus perhaps one of the most effective ways of ensuring learners' motivation is to make certain that they are on the right course for them in terms of level, content and outcomes. This deduction is certainly congruent with the finding from surveys of withdrawn students in the U.K. Open University, which consistently present "wrong course choice" as the second most important reason for dropping out after "insufficient time." It supports the contention that merely using course descriptions to try to get potential students on the right course may not be nearly enough to ensure their motivation (Simpson 2004a). I will return to this topic in Chapter 9.

(iii) Achievement Goal Theory (Skaalvik 2004) may also have useful findings for distance educators. According to this theory there are three different types of goals:

- *Mastery Goals*—associated with reaching competence;
- *Performance Goals*—associated with demonstrating competence to others;
- *Performance Avoidance Goals*—associated with avoiding looking inadequate.

Research suggests (Skaalvik 2004) that students with Mastery Goals tend to do best. Such goals are promoted by having short-term objectives, "private" assessments (i.e., assessments not seen by other students) and training in planning and self-motivation. Performance and Performance Avoidance Goals are those associated with overt competition, perhaps with other students. They may be less helpful in promoting motivation for some students (although there may be cultural differences here), but the theory as yet does not seem to suggest other ways in which students might be encouraged to change their goal strategies, apart perhaps from the use of formative assessment—see Chapter 4.

(iv) "Self–Perceived Competence Theory" (Pajares 2004) may also have lessons for distance educators. Students were asked how competence might be achieved, whether through effort, ability, luck or unknown causes. Researchers found that roughly 20% of students had illusions of their own incompetence—they felt that success was due to luck and unknown causes and felt generally helpless. Roughly 60% of students had realistic views of their competence and another 20% held illusions that they had high levels of competency. Perhaps helping students with unrealistic views of their competencies to develop a more rational view of themselves would help their motivation. But the theory does not seem to suggest ways in which this might be achieved.

(v) The Self–Concordance Model (Kasser and Ryan 2001) suggests that there are four different kinds of motivation:

- external—driven by outside forces;
- introjected—acting in order to avoid guilt and anxiety;
- identified—based on subscription to the underlying values of the activity;
- intrinsic—driven by curiosity and pleasure.

Findings suggest that external and introjected motivations are associated with lower self–esteem, more drug abuse, more television consumption and acting in a narcissistic and competitive manner. Examples from current TV reality shows may come to mind. Ryan and Deci (2000) suggested that, for learning, it is intrinsic and identified motivations that are the most effective: that, while external and introjected motivation might *start* a student studying—for example to gain a qualification (external motivation) or out of guilt because they feel they ought to be doing something useful with their time (introjected motivation)—it is believing in the value of education (identified motivation) and actually enjoying learning (intrinsic motivation), that will *keep* a student studying. This may well accord with your own experience—that it is students who enjoy what they are learning who are the most motivated.

(vi) Expectancy Value Theory (Wigfield and Eccles 2002) has already been mentioned in connection with assessment in Chapter 4. As noted there, it suggests that a student's learning motivation is equal to their assessment of their chances of succeeding at a task multiplied by the importance of the task to them. If either of those quantities is zero, then their motivation to learn will be zero. So it is important to ensure that, while students can be set challenging learning tasks, they perceive that those tasks are relevant to their final goals and not impossibly difficult for them.

Theories of Learning Motivation—2

However, while these theories often give good explanations of learning motivation and sometimes show causal links between some student characteristics, such as the evidence that students with a high sense of self-efficacy tend to do well in study (Zajacova, Lynch and Espenshade 2005), they do not necessarily explain how that motivation might be actually enhanced, apart perhaps from exhortation and example. Certainly example and exhortation must have some effect—it's just that, as any teacher knows, their effects can be limited. Importantly we need theories of learning motivation that might enable us to find ways of enhancing that motivation. As Karl Marx (1845) once said, "The philosophers have only interpreted the world, in various ways; the point is to change it."

However, there are more recent theories that may suggest ways in which distance educators could enhance students' learning motivation. These are "Self-Affirmation Theory," Keller's "ARCS Theory," "Positive Psychology" and "Theories of Self."

(i) Self-Affirmation Theory

A theory that may have implications for distance student support has no name that I'm aware of yet—I think of it as "self-affirmation theory"—and is due to Cohen et al. (2006). It suggests that students who see themselves as disadvantaged can improve their learning by enhancing their "social identities" through "self-affirmation" exercises—activities that allow them to identify and assert their values. In the United States, a group of disadvantaged Afro-American students undertaking self-affirmation exercises reduced the achievement gap between themselves and a group of European-American students by about 40 percentage points. One of the researchers described the technique as "like flicking a light switch, releasing the motivation and abilities that the students had had all along" (Garcia, in Cohen et al. 2006, p. 1307). I like this description as it suggests that a student supporter's role is not to try to generate a motivation to learn from scratch, but merely to allow the motivation to learn (which all children are born with) to be liberated again.

However, there has been no attempt to apply this theory to distance learning yet as far as I'm aware.

(ii) Keller's ARCS Theory

Keller's ARCS Theory (Keller 1998) is so called because the letters stand for the four critical elements that Keller believes are needed in activities designed to enhance a student's learning motivation. They are:

- *A* = *Attention*—any motivational activity needs to get the learner's attention;
- *R* = *Relevance*—a motivational activity needs to be seen to be immediately relevant to the learner's needs in order to maintain their attention;
- *C* = *Confidence*—an activity needs to engage and enhance their confidence;
- *S* = *Satisfaction*—students need to feel a sense of satisfaction as a result of the activities.

There is some evidence for the efficacy of Keller's theory, particularly in the design of "motivational messages" and course material—see Chapter 12.

(iii) Positive Psychology and the "Strengths Approach"

Positive Psychology is the study of people's happiness and strengths, contrasting with classical psychology's concentration on the causes of people's unhappiness and weaknesses. Positive Psychology takes as its starting point questions, not of what makes people miserable, but of what makes them happy. "Positive Psychology . . . is the scientific study of optimal human functioning [that] aims to discover and promote the factors that allow individuals . . . to thrive. [It is the] psychology of happiness . . . and personal strengths" (Seligman 1998). One of the best short guides to Positive Psychology is Boniwell's (2005) "Positive Psychology in a Nutshell."

The "Strengths Approach" to learner support arises from findings from positive psychology and is partly based on studies by Anderson and Clifton (2001) in the United States. It centers on enhancing learner motivation by emphasizing the importance of recognizing personal strengths as a vital factor in the learning progress. Its fundamental tenets are that:

1. Research suggests that people do best when they focus on their strengths rather than their weaknesses.
2. Focusing on weaknesses and trying to improve performance by trying to overcome them is not a particularly effective way of improving success.
3. Rather, the key to success is to identify and build on existing talents and see how they can be transferred to the skills that are needed for effective study.

The Strengths Approach is also derived from findings in the field of positive psychology about how successful people work:

1. High achievers fully recognize their talents and develop them into strengths.
2. They apply their strengths in roles that suit them best.
3. They invent ways to apply their strengths to their everyday tasks.

It is also derived from findings from research into the value of following strengths, which:

- encourages insight and perspective on your life
- generates optimism and provides a sense of direction
- helps to develop confidence, resilience and a sense of vitality.

(Anderson and Clifton 2001)

Anderson and Clifton use the strengths approach in face-to-face groups, using group discussion techniques and worksheets to help students identify and explore their strengths, and then apply them to their situation.

Implications of the Strengths Approach for Learner Support in Distance Learning

The Strengths Approach may suggest ways in which students' learning motivation may be enhanced as an alternative to exhortation and example, or putting an emphasis on the development of learning skills. The approach suggests that learners should be encouraged to identify their strengths and should apply them to their learning. However, there are a number of difficulties in identifying a learner's strengths, such as:

1. They may not be aware of their particular strengths. For example, a woman with few formal qualifications at home looking after children may well have developed high levels of stress and time management skills, but may be unaware of them, or of how important such skills are to successful learning and how they might be transferred to the study environment.
2. They may see strengths as weaknesses. For example, a person who finds that they frequently need to ask for help may see that as being dependent and weak, when in fact such a talent can be very helpful in learning.
3. They may have been told by authority figures that a particular strength is a weakness, or at least not a strength. For example, a person who is good at networking may have been told as a child to stop chatting in class and not realize that collaboration with others can be a very useful talent for study.

Anderson and Clifton identify a list of about 30 strengths, but not all of these are necessarily relevant to learning, and in any case what can be explored in a face-to-face course over several weeks is not going to be possible in the very limited contact available in distance education.

Boniwell (2003) suggests that the key to a combined Positive Psychology and practical Strengths Approach is via an initial contact with a new learner, emphasizing the positive during that contact. According to her, an adviser should adopt a nine-point approach:

1. Emphasize the positive during initial contact.
2. Focus on existing assets and competencies.
3. Draw out past successes and high point moments.
4. Encourage "positive affect" (hope and elevated thoughts).
5. Identify underlying values, goals and motivation.
6. Encourage narration (life story, putting life in perspective, making sense of it).
7. Identify resources, protective factors and potentials of learners.
8. Validate effort rather than achievement.
9. ONLY THEN, if possible, talk about uncertainties, fears and lack of skills.

Boniwell suggests as an example that a practical way of using this approach might be for an adviser to ask a student, "Would you be willing to tell me a little about yourself? Tell me a bit about your life history. I'm particularly interested in things that you've done that you thought were successful—things that you felt you did well." Once someone has opened up on this topic a little, the adviser will hopefully be able to identify a student's strengths (perhaps even those they weren't aware they had) that relate to learning.

Putting the Strengths Approach into Practice

As yet, there is limited evidence for a strengths approach in distance education. A pilot project, the Proactive Student Support (PaSS) project, using a Strengths Approach to learner support, was conducted from 2002 in the UKOU and reported in Open Learning (Simpson 2004a: 2). The project consisted of a short (less than 10 minutes) proactive telephone contact, using a Strengths Approach, to an experimental group of new students before the start of their first module. The report noted that this contact increased retention at the end of the course by an average of nearly 4% over a balanced control group (a group with the same "predicted probability of success" (see Chapter 7) as the experimental group).

The experiment was repeated in the years 2003, 2004 and 2005 and the overall results are shown in Table 6.1.

Table 6.1 Results of the U.K. Open University Proactive Student Support (PaSS) Project

Year	Total students in trial	Increase in retention rates—experimental group over control group (% points)
2002	2,866	3.9%
2003	1,363	5.1%
2004	987	4.3%
2005	10,130	7.6%

The 2005 result is included here for completeness, but the trial was a little different from the others in that it was the result of an attempt to mainstream the project across the university—hence the much larger student numbers involved. However, the result may be less reliable, as the control group in this trial was not balanced in the same way as previous trials. They were simply the students who could not be contacted after two attempts. It may well be that these "elusive" students are already more likely to drop out than contactable students.

Nevertheless, the results are statistically significant to considerably less than 1%, which suggests that the effect of the contact is a very real one and that it produces at least a 5% improvement in retention. However, we must be cautious in ascribing these results solely to the Strengths Approach. The project used a wide range of advisers to make the contact and they were briefed to use a simple Strengths Approach using the suggestions from Boniwell noted above. But it was not possible to monitor their activities in sufficient detail to be sure that they were using the approach exactly as briefed. And it is perfectly possible that any contact of a reasonably friendly nature would have had a similar effect.

Thus, although we can be sure that the proactive contact increased retention by approximately 5% on average, we cannot yet ascribe the increase with certainty to the use of the Strengths Approach. Perhaps, for example, the main effect of the Strengths Approach was to increase the advisers' confidence through having a theoretical framework in which to place their perception of proactive contact. Further work is needed to be sure that it is the Strengths Approach that is making the difference to learners.

(iv) Self Theory

There remains another theory of motivation that may be important not just to learners but to learner support staff as well. This is the "Self Theory" due to Carole Dweck (1999), which may be illustrated by asking you, the reader of this book, to respond to two statements:

Q1. *You have a certain amount of intelligence and can't do much to change it.*
Answer Yes (Agree) or No (Disagree).

Q2. *Success is made up of X% intelligence and Y% effort.*
Give values for X and Y.

The answers to these questions can illustrate the reader's "Theory of Intelligence":

(i) If you said Yes to question 1 and your value of X was greater than your value for Y (i.e., you think that on balance your intelligence is more important for success than effort), then you are an "entity" theorist. "Entity" theorists believe that their intelligence is largely fixed and cannot be changed by effort.

(ii) If you said No to question 1 and your value of X was less than your value for Y, then you are an "incremental" theorist. "Incremental" theorists believe that their intelligence is malleable and can be increased by effort.

This, of course, is a huge oversimplification of a highly developed theory. In particular, it leaves the terms "intelligence" and "success" undefined. In the former instance, Dweck appears to be using the word "intelligence" very much in lay terms as a person's perception of their innate ability, rather than in any technical or psychological definition. Success seems to be similarly defined in terms of a person's realization of their potential rather than in terms of external achievement.

But, whatever the definitions involved, the theory may have implications for both students and academic and support staff in distance higher education. It suggests that both students and staff may tend to fall into entity and incrementalist groups, with implications for both the way students study and the way staff support students.

(i) For distance students:
Entity theorists—students with an "entity" theory may have high self–esteem and expect easy achievement (they may feel that they have an "entitlement" to success). They may be less likely to undertake preparation (they may behave as "dreamers"—that things will come out right by luck), but when they run into difficulties they may feel they have reached the limits of their abilities and may give up more easily.

Incremental theorists—students with an "incremental" theory may have a lower self–esteem, but may be more resilient and persevering. When they run into difficulties, they will see them as reasons to try harder. They may still fail in the end but their overall chances of success will be higher because they have kept trying. There is indeed general agreement amongst psychologists that, as Hoppe and Stojanovic (2008, p. 62) remark, "People often overestimate the important of intellectual ability. Practice and perseverance contribute more to accomplishment than being smart."

(ii) For distance staff:

There seem to me to be three basic attitudes that staff in educational institutions can display to students. The first two are

"Darwinistas"—for Darwinistas, education is about the survival of the fittest. They believe that students drop out because they're simply not intelligent enough, unmotivated or just plain lazy, and so it's the role of staff to weed out the students unfit to graduate.

"Fatalistas"—Fatalistas believe that students are doomed to pass or fail, and while it's their duty to provide the best teaching they can, it's up to students to make the best use of that provision. If students lose motivation to study, then Fatalistas will probably believe that there is little they can do about it.

It seems to me that both these categories of staff have an entity theory of intelligence and tend to believe in an educational bimodality—that there are two kinds of students: those who will pass with good teaching and those who are doomed to fail, whatever you do. But, as the Cambridge psychologist Felicity Huppert (2004) says, there is "no . . . evidence of bimodality" and people's abilities and personalities do not fall into neatly defined groups; we are all—students, educators, readers of this book—on continuous spectra of various characteristics.

I have asked the "Dweck questions" of various groups of distance educators in institutions where I've worked, and worked out an "entity theorist score" based on their answers—the higher the score, the higher the entity theory belief—see Table 6.2.

You can see that distance educators from the Korean National Open University tend to be entity theorists—possibly as a consequence of the strong Confucian beliefs in that society—and that university staff working in the U.K. widening participation in higher education area and staff at the University of South Africa are the most incrementalist. (To calculate your own score: if you answered "Yes" to question 1, count 100; if you answered "No," count 0 and then add your value for X and divide the result by 2.)

Staff with an incremental theory are more likely to believe that students failing through lack of motivation can be helped through increased support.

Table 6.2 Distance education staff "entity theorist scores"

Distance educators from:	"Entity theorist" score
Korean National Open University	131
UniTech—Papua New Guinea	84
U.K. Open University part-time tutors	70
Leicester postgraduate programme staff	67
U.K. Open University full-time advisers	60
University of London international programme staff	59
U.K. widening participation in higher education staff	49
University of South Africa tutors	42

In contrast to Darwinistas and Fatalistas, I like to think of them as the third kind of staff—"Retentioneers." Retentioneers are more likely to feel that the difficulties that students can face in motivation may stem from (say) their previous educational experience and not be an inherent and unchangeable part of their personality.

Anderson (2006) points out that institutions with high prestige often have Darwinista or Fatalista tendencies (Anderson used the term "survivalist" to describe both characteristics) because they can afford to do so. There can therefore be a tendency amongst staff in other institutions to be drawn into such attitudes as they are identified with institutions having a higher status. Thus one of the most difficult problems in applying a Strengths Approach to learner support is the possibly ambivalent attitudes of support staff. Or, as Johnston and Simpson (2006, p. 32) put it, "The biggest barrier to student retention is the institution itself."

Dweck and colleagues used her approach in an experiment in a New York school. She took two groups of disadvantaged adolescent students, and taught one about how the brain works and taught the other that their intelligence was malleable. The second group showed significant increases in grades and study motivation over the first group, maintained for at least two years (Dweck, Blackwell and Trzesiewski 2007).

What was important about this project was that the intervention was very short and yet the effects were marked and long-lasting. As Dweck noted (quoted in New Scientist 13 Jan. 2007, 17), "the effects are far beyond what you might expect from the simplicity of the interventions."

Proactive Motivational Support

It may be that the best way forward for distance educators to help enhance the motivation of their students will be to use an eclectic mix of these two theories, concentrating on using a mix of techniques suggested by the theories according to the students in front of them.

But there is one further element that must be taken into account—the need, as will be suggested in Chapter 7, for contact to be proactive; that is, the institution needs to take the initiative to contact its students rather than waiting for students to contact it. As Anderson (2006) says, "Student self-referral does not work as a mode of promoting persistence. Students who need services the most refer themselves the least. Effective retention services take the initiative in outreach and timely interventions with those students."

If we take these elements all together—Dweck's Self Theory, Boniwell's Strengths Approach and Anderson's taking the initiative to contact students—we might have a theory of distance learner support that I have tentatively called "Proactive Motivational Support" that could be developed and tested against more conventional student support techniques. I do not claim that this theory is particularly original—for example, it strongly resembles the concept of "Appreciative Advising" (Bloom and Martin 2002) in which student advisers focus on using positive open-ended questions to elicit students' strengths and passions to help them develop their goals.

There are also a number of other theories, some aimed at the online experience, and sometimes "acronym–based," such as Bonk's (2012) "TEC–VARIETY" theory, standing for "Tone, Encouragement, Curiosity, Variety, Autonomy, Relevance, Interactivity, Engagement, Tension, and Yielding Products." But it is not often clear how evidence-based such theories are and how far they are in fact about teaching, rather than learning.

Proactive Motivational Support has the following characteristics:

- *individual*—it would try to be focused on individual student needs rather than a top-down, one-size-fits-all approach;
- *proactive*—it would take the initiative to contact students;
- *interactive*—it would allow learners to interact with their support rather than be a take-it-or-leave-it approach;
- *motivational*—it would be informed by current psychological theories of learning motivation and use both Self Theory and the Strengths Approach.

Evaluating Proactive Motivational Support

I have been conducting a very small-scale experiment with students that I teach on an introductory U.K. Open University math course. The normal strategy for supporting students on this course is to teach them through relatively lengthy, and therefore necessarily infrequent, telephone tutorials. I have largely discounted this approach and used much more frequent and much shorter proactive motivational contacts using phone, email and letters, after starting by attempting to persuade students that they were all "hard-wired" for math and that (after Dweck) their mathematical intelligence was malleable and could be developed by effort. An example of the "motivational email" I used is shown below (see Chapter 8 for a link to further examples of motivational emails).

Example of a "motivational email" based on the Dweck theory:

Subject: Study Tip 1—Are You "Fixed" or "Malleable"?

Dear

As I promised I'm sending you my first study tip. I hope you find it useful!

Are you Fixed or Malleable?

Recent findings in psychology suggest that what we think about our own intelligence or IQ is the most important factor in how successful we are when we try to learn something. Psychologists say that people fall into two groups—

- "Fixed" intelligence people—these people believe that their intelligence is fixed at birth and can't be changed by external factors or their own efforts.
- "Malleable" intelligence people—these people believe that their intelligence is not fixed and that it can be changed through effort.

These beliefs affect how people learn, particularly when they run into difficulties or fail an exam. People who believe that their intelligence is fixed may work hard. But when they run into difficulties or failure, they tend to believe that they've reached the limit of their intelligence and give up.

People who believe that their intelligence is malleable will see difficulties as a sign that they need to try harder. This is because they believe that effort will overcome such difficulties in the end. Failure is feedback that says that they need to make more effort.

Your IQ is not Fixed!

We now know (despite what psychologists used to believe) that intelligence is not a fixed quantity for life. We know that it can be developed by a good environment and by personal endeavor. In other words, the malleable people are right.

We also know that this may apply particularly to learning math. We are all hard–wired to be able to do math at birth. Unfortunately, sometimes we're put off math at school or elsewhere and come to believe that we can't do it. That's not true—with enough effort math can be learned, even if you've been put off it previously.

Malleability is the Key

Malleable people don't see something hard to understand or a poor grade as a comment on their basic intelligence. They just see it as a sign that they can ask for help and try again.

So remember—your intelligence is malleable! With effort and support you will succeed on this course.

Good luck!
Ormond

Table 6.3 Results of using Proactive Motivational Support on an introductory U.K. Open University math course

	My tutorial group *% pass* *(number of students)*	*Whole course* *% pass* *(number of students)*	*Difference in retention* *% points* *(my group—whole course)*
2006	93.3% (15)	71.1% (398)	+22.2%
2007	92.3% (13)	62.3% (403)	+30.0%
2008	73.3% (15)	58.4% (483)	+14.9%
2009	62.5% (16)	65.8% (418)	−3.3%
2010	76.5% (17)	61.9% (381)	+14.6%
Av.	**79.6% (76)**	**64.4% (2,083)**	**+18.9%**

In follow-up proactive motivational emails, I tried to persuade them that the more effort they had to make (including making mistakes), the better their long-term mathematical development would be. To an extent that surprised me, I found that I was not attempting to teach them, although of course I answered their questions where they arose.

Then, after starting with Dweck's approach, I focused all the time on their motivation using the Strengths Approach advocated by Boniwell. The results are shown in Table 6.3.

It can be seen that, in this study, the Proactive Motivational Support approach showed an increase of an average of more than 15 percentage points over the conventional approach. The group sizes here are too small to draw definitive conclusions from this study. Neither was it possible to balance the groups for predicted probability of success. However, the results do suggest that there may at the very least be a case for focusing proactively on distance students' learning motivation, whatever the theory is called.

Chapter 7

Designing Student Support for Success

We must reach the quiet student.

(Bogdan Eaton and Bean 1995)

So far in this book I've looked at the theory and various characteristics of student support. But as I argued at the outset of the book the aim of student support is to enhance student success, to increase student retention and reduce student dropout. In this chapter I will look at what works in student retention and—as importantly—what doesn't work. Before starting on that, there are several questions to ask about student retention and dropout:

- When do students drop out?
- Why do they dropout?
- Who drops out?
- What does research tell us?
- Student support for success—what might work best?
- What media to use for support?
- What's the evidence for proactive contact?

When Do Distance Students Drop Out?

The question of when students drop out of distance education may seem not the most important issue in student retention. However, if we want to change retention for the better through interventions, it turns out that this is actually a vital question to answer.

We already know a little about when students drop out from distance education from the "rivergrams" in Chapter 4. Those rivergrams suggest that at least in the U.K. Open University new student dropout is very heavily loaded into the first few weeks of a course module. Some 40% of new students leave in the first two months of the course. This may in part be due to financial organization (students who leave before two months has passed receive a larger refund of tuition fees than after that time), but it accords with experience in other distance institutions. Powell (2009), in his study of four institutions, noted that "most dropout at a program level occurs very early."

Of course, even after the initial dropout, students continue to pour out of every institution, leaving, as we saw, graduation rates of the order of only 10% at the end of a degree program. Figure 7.1 shows the rate of active withdrawals (students who tell the university that they are withdrawing, rather than "passive withdrawals," who simply stop studying and do not tell the university) of new students in the U.K. Open University. Recruitment to course modules starts in the March preceding module start in February the following year, with the module exams starting in the following October. Clearly dropout is very

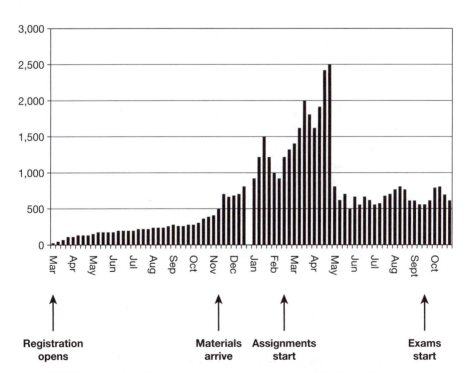

Figure 7.1 Weekly active withdrawals of new students in the U.K. Open University

front-loaded, with a peak of withdrawals in the April after module start, which can clearly be seen, as can the smaller peaks over the summer and before the exams in October.

I identified at least eight points at which students could leave the U.K. Open University during their first course module. These eight were:

1. new students who register but withdraw before the course module start—it can be seen from Figure 7.1 that this is a considerable number from March in the year before module start. It represents a substantial financial loss to the institution because of recruitment costs—see Chapter 11 on costs and benefits;
2. new students who register, fail to submit an assignment but do not formally withdraw (passive withdrawers);
3. new students who are withdrawn by the University for administrative reasons (failing to pay tuition fees, failing to attend a mandatory residential school requirement and so on);
4. new students who withdraw before the final exam because they think they will not pass it;
5. new students who fail the exam and do not continue;
6. new students who are offered a resit exam at the end of their module but do not accept the offer;
7. new students who fail the resit exam and do not continue;
8. new students who pass the course but do not continue onto the next module.

A "rivergram" whose width at any point indicates the number of students at that point, and which shows these various entrances and exits for continuing U.K. Open University students, becomes very complicated but will give some idea of the proportions involved (see Figure 7.2).

The various routes by which students enter and leave the module are:

1. students entering from their previous module
2. students retaking the course
3. previously inactive students re-entering
4. students transferring credit
5. students resitting the exam
6. students completing the module
7. students failing the exam but accepting resit offer
8. students failing the exam and not accepting resit
9. students dropping out but returning to a later presentation
10. all students dropping out $(11 + 12 - 9)$

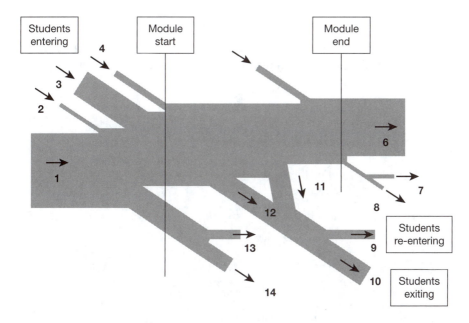

Figure 7.2 A "rivergram" for the U.K. Open University continuing students showing the various routes by which they enter and leave a module

11. active withdrawals
12. passive withdrawals
13. students declining the offer of a module but returning to a later module
14. students declining the module and not returning later

The students succeeding at the end of the module as a proportion of the number entering is around 70%. The complexity of the various routes that students take through their studies and the number of ways they can drop out is very apparent. The difficulty of tracking them and taking appropriate action is also apparent. Other institutions will have different "escape" points and the proportion of students who leave at those points will also be different. All these "escapees" fall outside retention activities, so as well as support for retention there also needs to be "retrieval" strategies—see Chapter 10.

Why Do Distance Students Drop Out?

There are three possible perspectives on the reasons students drop out from distance education: what students say, what staff in institutions believe, and the reality.

What Students Say about Why They Drop Out

Many institutions attempt to survey their dropped out students using various questionnaires. An excerpt from one such questionnaire—from the U.K. Open University—is below:

Student Withdrawal Questionnaire

Reasons for withdrawal—please put a cross in the box alongside each reason that applies to you:

- ☐ The course was not what I expected
- ☐ I found the course too difficult
- ☐ I fell behind with my coursework
- ☐ I did not find the course material interesting
- ☐ The pace/workload was too great
- ☐ Not happy with my course tutor

There are a number of difficulties with such questionnaires. Woodley and Parlett (1983) note that difficulties arise from:

1. *Non-respondents*. The proportion of non-respondents to withdrawal surveys can be quite high, typically 75% or more. Some students who have withdrawn may feel a sense of failure and not wish to have any more contact with the institution. The length of the questionnaire (there were more than 60 questions in the one shown in part above) may intimidate others. It is difficult to guess how this might skew the results.
2. *Rationalizations*. Inevitably there is a chance that the reasons that students give for withdrawing from the course are post-event rationalizations. This doesn't suggest an intention to deceive merely that (for example) it is easier to give a (genuine) illness as the precipitating factor rather than (say) underlying ability to cope with the course concepts.
3. *Underlying causes*. Even when the reasons given are true, they don't necessarily reveal underlying causes. For example, the most common reason given for withdrawal in distance learning schemes is insufficient time. But lack of time is sometimes about choice of priorities, so in a particular case it may be that loss of motivation may have led to a subsequent reordering of priorities and consequent downgrading of study.

4. *Questionnaire design.* The way a questionnaire is designed can also affect responses by (for example) offering a limited range of reasons in the form of boxes to tick. But questionnaires that are more complex—allowing more than one reason to be ticked, for example—become increasingly difficult to interpret.

5. *Combinations of factors.* The decision to drop out may be due to a combination of factors. Students might say, for example, that work pressures made them drop out, when in fact had the course interested them more, or had they been more resilient, they might have continued.

The responses to the UKOU Student Withdrawal Questionnaire illustrate some of the difficulties inherent in using questionnaires.

1. A total of 77% of students are "very or fairly satisfied" with the services and course components—but it is not clear whether this is a high or low figure.

2 Students are least satisfied with:

   (a) the amount of study time required (23% said that they were "fairly or very dissatisfied')
   (b) the guidance received (22%)
   (c) tutorials (20%)

   but it is not clear what the specific reasons for these dissatisfactions are or how they relate to the decision to withdraw.

3. The most commonly cited reasons for withdrawal are:

   (a) fell behind with coursework (41%)
   (b) increased pressures at work (29%)
   (c) general work/home pressures (26%)
   (d) increased pressures at home (26%)
   (e) personal illness or disability (23%)

   This clearly indicates that lack of time is a very potent cause of dropout, but (as suggested above) does not necessarily allow clear conclusions to be drawn. For example, it may be that courses are overloaded, or students are not being given accurate estimates of the study time needed, or that they do not themselves have prioritization skills.

Can useful clarification be derived from the comments that students make on the questionnaire form, where allowed to do so? This is a selection of comments taken at random from the "comment" section on the questionnaire above.

"The reason I withdrew from the course was personal/marital breakdown which has left me emotionally drained and unable to concentrate. This situation is on-going."

"I did not take the decision to withdraw lightly—I hate to give up. I was in no way dissatisfied with the course—once the books, etc. arrived I realized I had seriously underestimated the amount of reading required."

"I found the form of study too stop and start. If I had a problem I had to stop, try and contact someone and wait for a reply. By this time all impetus had gone. It even took me 4 days to speak to an advisor when I decided to withdraw."

"My long-term relationship broke down."

"The pace of the course was overwhelming. There was so much new grammar included in every session that did not allow for consolidation of previous sessions. I was devoting at least 20 hours a week and still not managing to learn everything."

"The work content was fine but I don't have easy acsses to a computer and I don't have enough essay exspereance my spelling is terrible even if I use a dictonary I still have mots of mistakes which also adds more time to the task. Spelling and punctuation is my downfall." *(transcribed literally—possibly a case of undiagnosed dyslexia)*

"I had to spend too much time on study; the assignments also needed a lot of time to complete. With the course being very intense I was suffering with personal difficulties and I was just not enjoying it."

"I must admit that I did choose my course in a hurry, but chose it on the basis that it was a subject that I had a long term interest in, so I was extremely disappointed to find that I was not stimulated by the course material."

"I completely underestimated the amount of study time required for a language course. I also underestimated my ability to concentrate and study when I had finished a day's work. I thought I would be able to fit study time in after work or maybe during the day when I had a free hour, but the reality of doing this did not work out and I felt myself becoming frustrated and isolated at my inability to study and concentrate. I am keen to try again but I need to find a more effective way of arranging my study time."

"A personal domestic problem arose at almost the time I commenced studying. Although I completed the first month and got a good grade for my assignment, the increased stress destroyed my concentration and I was unable to catch up. My situation has eased now, but I do not feel sufficiently motivated to try to catch up with this course."

". . . also another irksome point is the continual misprints. The first question on the first assignment had a mistake in it, not conducive to a good start. For students who are not capable of spotting mistakes it is devastating."

"My job requires me to learn 2 new software programs and I just couldn't devote enough time to my study. When I did sit down and study my course materials, I couldn't get my head around the programing as it is very different from the other programs I am studying."

"I didn't realize how much time the course would take up. I didn't have time to watch all the videos well as study the books. I found the material interesting but after having my blood pressure diagnosed as high due to stress I decided something had to give. I was constantly worrying that I wasn't studying when doing other things and vice versa. Maybe in the future I will be able to study but at the moment I need to slow down and do a lot less."

I've quoted from these questionnaires at length not only to illustrate the importance and interest of such material in retention studies, but also the difficulty of making sense of it in large quantities.

Devices that allow for more organized responses such as interviews and focus groups, can give a better insight into reasons for withdrawal (although it appears that in distance learning systems it is particularly difficult to assemble focus groups of dropped out students perhaps for the same reasons as the low response to questionnaires). Such data is still obviously difficult to interpret.

These inherent difficulties in withdrawal questionnaires are important. If (as currently) nearly two-thirds of students give running out of time due to work and domestic issues as reasons for withdrawal, then the inference can be (and is) drawn that there is little that institutions can do about withdrawal. This may be a mistake. Morgan and Tam (1999) interviewed a large number of students in depth and looked at the barriers to progress that might lie behind their first response. For example, the answer "not relevant to my work" appeared to have behind it issues to do with changes in personal situation, lack of study skills and communication problems with the institution for the student concerned.

Morgan and Tam then classified the barriers into four types:

- Situational—e.g. poor family support
- Dispositional—e.g. personal study problems
- Institutional—e.g. late arrival of materials
- Epistemological—e.g. difficult course content

They noted that even if students' responses were taken at face value, all students reported at least one barrier that institutions could remove. Whether students would have continued if their one particular barrier had been removed was not clear, but it is obviously wrong to assume that all dropout is beyond the reach of institutional action.

If, as Anderson suggests (2006), students drop out because they lose the will to go on, and if that is sometimes because of events beyond our control, then rather than focus on the many instigators of that loss of will, perhaps we need to try to enhance students' learning motivation in order to strengthen their ability to persist and to be in the face of such events.

Who Drops Out?

It is clearly in both a student's and an institution's interests to have as clear knowledge as possible of the student's background and how that affects his or her chances of success in a distance education setting. In an admission system determined by entry qualifications, the more accurate the forecast of students' potential, the fewer the number of students selected who will go on to eventually drop out—the "false positives". Such false positives represent a waste of resource for both the institution and the students themselves. But equally important for social justice and the long-term value to a country, the more accurate the forecast, the fewer the potential students excluded who could have succeeded had they been admitted—the "false negatives". For example, in a U.K. study about 5% of students given the U.S. SAT (Scholastic Assessment Test) scored high enough for entry into a top U.S. university. Yet almost all failed to get a U.K. "A level" qualification good enough for entry to any leading U.K. university (*Times Higher Education*, 5 November 2004, 2).

In a distance open entry system the considerations may be a little different. If there are no entry qualifications then students are, in a sense, studying at their own risk and they will pay the price (in terms of their own tuition fees, time expenditure and the other possible negative effects outlined in

Chapter 1) if they fail. However, the institution itself should be interested in being able to predict its new students' chances of success. If it is possible to identify students with a low chance of success, then it might be possible to focus student support on such students and increase overall retention rates as a result.

Predicting Student Success

There have been a number of attempts at predicting which students will succeed, both in conventional and distance education. Some have been very simple, such as the research by Wright and Tanner (2002), who gave 393 new medical students a simple administrative task of providing a passport photograph. They found that of the 93% of students who complied, 8% went on to fail their first year exams. Of the 7% who did not provide the photograph 48% went on to fail. Such a finding shows the difficulty of using socio-psychological tests of various kinds to predict dropout, such as Shin's (2003), who used a questionnaire to measure a student's "Transactional Presence"—the psychological distance between a student, the institution, tutors and other students. The problem with such studies is that students who are most likely to drop out are those most likely not to complete the questionnaires.

But in any case the accuracy of questionnaires in predicting success may not be that great. DeTure (2004) found that scores on cognitive style and self-efficacy were poor predictors of student success in online distance education and Bernard et al. (2004) found that while it was possible to develop questionnaires to forecast student success, the student's previous course grade was usually a better predictor than any questionnaire.

It is possible that tutors may be better at predicting vulnerable students. Thorpe (1988), asked U.K. Open University tutors (adjunct faculty) to identify students they thought were "at risk" of failure on initial entry courses. Tutors were then funded to offer extra support to such students, generally in the form of one or two hours' extra tuition. The identification of such students was left to tutors largely on the basis of their experience, although it subsequently became clear that the main criterion they were using was students' previous educational qualifications (peqs). In fact predictions based on peqs turned out to be reasonably accurate, and interventions based on those predictions had a marked effect on student success. There were clear differences between students who had received extra support and those who had not—see Figure 7.3 (the range of previous educational qualifications in the graph is from none, through increasing U.K. school level qualifications to previous degree).

The results show not only a clear link between previous educational qualifications and subsequent success, but that also early support interventions could have significant effects on student success.

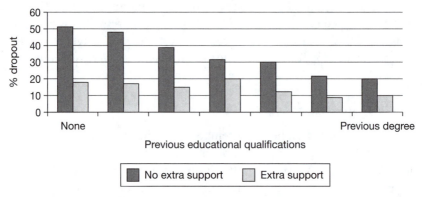

Figure 7.3 Dropout rates for new U.K. Open University students receiving extra early support compared with students receiving none

It can be seen that the extra support increased success, even including well-qualified students. However, overall the retention increase was only of the order of 3%. This was probably due to at least two factors (there may well have been others):

1.　Some 30% of tutors failed to take part in the scheme (suggesting possible problems with tutor briefing, supervision and attitudes).
2.　The identification and extra support could only take place after allocation of students to tutors—making remedial interventions probably too late in the module to be very effective.

Typically for a retention initiative, the project faded out after a few years (see Chapter 15) and is largely unremembered in the institution.

However, it is clear that there are many more factors in student success than just their previous educational qualifications and that statistical methods may be more useful.

Indeed statistical methods of predicting student success have been in use for a number of years in conventional higher education. The Noel-Levitz Corporation in the United States (www.noel-levitz.com) offers a service that will identify new students' chance of withdrawal based on a logistic regression analysis of previous students' records. Such an analysis uses previous students' known entry characteristics (such as sex, previous educational qualifications and age) to relate to their subsequent success. The analysis produces an algorithm weighted for different factors that can be applied to new students entering the institution to predict their chances of success in turn, assuming that the dependency of success on the various factors does not change substantially from year to year.

In the U.K. Open University a statistical analysis was undertaken (Woodman, 1999) and it appeared that the most important factors linked to success for new students were (in order):

1. their chosen course level; students entering on level 1 (first year of an undergraduate degree equivalent) tended to have a higher success than students entering on level 2 (second year of degree equivalent) courses
2. the credit rating of a course; students entering on 15 credit point courses (equivalent to one-eighth of full-time study) were more successful than students entering on 30 or 60 point courses
3. a student's previous educational qualifications
4. their course choice (arts students were more likely to be successful than maths and science students, for example)
5. their socio, economic status (the higher the status the more successful)
6. sex (women were more successful than men)
7. age (middle-aged students were more likely to be successful than younger or older students).

Ethnicity was not significant, possibly because the numbers declaring it were too small for analysis.

These factors were then used to predict the probabilities of success of the succeeding year's cohort of new students. These predicted probabilities of success (pps) varied, for example, from around 83% typically for a middle-aged woman at home wanting to study arts modules, to 9% for a young unemployed man wanting to study math. The overall distribution is shown in Figure 7.4 for the 30,000 new students entering the U.K. Open University in 2002.

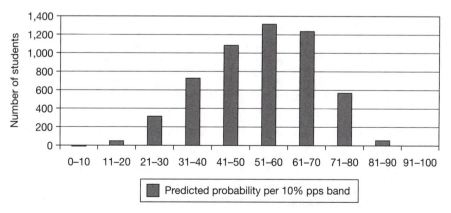

Figure 7.4 The number of students in each 10% "predicted probability of success" band

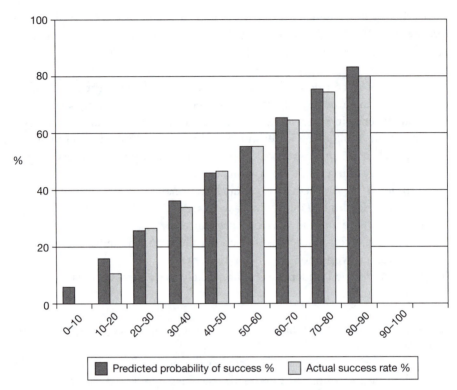

Figure 7.5 Comparison of predicted pass rates and actual pass rates in 10% bands

These predictions were surprisingly accurate given the relative sparseness of the data. Figure 7.5 shows the agreement between predictions and actual outcomes to be quite good except at low probabilities where the student numbers are fairly low and the predicted success rate was more than the actual.

I have focused on this predictive model partly because it is an illustration of the relatively new field of "learning analytics"—the collection of data about learners, partly in order to identify the conditions that might cause them to disengage before they actually do (Siemens 2012). But the importance of predictors is that it allows institutions to focus their support efforts on the most vulnerable, as we shall see later in this chapter. This is particularly important as these are the "quiet students" who do not ask for help, the students who, as Anderson (2006) says, "need help the most but seek it the least" and so often become victims of the "inverse care law" (Tudor Hart 1971), that the availability of good care in a population tends to be inversely proportional to the need of that population.

Student Support and Student Dropout—What Does Research Tell Us?

Before asking what can be done to reduce distance student dropout, we should ask what has been discovered in the distance learning research literature about student success and retention. I would suggest that there are three particular issues:

1. *Little retention-focused research.* There seems to be surprisingly little retention-focused research literature in international distance education. There is certainly a great deal of reported research, but a large amount—I estimate more than 70% of publications—is to do with e-learning developments of one kind or another. Furthermore, much of the research appears to be aimed at "enhancing the students' learning experience," a phrase which in various forms occurs in many places. There is nothing wrong with that, *except that enhancing the learning experience is not the same as increasing student retention and success.* Given that student dropout is so heavily front-loaded in distance education, much of the effort given to that enhancement is focused on the remaining students who are often progressing satisfactorily. It is rather like going to a battlefield site and offering the survivors manicures. After all, the best learning experience you can give a student is *to pass their course.*

2. *Much research is of limited value.* Distance education has been a fertile field for research publications for many years. However, it has been criticized for almost as long, starting with Moore (1985, p. 46) who wrote that there was then "a massive volume of amateur, unsystematic, and badly designed research producing information of very little value." These criticisms have continued, most notably by Perraton (2000) and Zawacki-Richter, Bäcker and Vogt (2009), who maintain that despite the huge growth in the literature not much has changed, and that many important areas are badly neglected. The otherwise excellent Zawacki-Richter paper also illustrates my first point above by only mentioning student retention once, and then only as a subcategory of quality assurance.

   To irretrievably mix metaphors, looking for articles on student retention amongst the many on topics such as "tuition quality," "learning skills media," "online communities" and other worthwhile but essentially contributory topics, feels rather like "attending a soccer training session where the emphasis is on ball-control skills or ball-turf interactions, but which fails to note that the whole point is to score goals" (Simpson, 2003).

3. *Evidence for the effectiveness of e-learning.* Finally, despite all the effort and resource that has gone into the many modes of e-learning, blended learning and mobile learning, there is not much evidence that they have had much effect on student success and retention—see Chapter 8.

Student Support and Student Dropout—What Might Work

If it is the case that there is little good research on retention around, what does that which is available tell us about what works?

There are two apparently conflicting suggestions: Johnston (1998) says that "Trying everything that works doesn't work," while Hattie (2010) says that "Almost everything works." I believe that these two contradictory propositions are actually saying much the same thing—that there are many things that can increase student success in all kinds of learning, but that in trying to do everything there is no way of prioritizing activities and finding what works most cost-effectively in a situation where funding is always limited. The result is that many institutions set up retention projects with many recommendations, but with no central focus. The result is, as Tinto (2008) points out, that they tend to fade out after a few years. In student support for retention and success "the main thing," as the businessman Stephen Covey says, "is to keep the main thing, the main thing."

What, then, is the main thing for support for student success? As I suggested in Chapter 6, I believe that it is helping students to develop and maintain the motivation to learn. But how to focus on that?

The "Retention Formula"

Dr. Alan Seidman, editor of the U.S. *Journal of College Student Retention*, suggests that there is a formula for student retention (Seidman 2006):

$$RET = EId + (E + I + C) Iv$$

That is, Retention = Early Identification of vulnerable students + (Early + Intensive + Continuous) Intervention. I would amend the formula to read

$$S = AC + EId + (E + C) PaM$$

where S = Student Success, AC = Appropriate Course Choice , EId = Early Identification of vulnerable students, E = Early, C = Continuous and PaM = Proactive Motivational Support.

This is not to say that there are no other activities in student support that work in increasing student success. But it is to say that the activities of getting students on to the right course for them, and making early and continuous proactive motivational contact with them, must be absolute priorities in any retention strategy.

Taking the individual terms: AC (Appropriate Course Choice) is covered in Chapter 9, EId (Early Identification of vulnerable students) was covered earlier in this chapter, PaM (Proactive Motivational Support) was covered in Chapter 6, leaving E + C (Early and Continuous Contact) to be covered below.

Early and Continuous Contact

Clearly we need to define what we mean in the formula by early and continuous contact, both in timing and the media used. The media for contact is covered in Chapter 8, so here I will ask only what early and continuous contact means.

Early Contact

As noted earlier, it can be seen from the various rivergrams and weekly dropout figures that student dropout is very heavily front-loaded, often occurring in the first few weeks from both before a module starts and shortly after the start. This means that any efforts to increase retention must begin at the very start of a module or even before the start.

That in turn raises financial issues—it obviously costs more to intervene with the larger number of students at the beginning of a course than to wait and focus efforts on the smaller number who survive after the first few weeks. Powell (2009) argues that this early dropout is not really dropout but "non-engagement" and that, as such, the early dropout does not really matter. He remarks: "High program dropout rates may not be educationally a bad thing for distance education. After all, the expense to students and society is minimal even if the 'water is cold'." But as we saw in Chapter 1 this is simply not true—the expense to students and society is anything but "minimal," and I firmly reject the "Passchendaele" attitude to distance education (named after the First World War battle in which thousands of soldiers were thrown "over the top" and across No Man's Land in the hope that a few would get through past the machine guns in the other trenches). It seems to me to be entirely unethical to adopt this approach in distance education.

In addition there is clear evidence as we shall see that very early contact—even before module start—does have a retention effect, so non-engagement, if it exists, can at least be partly overcome through such contact.

On the other hand, the early dropouts are most likely to be the most vulnerable, so there are ethical considerations to be brought in as well. Thus the decision about early contact needs to be taken on cost, political and ethical grounds.

Continuous Contact

Every extra contact made has an extra cost, so even where there is a financial surplus for the institution on the first contact (Chapter 11), this will diminish with each further contact, unless that contact increases retention proportionally. So it will be important to try to establish the optimum number of contacts in terms of increasing retention cost-effectively.

This is a challenging piece of research to undertake and there is limited evidence. Case and Elliot (1997) found that from two to five contacts per module gave them the optimum retention effects, but this was a small study and it is not clear how much variation in contacts was allowed. A different perspective comes from Burt (2007), who conducted "thought experiments," asking groups of students to imagine how satisfied they would be at various levels of proactive contact from their tutor on a scale running from 0 to 100, where 0 is "not all satisfied" and 100 is "extremely satisfied." His results are shown in Figure 7.6.

If there is no proactive tutor contact, then the mean student satisfaction is very low. One contact almost triples the satisfaction level, and as the number of contacts increases, so satisfaction continues to increase. With three contacts,

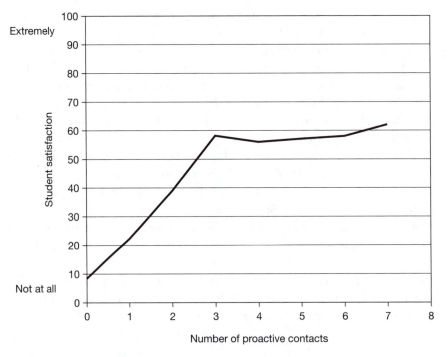

Figure 7.6 Student satisfaction for different amounts of proactive tutor contact

satisfaction reaches 59 on Burt's scale, and satisfaction then stays at much that level for subsequent increases in the number of contacts.

We cannot, of course, assume any link between student satisfaction in a small-scale imaginary experiment and any increase in a student's success as a result of that number of contacts. But taken with the Case and Elliot findings, and the comment from Dweck (1999) about her own study, "the effects are far beyond what you might expect from the simplicity of the interventions," it may be that for many students the proactive contact from the institution need not amount to a kind of academic harassment; a relatively small number of well-designed and timed contacts may have significant success effects.

Who Makes the Contacts?

If proactive contact has some success effect, than the question of who makes that contact from the institution arises. My personal belief is that contact needs to be personal, that students are most likely to be motivated when they feel that there is an individual in the institution—a tutor, adviser, any human being—who takes some interest and responsibility for their success.

It is difficult to find research evidence for this view—indeed it would be hard to design a research study to test the hypothesis. Perhaps the only way would be to undertake a "medical" trial in which two groups of students of similar characteristics were compared, one group receiving no personal tutoring (or a placebo, although it's difficult to imagine what form that might take) and the other receiving some kind of personal tutoring. Such a trial would hardly be ethical. Another way might be to introduce a personal tutoring scheme into a student support system that had hitherto not been organized that way and see if there were subsequent differences in student performance. Such "experiments" would still be difficult given the many variables that make up student success. But inadvertently the U.K. Open University set up the conditions for such a trial when it changed its student support systems in around 1996, in effect abolishing its previous personal tutoring system.

Prior to 1996, students in the U.K. were allocated a "tutor-counselor"— someone who taught them on the first module of their course and remained in a personal non-academic support role for their remaining modules, for which they had separate tutors. This system appeared to be popular with students.

I had previously found (Simpson 1977) that students overwhelmingly agreed with the statement "there should be a person in the O.U. system who has a personal knowledge of their progress and to whom students could refer." But this finding could be criticized on the grounds that this was a difficult statement to disagree with and that no alternatives were offered. Thus, when change to the role was proposed, there was little objective evidence of its value.

Change was proposed in 1996 at least partly because it was felt that the personal tutor system was too expensive. Typically for a distance education institution, no cost-benefit analysis was undertaken, as student support was seen as pure cost. The personal tutor was abolished and replaced by a reactive system based in regional centers with team of half a dozen staff serving the needs of up to 10,000 students using a "Customer Relationship Management" system.

No attempt was made to evaluate the effects of the changes on student success. Admittedly such evaluations would have been difficult given the multivariate nature of the causes of student dropout (Woodley 1987), but given the sums of money involved and the self-styled character of the university as a "learning organization," it is surprising that no attempts were made to see if the modifications had been effective. However, data collected since the change may suggest some effects:

1. *Student retention on module.* As suggested in Chapter 1, U.K. Open University retention rates had been drifting down for a number of years. But the rate of decline appeared to accelerate somewhat over the period of the change—see Figure 7.7 for the long-term figures for retention on the technology foundation module.
2. *Student re-registration after year 1 module completion.* In 2003, nearly 30% of new students completing their first year did not carry on to a second: in fact, the proportion of students carrying on after their first year had been dropping since the early 1990s—see Figure 7.8.

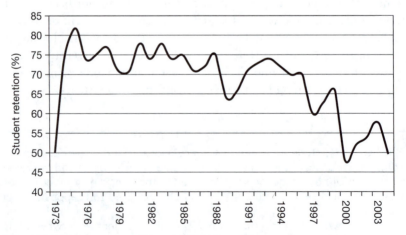

Figure 7.7 Student retention (%) in the U.K. Open University on successive technology foundation modules

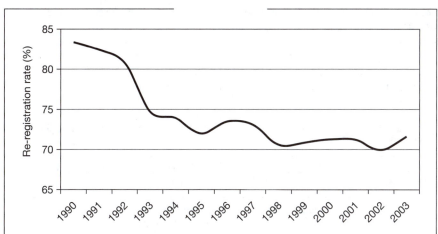

Figure 7.8 Re-registration rates (%) of new students completing a module the previous year

There is a small but definite drop in re-registration rates from 1996 onwards, although admittedly small in comparison with the long-term drop from 1992. However, the personal tutor model was gradually falling into disuse from that year for other policy reasons, so that drop may still be an indication of the loss of the personal element.

Thus on two measures of retention there are some signs that the loss of a personal link may inhibit student success. This is particularly true for a student moving from one module to another with no personal support link between them. So it is interesting to note that in a new policy the U.K. Open University is now reintroducing a personal support element with the intention of supporting students through a series of modules to a degree— a "Student Support Team" based in a curriculum area and containing tutors, administrators and Faculty staff—see Chapter 16. It remains to be seen if a team can provide the element of long-term personal support that may apparently be needed for student success.

What media to use for support? The last question to consider will be which media can be used for proactive motivational support, be that phone, email or text messaging, or one of the other new modes, or a combination of several modes. We'll look at this in detail in Chapter 8 on the media for support.

The Evidence for Proactive Contact

There is accumulated evidence from a variety of studies that proactive contact of various kinds using a variety of media does have significant effects on student success. These are summarized in Table 7.1.

Table 7.1 A summary of the retention effects of some international proactive student support studies

Study	Method	Finding	Notes
Rekkedal 1982 Norway	Postcards	46% increase in retention	
Case and Elliot 1997 US	Phone calls	15–20% increase in retention	From 2 to 5 calls most effective
Visser 1998 UK	Postcards	27% increase in retention	Small-scale study
Chyung 2001 US	Phone calls	Dropout reduced from 44% to 22%	
Mager 2003 US	"Telecounselling"	5% increase in retention	Cost-effective 625% return on investment
Simpson 2006 UK	Phone call before course start	5.1%	Cost-effective 460% return on investment
Twyford 2007 Australia	Motivational emails	11.7% increase over control	
Huett et al. 2008 US	Motivational emails	23.4% increase over control	Significant at 0.5%
Simpson 2011 UK unpublished	Phone calls plus motivational emails	18.9% increase over control	

It is hardly possible to average these trials in any significant way, as they are so different in the student targets, the timings, the media used and the style of the contact. And, as in any research, it is important to be aware of the "funnel" effect, whereby only trials with positive outcomes are published. Nevertheless, in most of the cases increases in retention of the order of 20% points or more have been achieved.

The evidence about the use of motivational emails may be particularly interesting and this is examined in more detail in Chapter 8, on the media for support.

Chapter 8

Media for Support

E-learning

There's more to a party than issuing invitations.
(author unknown, quoted at the San Diego Retention Conference, 2006)

The biggest development in distance learning in the last 20 years has been the growth in the media by which distance education can be delivered. From a system that originally distributed course materials largely by post in text form and support through face-to-face, phone and letter, there is now a bewildering array of media through which both can be delivered. In particular, we now have the internet and Information and Communication Technologies (ICT) in their many forms—CDs, DVDs, search engines, virtual learning environments (VLEs), emails, instant messaging, social media such as Facebook, podcasts, webinars, computer forums, wikis, blogs, vlogs (video blogs), YouTube, pencasts, Twitter, Cloud computing and so on. The use of these devices and systems for education is covered by the blanket terms "e-learning", "blended learning" or "mobile learning".

For, along with developments in the internet, there have been developments in the technology used to access it—now not just computers, but smartphones, allowing the internet to be accessed on the move (hence the term "mobile learning"), and e-books, which allow thousands of texts to be accessed on one portable device. And many educational developments are using a mix of text and online systems in a mode called "blended learning."

But how has this proliferation of delivery systems affected distance education, both in terms of the delivery of course materials and student support for success?

Media for Course Material Delivery

While course materials can be delivered over the internet, paper texts still have many supporters. Where students have a choice, as at the Open Polytechnic of New Zealand, they still often prefer paper texts. And texts do have many advantages—independent of a power source and internet connection, relatively portable, and (as we will see later in this chapter) possibly more learning-friendly and easier to read as well as to annotate. There are disadvantages in terms of delivery and cost, although—again as we will see later—these are not as great as is sometimes thought. Indeed I forecast that the paper text, whether in the form of a book or printed course unit, still has an enduring future in distance education.

Obviously course material can be delivered by methods that do not necessarily involve the internet but which still need a computer, such as DVDs and CDs. And more recently the advent of the e-book and iPad may be more of a revolution in course delivery, although as yet there seems to be little evidence that such devices either increase student success or reduce costs, as we shall see later.

Of course, the huge advantage of ICT and internet course materials is the huge variety of learning activities that they can introduce into plain text, particularly the interaction between students and their tutor. But this variety can be a pitfall as well as a springboard—see later under "E-learning Choices."

Media for Student Support

The real revolution in media comes in the form of student support. And yet some older media are still effective.

Correspondence Text Support

In some situations, particularly in the developing world, where there is little internet and poor phone connections, distance student support through correspondence text by post may still have a role to play. For instance, as well as course materials it is possible to send leaflets covering support topics to students, such as the examples in the "StudyAid" pack (www.ormondsimpson. com). Equally it is possible to maintain their learning motivation using letters and postcards—both Rekkedal (1992) and Visser (1998) used "motivational postcards" and found increases in distance student retention. The "motivational emails" (see later) could also be easily adapted into text for the same purpose.

Face-to-Face Support

To some extent face-to-face support in the form of face-to-face tutorials at local locations has fallen out of use in some distance education institutions, or for other institutions it was never part of the support system in the first place. Nevertheless face-to-face support is still used by distance institutions as varied as the University of South Africa, the Chinese Open University, the Korean National Open University and others.

Advantages and Disadvantages of Face-to-Face Support

Face-to-face support certainly has several advantages. Amongst the most obvious are:

- the speed and richness of the medium—points can be raised and questions answered quickly;
- students being able to work with each other easily;
- and—not unimportantly—for many tutors face-to-face contact with their students is more rewarding and morale-maintaining than any other medium.

When it comes to evidence of student retention and success, it is not difficult to show that students who attend face-to-face activities are more likely to succeed. But this in turn illustrates one of the main disadvantages of face-to-face support—that it may well be inaccessible to many students who are disadvantaged by remoteness, transport difficulties and lack of child-care facilities—in other words, students who are already vulnerable to dropping out.

The other disadvantage of face-to-face support is that it is likely to be an expensive medium per student supported unless student attendance is very high, which in turn possibly lessens its other advantages and makes it a less effective medium. Thus the question of where a distance institution should focus its limited student support resources is a complex one that depends on measuring how effective various media are in increasing student success set against the cost of those media for that institution (see Chapter 11).

Skills for Face-to-Face Support

The kinds of skills needed for effective face-to-face support are very much those described in Chapters 3 and 4, and it would be very easy to write another book on the techniques that could be employed. For some suggestions for support and video examples of face-to-face support in action, see the booklet "All Together" and check out the videos "Face-to-Face Tuition Parts 1 and 2" on www.ormondsimpson.com/page4.htm or watch them direct on YouTube at http://tinyurl.com/distance-tutoring1 and http://tinyurl.com/distance-tutoring2.

Phone Support

The phone is still a very effective medium for student support for success, not least because more people have phones than computer internet access, both in the developed and developing worlds. Phones can also be used in a variety of ways:

- speech—one-to-one and conference calls including video-conferencing;
- text messaging (SMS), including Twitter;
- audiotext services—see Chapter 15;
- voicemail support—see Chapter 15.

Phones can be combined with internet access to make VoIP (Voice over Internet Protocol) calls, such as the Skype program that makes calls and video calls free and which can be made on internet-connected smartphones or via computers.

Advantages and Disadvantages of Phone Support

Phone support has a number of advantages:

- There is evidence that proactive phone contact can have good retention effects—see Chapter 6 for an example.
- It is immediate and individual if used in speech mode.
- Accessibility—as noted above, most distance students will have access to a phone of some kind.
- Costs of the medium can be low, especially if VoIP can be used.

The disadvantages of phone support can be the opposites of its advantages:

- If used in individual speech mode, the cost of a tutor's time can be considerable—compare the time taken to phone 20 students individually (as I have to do on a distance course I teach) with the time taken to send them an email. This adds considerably to the cost. And there's some anecdotal evidence that younger people tend not to take synchronous calls—they let calls go to voicemail.
- Using the phone well probably needs some specific skills, especially if teaching a numerate subject such as math.

Some of these disadvantages might be overcome by using the phone in multiple mode in conference calls with a group of students, or in asynchronous mode such as text messaging, audiotext and voicemail support. However, although there are examples of the use of text messaging in support—for example, at the University of South Africa—this has not been evaluated for retention as far as I know, and the other modes are not in widespread use in distance education.

Skills for Phone Support

Again it would be possible to write at length on the skills useful for phone support, especially motivational support. There is a short training pack, "Supporting Distance Students By Phone," available on www.ormondsimpson. com/page4.htm, which covers some of the key skills.

Support through E-learning

Of course, the main thrust of effort and research in distance education at the moment is in various forms of e-learning. But it is worth asking what we know about this still comparatively recent development in distance education.

E-learning—What Does Research Tell Us?

One thing that the research suggests is that the term "e-learning" should really be replaced by the term "e-teaching," since it is clear that institutions are putting a huge amount of effort into using the internet and ICT in all its forms, mostly for teaching. As we shall see, it is not yet clear just how much of that e-teaching by institutions translates into e-learning by students. Furthermore, the emphasis appears to be on e-teaching (e-academic support) rather than "e-support (e-non-academic support)." However, the term "e-learning" is in too widespread use to be ignored and I will use it loosely to cover all the kinds of communication media and activities now used in distance education.

Certainly the e-learning trend has been good for academics researching in distance education; I estimate that more than 70% of the articles published in refereed distance education journals are about e-learning (that is, e-teaching) in one form or another. And yet this evidence is largely about "enhancing the quality of the student's learning experience," which, as I have argued previously, is not necessarily linked to student retention and success. So what is the evidence for e-learning and student success?

E-learning and Student Retention and Success

While there have been many studies into aspects of e-learning, there have been few that have shown clear evidence for increased student retention and success in conventional education. Indeed, some studies of conventional education have shown an opposite effect such as a study based on Programme for Internaional Student Assessment (PISA) data (Fuchs and Woessmann 2004)—

a large-scale trans-Europe meta-survey—that found that students who use computers a lot do worse than students who use them less. More recently in the United States, a study released by Colombia University of community college students (CCRC 2012) found an 8% gap in completion rates between traditional courses and online courses in favor of the traditional.

So, does e-learning increase student retention and success in distance education cost-effectively? There is, as yet, apparently little evidence either way that it does so. Most of the research seems to be inconclusive and findings often seem to be along the lines of "this project increased the quality of the students' learning experience," often evaluated through a questionnaire given to the surviving students. It is very hard to find good research that demonstrates conclusively that some project in e-learning has actually increased student retention and success.

Where direct comparisons have been made, they seldom show an e-learning advantage and sometimes the opposite, such as the example in Table 8.1 below. This shows a comparison between U.K. Open University course modules in which computer use was compulsory and those for which, at the time, it was optional.

But, apart from questions of student retention and success in e-learning, there are issues of access, popularity and cost that are also important.

E-learning and Access

Working as an academic in the affluent West, it is sometimes hard to remember that not everyone has good internet access. I've noted this before in Chapter 1, but it is worth reiterating that this is true even for the United States and U.K.—see Table 8.2, drawn from the U.S. Census Bureau and U.K. Office for National Statistics respectively.

In both countries the lack of internet access is very heavily concentrated in poorer and rural areas—in the United States in 2009, some 73% of people on less than $40,000 per year had no household access. While access is still growing, large increases seem unlikely to be rapid in current economic circumstances. Of course, many people now access the internet via a smart-phone, but it seems likely that this is again mostly concentrated amongst the

Table 8.1 Completion rates of U.K. Open University course modules with compulsory and optional computer use (Open University Institute of Educational Technology Student Statistics Team 2005)

	Compulsory computer use	*Optional computer use*
Completion %	58.4%	63.1%

Table 8.2 Household internet access, United States and U.K.

	No internet access at home	Dial-up access only
United States (2009)	31.3%	4.7%
U.K. (2011)	23%	2%

better off. And equally, some people can access the internet via internet cafes and other public locations, but it is not clear how easy it is to study with that level of access—one small project I ran myself using access through a local library proved a failure because of difficulties of physical access for the amounts of time required.

Access in the developing world is, of course, much more restricted. In sub-Saharan Africa, for example, household access is often less than 5%, and even in the most advanced African country, South Africa, only 14% of households have internet access.

Thus, when a distance institution makes the decision to move to an entirely e-learning environment, it has to be aware that it is excluding some proportion of the population that is often already educationally disadvantaged. The U.K. "Open" University is now, in effect, closed to a quarter of the most educationally disadvantaged of the UK population, a situation which I regard as frankly ethically unacceptable.

Costs of E-learning

Of course, two great justifications for e-learning is that it is thought to be both cheaper and more sustainable than conventional distance education. But not all the experts agree. First of all you have to ask, "Whose benefits and whose costs?" (Rumble 2004, p. 48). It doesn't always seem cheaper to students who have to invest in computers, internet access and peripherals and update them, and two international experts (Rumble 2004; Huelsmann 2000) have found that, when all the overheads are taken into account, it is not cheaper for institutions either. And, as noted in Chapter 1, in times when we need to be concerned about sustainability, Roy, Potter and Yarrow (2007) found that e-learning was less "green" than conventional learning.

Popularity of E-Learning

One argument for investing in e-learning is that it is demanded by students. But it is not clear from the records that e-learning is especially popular with potential students. Consider the following list of institutions that have invested heavily in developing e-learning ventures in the last 15 years or so and that

Table 8.3 E-learning ventures that have downsized or closed

Institution	Result
NYU Online	Loss $21.5m
Cardean University	Loss $100m
Columbia University	Loss $25m
U.K. e-University	Loss £62m ($99m)
Scottish e-University	Loss unpublished

have subsequently downsized or closed, sometimes with considerable losses—see Table 8.3.

A number of reasons were given as to why these institutions were closed, but I believe in the main it was because they failed to recruit enough students to compensate for their setting-up costs and to become financially viable.

In addition, where students have a choice they often appear to prefer reading paper text rather than reading on screen. This may be because there is some evidence that reading online is up to 30% less effective (O'Hara and Sellen 1997). There appears to be similar evidence for the use of e-books for study, where Garland (2012) found that students using conventional books tended to learn more effectively than students using e-books. In a recent survey of the use of e-textbooks in a campus situation, for example, the savings for students were found to be minimal and there were technical problems that made them unpopular with some students (De Santis 2012). E-books, it seems, are good for reading consecutive text, but they are less good for annotating and moving forward and backward in a text in the way some students want.

This possible unpopularity may also be a measure of how complex computing has become, with the growth of spam, viruses and fraudulent websites, as well as computer crashes, loss of data, software difficulties and so on, all of which can mean that sometimes a computer will be a barrier to learning rather than an aid. And, while young people are often very good at using computers for socializing and playing games, it is not clear that they are necessarily good at using computers for learning.

Using E-learning for Student Retention and Success

So far I have deliberately—and quite unfairly, you may think—loaded the case against e-learning. This is because I think it is important to contest some of the hype that has surrounded so much of its development in distance education.

But of course e-learning is very much here to stay, with its one overwhelming advantage of allowing students to study from wherever they are, with whatever institution they fancy (although, as I mentioned previously, this is not an unmitigated advantage, given the growth of fake universities in the last few years).

So we must make the best of it and ask what are the most effective ways to use e-learning to enhance student retention and success. One of the difficulties of doing this is that e-learning offers the distance educator so many options. See the array of possibilities in the opening paragraph of this chapter. How can we choose which of these is most effective?

E-learning Choices

In Chapter 12, on course design, I will mention the possibility of "Course Exuberance Syndrome"—the idea that, in their enthusiasm for their subject, the writers of a course might so overload it with topics and media that it would, in turn, overwhelm students. Given all the possibilities offered by e-learning, it is an easy temptation to fall into. But Cognitive Load Theory says that presenting material in redundant ways is undesirable, a view endorsed by Rickwood (1998), who found that students often prefer only a limited set of media to use and that a proliferation of possible media is both confusing and threatening. This might be a distance education version of Ockham's Razor— "that you should not multiply hypotheses beyond necessity"—that is, you should not use more media than is necessary. So, how to proceed?

Learning Value versus Learning Time

One way might be to consider the concepts of the "learning value" and "learning time" of various media:

- *learning value* is the quality and amount of learning that a student gets from a particular learning medium;
- *learning time* is the amount of time that it takes to access and use that medium.

We can then plot learning time against learning value. For example, perhaps the highest learning value still comes from reading paper text (O'Hara and Sellen 1997), which needs very little time to access, so that might be close to the origin on both axes. If the research quoted above about reading online is correct, then online text takes a little longer to read for the same learning, so appears slightly higher on the learning time axis. I have placed some other media quite arbitrarily on the chart (see Figure 8.1) to illustrate the point.

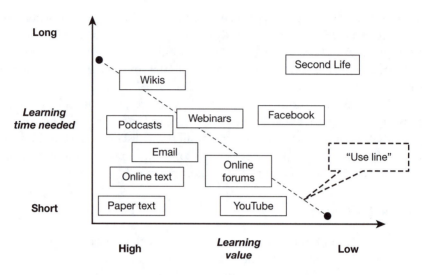

Figure 8.1 Learning time versus learning value (N.B. these are arbitrary placings)

Media close to the origin will be richer in terms of the fastest learning for the least time. Since distance students are typically chronically short of time they will choose the learning media that are most efficient from their point of view. So it may be possible to draw a "Use line"—media outside this line are less likely to be used than media closer to the origin, which are therefore seen to be more efficient.

This perspective is supported by a paper (JISC 2010) that surveyed students' attitudes towards the use of social media such as Facebook and Twitter by their institutions. The survey found that students did not particularly want their institution to be in "their" social spaces, which they used—naturally enough— for socialization. Presumably such a presence was a little too much like having lectures in the student coffee bar . . .

In teaching a blended learning course (a mix of text-based materials with phone and email contact), I use the phone and email—and an occasional postcard—in making proactive motivational contacts with my students. I also occasionally use YouTube to post short videoclips on particularly difficult points or refer to videoclips on the web such as "Khan Academy" (www.khanacademy.org), but I try to be careful to make sure these are not redundant and don't overload students. I also assume that not all students will visit such clips. After all, the first thing a student does when getting too far behind or losing motivation is to stop visiting module websites.

Learning Time, Value and Costs

The two-dimensional chart in Figure 8.1 ought to have a third dimension of cost to the institution, as every additional communication mode will have an extra price tag for the institution. As such it will be important for the institution to decide which of the many modes it chooses to use—teaching resources are not unlimited. And perhaps there ought to be a fourth axis for cost to the student. But a four-dimensional chart is certainly beyond my imagination . . .

E-learning and Non-Academic Support

How does all the preceding apply to the business of using non-academic support to increase the retention and success of distance students? There could be a number of ways, depending on the various e-learning channels being used. But the important thing to remember is that, as I've suggested previously, the first thing a potential dropout does is stop visiting VLEs, websites and forums and stop following Twitter. At that point it doesn't matter how good the teaching materials are; the student has gone. So, to be effective in increasing retention, an e-learning channel needs to be proactive and motivational. One example of a proactive e-learning channel is the use of motivational emails.

Motivational Emails and Texts

As I suggested in Chapter 7, non-academic support should be early, proactive and motivational. One way of achieving that is to use a system of "motivational emails" or text messages (SMS), sent at regular intervals to students. Here, using emails or texts has clear advantages over other communication channels—they are quick, economical in time and money and can encourage responses. And there is accumulating evidence that motivational emails can increase success and retention—see Chapter 7. In addition to the examples quoted there, Balaban-Sali (2008) claimed evidence to the effectiveness of motivational emails, and Huett et al. (2008, p. 171) found differences in overall motivation and argued that "simple, cost-effective, and easy-to-design email messages show potential for addressing distant students' motivational needs."

Designing Motivational Emails

In designing motivational emails, I use both Dweck's and Keller's theories, as well as a Strengths Approach, so that the emails are short (fewer than 400 words), written in an informal, friendly style using humor where appropriate (Keller's "Attention"), but always containing serious ideas about learning and overcoming learning problems (Keller's "Relevance"). The humor is an essential part, as it increases the likelihood of the messages being read, demystifies learning and acts to lower stress levels. I also use short anecdotes— some psychologists suggest that stories are a particularly effective way of communicating points and getting them remembered.

The emails do not set out to give conventional study skills advice. As suggested earlier (Morgan, Taylor and Gibbs 1982), there is evidence that such advice has little effect unless students are first well motivated to learn. The aim of these emails is to "turn on students' learning motivation as though 'flicking a switch'" (Cohen et al. 2006, p. 1309) through encouragement and by recognizing and addressing barriers to that motivation. However, the emails are not mere exhortation; they are based in recent psychological findings.

Customizing and Personalizing Emails

There is evidence from psychology studies that emails that are "personalized" (i.e., personally addressed, preferably by first name) are more likely to be read than those addressed to, for example, "Dear Student." So I use an email merge system.

Evidence also suggests that "customized" emails (i.e., containing materials specific to that student) are even more effective. Kim and Keller (2008) used what they called "Motivational and volitional email messages" (MVEM) combined with personal messages, and found increases in motivation over a group receiving just the MVEM. However, that level of sophistication is likely to be costly and to require a higher level of knowledge of individual students than is often available in distance education.

The Email Topics

There is an introductory email that explains that I will be sending a series of email "study tips." Then the following emails are sent at roughly fortnightly intervals:

1. "Are you fixed or malleable?"—Dweck's learning theory
2. "What can you expect from distance study?"
3. "Motivating yourself to learn"
4. "Getting organized for study"
5. "Finding your best study methods"
6. "Finding the time when getting behind"
7. "Making lists"
8. "Losing motivation?"
9. "Family support"
10. "Managing your 'procrastinitus'"

11. "Self-discipline"
12. "Learning to concentrate on learning"
13. "Being a lucky student"
14. "Study anxiety syndrome"
15. "Exam tactics"
16. "Don't stop now!"

The first of these emails—"Are you fixed or malleable?"—can be found in Chapter 6. One more example of the emails follows to give a flavor. The full texts of all the emails can be found on www.ormondsimpson. com/page4.htm and are freely available for redrafting and use by anyone.

Email 6

Dear

Subject: Study Tips

Study tip 6—Finding the time when getting behind

Distance students tell me that time is the biggest issue they face with their studies. There's finding the time in the first place and what to do when—as almost always happens occasionally, they get behind.

Finding the Time
You can find all kinds of "time management advice"—making diaries, filling in time charts and so on. But psychologists have found that time management devices often only tend to work for a while before people revert back to their previous ways.

So here's a different way of doing things—the *4D method* for finding time:

- *Defer*—there may be things you think you must do but which you can put off for a while;
- *Delegate*—there may be things you do that you can get someone else to do;
- *Downgrade*—there may be things you don't have to do to such a state of perfection;
- *Decommit*—a fancy way of saying there may be things you don't have to do at all!

Catching up

Almost every student gets behind with their studies at some point. Life just happens! So here's the world's shortest guide on how to catch up—*the 3S model.*

- *S = Skim.* Sometimes when you need to catch up, it's OK to skim what you're reading and just get a feel for it without reading it word for word.
- *S = Skip.* Sometimes it's OK to skip some material altogether if you need to, and if it's not vital for the next bit of study.
- *S = Scrape.* If you're behind doing an assignment, then occasionally it's OK to aim to just scrape through. You don't have to do everything perfectly!

Once you've caught up, you can study more carefully. But it's nearly always better to skim, skip and scrape than drop out. So remember: it's 4Ds for time management and 3Ss for catching up, and good luck!

Ormond Simpson

Motivational Text Messages

Given that, while not all students have access to the internet many have mobile phones, it may be possible to use text messaging in a similar manner, particularly as it is possible for an institution to send them centrally. Of course, the messages would probably need to be shorter—generally within the 140-character limit for one message, although the limit is set more by the capacity of the students' phone screens for easy reading. Pei-Luen, Gao and Wu (2008) found that the use of SMS messaging increased motivation, although this was not related to subsequent retention and success, so more work needs to be done in this area.

Other E-learning Channels for Non-Academic Support

As yet there is not a great deal of evidence for the effectiveness of other e-learning channels for student support for success. The main channel for most e-learning at most distance institutions is their Virtual Learning Environment (VLE—such as "Moodle," "Blackboard" or WebCT), which usually comprises course materials and teaching channels—podcasts (online presentations, often via PowerPoint with an audio commentary, which can be viewed asynchronously), online seminars ("webinars") that can be viewed and participated in synchronously using software such as "Blackboard Collaborate"—formerly "Elluminate"; see http://www.blackboard.com/Platforms/Collaborate/Overview.aspx)—and discussion forums, both student- and tutor-led.

Other channels that can be used are YouTube clips (short online video clips such as Khan Academy, mentioned previously), blogs (asking students to keep online diaries), "pencasts" (effectively like watching a tutor jotting notes on a whiteboard using a "smartpen"—possibly particularly useful for a subject like math, where visual explanations are helpful—see http://www.livescribe.com/en-gb/pencasts). Other channels appear from time to time and some institutions are trying to use social software such as Facebook to engage students. And, while it's hard to imagine anyone seriously using a smartphone to study, it hasn't stopped institutions offering courses such as "Move-on"—courses for business studies designed to be accessed via iPhones and consisting of 20 episodes (each 10 minutes long). See http://move-on.exodussa.com, whose progress it will be interesting to watch.

The difficulty when trying to decide how to use this panoply of e-teaching opportunities is to remember that, as Ramsden (2003) says, "No teacher can ever be certain that their teaching will cause a learner to learn." And, as I've suggested previously, it is very hard to find good evidence that the use of any particular channel has led to increased student retention and success. The one exception to that may be the use of discussion forums.

Discussion Forums

The use of online discussion forums (both student- and tutor-moderated) for academic support or teaching is too big a topic for this book. The way that discussion forums are used is in any case dependent on the topics being taught. While a discussion forum is helpful for discursive subjects, they may be of less help when teaching math-, science- and technology- based subjects (can the Second Law of Thermodynamics be taught through online discussion?). There are many texts available on online teaching—see the Select Bibliography section for some recommendations.

However, discussion forums are probably very important for maintaining students' learning motivation. As yet there seems to be little hard evidence about which particular models of forum interaction work best for retention, but it may be likely that there are several factors in a tutor-moderated forum that might make it retention-friendly:

● *Tutor response time to issues raised by students.* It may be useful to set expectations about response times at the outset, but in any case students left hanging for more than a couple of days for a response seem likely to begin to lose heart, especially at the beginning of a module.

- *Tutor style of response.* Again I suggest that the style of response should be modeled on the proactive motivational approach described in Chapter 6.
- *The kinds of activities (e-moderating or "e-tivities") a tutor might ask students to undertake in a forum.* Examples of such activities can be found in "All Together Online" at www.ormondsimpson.com or in books in the Select Bibliography.
- *Progress-chasing systems.* There needs to be a monitoring scheme so that students who fail to visit the forum are picked up and quickly and systematically responded to.

Given these relatively simple axioms, it may be possible to discover if forums can make a real contribution to retention and success.

Conclusion

I have been a little negative about e-learning—very much as a reaction to some of the hype that has surrounded it in distance education literature in recent years. My problem is that distance educators are naturally drawn to the idea that technical solutions exist to the very real issues of dropout in distance education. But it is important to be a skeptical technophile and, when offered any new solution, to ask the one word question, "Evidence?"

After all, there have been other technical solutions offered in the past. The great inventor Thomas Edison once said that "film will eventually supplant books in schools and universities" (McNichol, 2006, p. 39). It didn't quite happen. Some of my readers may be old enough to remember Educational Television, which was going to revolutionize teaching. Millions of dollars were spent, with very little result. Sadly (for me), very few of my readers will be as old as me and will be able to remember the electro-mechanical "teaching machines" of the 1960s that clanked their way into oblivion long before the computer arrived.

Critically, I believe e-learning has not yet been shown to be cost-effective in increasing student retention and success, and that the price of e-learning in excluding educationally disadvantaged people is high. A lot of effort is still needed to change both those states of affairs. But there are many developments possible that may change this picture. We don't yet know if the smartphone and iPad have anything to offer in the way of "apps" that could be used for enhancing learning motivation. There are already apps for learning, such as the mind-mapping app "Mindmeister" (http://www.mindmeister.com/ipad), which students could use for organizing study topics. But it will continue to be important to identify what is actually e-teaching and whether that is generating real e-learning.

Chapter 9

Enrollment, Induction, and Preparation

> I never heard that it had been anybody's business to find out what his natural bent was, or where his failings lay, or to adapt any kind of knowledge to him . . . I did doubt whether Richard would not have profited by someone studying him a little, instead of his studying them quite so much.
>
> (Charles Dickens, *Bleak House*)

So far in this book I have focused on student support within a course module. But support for success must also encompass support during the enrollment process and after dropout.

Support for Enrollment

By enrollment, I mean the process of getting students registered on to the right course module and ready to start after their initial recruitment. I do not mean the initial recruitment of students to the institution via the marketing of its courses, an activity that consumes large amounts of resource in most distance education institutions (it is thought that, for many institutions, the cost of getting new students registered on a module often well exceeds the cost of supporting them once they are studying). Marketing is beyond the subject of this book, and indeed there can be a concern that it is almost antithetical to its theme; in some institutions the more successful a marketing department is in recruiting students, the higher the subsequent dropout, as students find that the institution, method of study or module is not what they thought or wanted. Sometimes there can be a "recruitment versus retention" ethical dichotomy, and some institutions, such as the Open Polytechnic of New Zealand, recognize this by giving their marketing departments a role in subsequent student retention.

But however recruitment and enrollment are organized, it is clear that support during the enrollment phase is crucial for a new distance student's subsequent success. That support usually takes two forms—getting students on to the right course for them and inducting them to distance learning.

Support for the Course Choice Process

There is considerable evidence from conventional education that students making the "wrong" choice of course—whether in level, pace or content—may be much more likely to drop out of study than students who are on courses that suit them (McGivney 1996).

Supporting evidence for this contention for full-time students comes from a variety of sources—for example, Yorke (1999) and Gibson and Walters (2002), who identified inappropriate choice of course as one of the four main reasons for dropout amongst students entering higher education after access courses. There is less evidence from distance education, but the annual surveys of both withdrawn and successful students in the U.K. Open University show that "inadequate course choice guidance" is the highest reason for dissatisfaction in both categories (Open University Institute of Educational Technology Student Statistics Team 2002). Some 21% of withdrawn students were "very" or "fairly" dissatisfied with this aspect of their studies, compared to 20% who were dissatisfied with the amount of study time required, 20% who were dissatisfied with tutorials and 13% who were dissatisfied with the cost of courses.

It is interesting to note that the whole area of choice is now the subject of attention from psychologists who suggest that the vastly increasing choice for consumers shows little benefits for them, creating anxiety and stress, and that poor choices are often the result (Schwartz 2004). This presumably may also apply to distance education choices where the massive recent growth in online institutions has made the choice of possible courses more and more perplexing.

So, given the importance of course choice, there is surprisingly little evidence as to how students make their choices of what to study at post-school levels. Of course, there will be intending students who have a clear idea from early in their careers as to the subject and level of their studies and whose choice is entirely appropriate for them. We can guess that such students are likely to go on to study successfully. But there will also be students who have equally clear ideas that are not, in fact, appropriate for them, and yet other students who have little idea of what their best choice should be. Such students are likely to rely on course titles and descriptions to make their choice. This will be particularly true for students in distance education; their opportunities to interact with their chosen institution and talk to staff are very limited. But just relying on using course titles and descriptions can have its limitations.

Course Titles and Descriptions

All institutions provide titles and descriptions of their courses to recruit potential students, but there are issues around the length and wording of descriptions, the conflict inherent in them between enrollment and retention, and about students' assumed entry behavior.

(i) Length

It is very likely that in any institution there will be pressure to keep course descriptions short, in part to minimize the expense of printed brochures. Even where descriptions are web-based there will be pressure to keep descriptions brief, as potential students may have short attention spans. This pressure will be particularly acute in a large institution with a large product range—I note that the U.K. Open University, with more than 500 modules, now has brochure descriptions of the order of about 100 words per course compared with around 250 words a few years ago.

However, short descriptions are very likely to be incomplete and therefore to be misleading. Longer descriptions of a course can be made available post-enquiry, yet my conversations with students suggest that (as Schwartz [2004] indicates) their choice is substantially governed by the short description and that the longer description is read selectively only to confirm that original decision.

(ii) Wording

Writers of course descriptions will generally have to use words such as "introductory," "advanced," "elementary," "explores," "describes" and so on, which allow intending students a wide range of interpretations. And where specific subject terms are used, it may not assist a student to have an outcome described in terms of a subject that they do not yet understand. It may be of little help to know that a course will give a thorough understanding of second-order differential equations if a student has little idea what such equations look like and why they are important.

(iii) The Conflict between Recruitment and Retention

Universities derive their funding not only from retention but from recruitment as fees are paid upfront. Courses that do not recruit will not run and may even result in the eventual closure of departments. There may be pressure to emphasize the accessibility of the course rather than its difficulty. This is not to suggest that there will necessarily be any dishonest intention here; rather that the right balance between encouragement and realism may be difficult to achieve.

(iv) Entry Qualifications

At conventional universities the entry qualifications required to study a course are some guide to its suitability for particular students. Open institutions that do not require entry qualifications can still suggest the sort of previous qualifications that would be helpful in their course descriptions.

However, it is not always possible to specify particular qualifications for a course, and entry behavior then has to be described in vaguer terms such as "potential students should have a basic understanding of numerical methods," which presents similar problems to the difficulties described under "Wording" above. And none of this helps mature students, who, while unqualified, may well have an appropriate background for a course but cannot tell that from the descriptions given.

(v) Outcomes

For many students the course they choose will be determined by the career they wish to follow. For mature distance students this will be some advantage when it comes to choosing courses. In many cases they have the maturity and knowledge to research their chosen direction and relate it back to the courses they wish to take. But as distance education becomes more attractive to younger students, it is not always clear that they have any better idea about what a particular career involves than what a particular course involves.

Thus it may not be enough for universities for distance institutions to rely solely on course descriptions to ensure that students enroll on the "right" course for them. There needs to be other ways of helping students find the best courses such as personal guidance, students' opinions, preview materials and diagnostic materials.

Personal Guidance from an Adviser

To some extent conventional universities can rely on personal and individual advice from faculty or student support staff. In mass distance education, however, such personalization may be prohibitively expensive. The U.K.

Open University employs a cohort of advisers who not only have to advise the annual 35,000 new students about all aspects of their studies but have an advisory responsibility to the University's 130,000 continuing students. My recent estimates from reviewing the University's adviser contact logs suggest that, not surprisingly, only around 10–20% of new students have any substantial contact with an adviser before starting study.

There are other issues around personal advice. Access to advice may not be easy for some students. Clayton and McGill (2000) suggest that students who could most benefit from advice are often those least able to access it because of lack of assertiveness, remoteness and other reasons. And students may not take advice when given. Johnson (2000), in a study of U.K. Open University students apparently registered for courses unsuited for them, reported that many did not take the advice to change to other courses. Since students are probably seeking advice having already started to fix on a particular course, this may be an example of choice fixation: what Schwartz (2004) describes as the way, once an initial choice has been made, changing that choice becomes more difficult. So, as suggested earlier, once students have made a choice they tend to be committed to that choice despite contrary advice.

Consequently there needs to be alternative methods of providing course choice, preferably through resources that potential students can use by themselves and that do not have to be mediated through an adviser (Simpson 2004a).

Students' Course Reviews

New students appear to value the views of students who have taken courses previously. This is not to say that students will be guided entirely by such views, but that they are likely to be factors in their decisions, just as people buying cars are likely to be influenced by previous purchasers' views.

In the U.K Open University in 1998, I invited a selection of students who had recently taken course modules to write a short note (100–200 words) aimed at advising new students considering taking the module they had just finished. These were lightly edited (largely to remove comments on aspects of the module, such as the tutor, which would not be common to all students) and collated into single sets for each module.

The comments are now on the Web—www.open.ac.uk/courseviews—and are freely available as a kind of "Trip Adviser" or "App Review" for courses. Each one of the university's undergraduate modules has a set of comments—usually containing about 10 or so individual comments from individual students—thereby giving a number of alternative perspectives on the module. It is hard to select typical comments from amongst so many, but displayed here are two (out of 10) for module A210 "Approaching Literature, Authors, Readers and Texts":

Students' Comments On Course A210

"A highly rewarding and stimulating course, but demanding in its reading requirement. An open mind is needed to make the most of the course. Those who resist the course's call to approach and explore literature in a variety of ways waste energy and miss out on some of its riches. Those who tackle the course in a positive way will find much that is both challenging and enjoyable, and have their literary horizons permanently widened."

"There is a very heavy workload with this course and a great number of texts. The Study Guides were on the whole helpful, although the first one seemed rather out of synchrony with the Reader and it was not clear where one stopped and the other took over. However, the range of texts was interesting, and the video performances thought-provoking. I would advise anyone taking this course to read *all* the texts before you start (except the anthology as only a few works are referred to in this) because it is nearly impossible to do as the guides suggest, to study the next text while completing work on the previous one and prepare the current assignment all at the same time."

There were initially some concerns that comments might be overly critical, negative or simply unfair. This has not turned out to be the case. There are negative comments, but they are almost always in the context of a balanced opinion. It is quite usual, for example, for students to criticize the workload of a course as being very heavy but to add in the same breath that, providing the load can be handled, it is an exciting and worthwhile course. Indeed, the overall tenor of the comments is usually positive while realistic about the challenges that the courses represent.

Do Students' Course Reviews Work?

Like other course choice resources, it is difficult to evaluate students' reviews for effectiveness. There are some indications of popularity—shortly after the site was set up, it was attracting some 300,000 hits a year. Feedback on the site itself was positive, with examples such as:

"I found this website an excellent resource. I'll be referring other students to it as well. It's particularly useful for those who are undecided on their course of study."

"As a tutor I think this website is a great idea; I shall refer current and prospective students to it."

"An excellent idea! I absolutely love this page and find it the most useful and interesting way to get a really good feel for the course and what is on offer. I shall soon compose and send my thoughts on a wonderful course last year."

"Great website, I'm going to be starting Diploma in Social Work next February, it would be nice to see course comments added on these type of courses to give us students like other students a feel for it before we start!!!!!!!"

In a typical recruitment–retention dichotomy, the Open University faculty were initially uneasy with the idea that students' reviews of their courses could be widely seen. They felt new students might be unduly deterred. However, it was accepted that an official site was probably preferable to one of the many unofficial sites that are available, such as Ratemyprofessor.com, particularly as the site now allows for faculty to reply to comments.

Since it was set up, the site also now contains the results of the "End of Module Survey," giving the percentages of students who answered questions with, for example:

"Overall, I am satisfied with the quality of this module"

"Overall, I am satisfied with my study experience"

"The module provided good value for money"

"I was satisfied with the support provided by my tutor/study adviser on this module"

"Overall, I was satisfied with the teaching materials provided on this module"

and so on. Of course, since the survey only goes to students who completed the course it is likely to give a positive and rather one-sided view.

Students' Comments in Forums

Online forums can allow potential students to ask questions of experienced students directly online. There is an example of this activity on the U.K. Bart's Medical School student site, which hosts an admissions conference where students in their last year at school thinking of medical studies can post questions that are answered by current medical students.

From Little-Samantha Status: Final Year School Pupil (Y11)

Hi everyone,

My boyfriend is interested in medicine, but seems to have a little phobia of the good ol' red stuff. Small amounts are ok (I think), but he watched a surgery program on TV once and felt sick to his stomach. So to those med students (or anyone with work experience): have you ever felt a little squeamish, and how have you dealt with it? Is it something you all just get used to?

From tig Status: Medical Student (Year 3)

I can't watch surgery on tv . . . in real life . . . fine! on tv everything is distorted and I am very squeamish!

From azy_cool Status: 1st Year Medical Student at Manchester

I was a little squeamish before I started, when looking at surgery on tv etc, but I used to watch it cos it was interesting and it got "easier" to watch the more you watch it . . . so he can try that. In medicine having to cut up dead bodies . . . that does sound quite bad, but really even the first lesson was fine,

I think tig is right its much easier in real life than on tv . . . if he really wants to do medicine then being squeamish shouldn't be a problem. I'm sure he'll be fine when he starts.

The U.K. Open University now has a similar forum (http://www8.open. ac.uk/platform/services/study-support) and, like many distance institutions, has a presence on Facebook and Twitter, although it is not clear how far these are effective in getting students on to the right module for them, or even how that could be assessed.

There are of course limitations to students' reviews. They cannot tell students that they have the right background for a course and, no matter how independent, they will always represent partial views of courses.

Course Preview Materials

Course preview materials were introduced in the U.K. Open University for its foundation courses more than 20 years ago, and were called "taster packs."

The original rationale was a simple one: students considering a particular module should have the opportunity of surveying the materials and undertaking a short "test drive" of that module. The reasons for using specifically designed materials for the purpose was to try to choose a selection of material that was reasonably typical of the module but sufficiently short for a potential student to read through in a realistic amount of time. A pack also contained typical examples of assessment materials, such as an assignment with a tutor's comments and grade, and a specimen exam paper, in order to give students some kind of feel for the level of work they would have to produce.

Once again there were recruitment–retention concerns. It was thought that such packs would deter students from studying a module. In order to deal with this each pack came with an explanation of its purpose and a "health warning" pointing out that the pack was typically less than 0.5% of the course, that it might contain material that relied on knowledge gained earlier in the course and so on. Of course, clearly one of the intentions of such packs is to deter students from taking a course if either the content is not relevant to their needs or at the wrong level. There would be cause for concern if it were found to be deterring students from a course that was right for them in both respects. In fact, Adams, Rand and Simpson (1989) found no evidence for that belief, and student feedback was uniformly positive:

Student feedback on taster packs:

"Interesting, informative. Challenges ahead thoroughly paraded. Thank you for the health warning!"

"I found the taster pack both stimulating and interesting. I now definitely want to study the Arts course."

"Very helpful—assisted in my decision to go ahead with this course this year."

"Many thanks for the taster pack. I found it very interesting, giving an insight as to the work involved. Enough to prepare—enough to scare!"

It is always difficult to evaluate such feedback, as it may be partial—students who have negative responses may not bother to feed back. But the uniformity of responses received is remarkable, so it seems safe to assume that at the very least there are few negative perceptions. The feedback also appears to reveal that potential students find the packs reassuring and motivating, rather than off-putting. To a potential student a course represents an intimidating unknown and there must always be the question in many students' minds—"Can I cope?" To see a typical selection from a course and realize that, although it may be challenging it is not completely impossible, must help overcome that fear of the unknown. Indeed from that perspective taster materials might well act as a marketing initiative.

Open Educational Resources as Preview Materials

One of the arguments for OERs is that they can act as tasters to encourage students to enroll on a complete module. While that must be true to some extent, most OERs do not usually have examples of assessment material—the most popular elements of the taster packs. And neither OERs nor taster packs can tell a student that he or she has the right educational background for the full course. That job must be the role of diagnostic material.

Diagnostic Materials

Diagnostic materials have long been used in open and distance learning to advise students about their study choices. There are essentially two kinds: generic, to test applicants' suitability for distance higher education, and course-specific, to test suitability for a particular course. Both can be externally assessed or self-assessed by the student.

Generic Externally Assessed Diagnostic Materials

In conventional higher education, these can range from the massive externally assessed 194 -point questionnaire used by the Noel-Levitz organization in the United States to identify vulnerable students, to simpler tests perhaps used in conjunction with an interview with an adviser. Such tests can be expensive to administer on a large scale and in an open-entry system may look like an entrance exam.

Generic Self-Assessed Diagnostic Materials

These have also been used. It should be remembered that, for many students, assessment can have negative associations. It is associated with competition, past failures and exams. In recent trials of externally assessed pre-course diagnostic materials in my own institution, there was only a 20% return rate, despite the fact that it was made clear that there was no connection between the assessment and the offer of a place. In addition, of course, the returns came overwhelmingly from students who were perfectly competent in the skills assessed.

Thus there may be some value in the concept of stand-alone self-assessment materials that encourage students to reflect on their own needs, aptitudes and motivations without any external assessment of any kind. This is a one-page excerpt from a booklet called *Taking Off*, which used to be sent to new students in my own institution. The whole booklet has 12 pages of similar "self-assessment" material.

There are many other such self-assessment programs, such as the Defense Activity for Non-Traditional Education Support (DANTES) Distance Learning

---

Taking Off—Section 1

How do you feel about being a new student? We hope that working through *Taking Off* will answer a few questions and provoke a few thoughts about your decision to study. You may already have a number of mixed feelings.

Tick those feelings below that seem to correspond to any of yours:

1. I am not sure whether I will be able to find the time for study.
2. I am not clear what university courses are like.
3. I am not sure I can cope with a specific topic, eg math.
4. I have not done any serious studying for a long time.
5. I feel excited about belonging to a university.
6. I think I'll meet some interesting people.
7. I expect the course to be interesting.
8. I hope I shall become more intellectually confident.
9. I hope I shall prove to myself that I am cleverer than I thought.
10. I will be better qualified and develop my career.

If this exercise raised any questions in your mind about your decision to start study then do contact us—we'll be happy to discuss any of your concerns.

Readiness Self-Assessment instrument, to be found at http://www.dantes catalogs.com and as used by the U.S. military.

The problem in using materials like these is that it is very hard to assess their value. Are the students most likely to drop out least likely to undertake them? Do students seriously undertake the activities? Do they seriously reflect on the results? Do they draw useful conclusions about themselves, whatever those may be? It may be more helpful to give new students more specific responses in the form of diagnostic quizzes and predictive feedback.

In 2003, I developed a test from the predictive probability of success system described in Chapter 7. It allowed a prospective U.K. Open University student to estimate their own probability of success through answering a series of questions that they could then score—see Table 9.1.

Table 9.1 Diagnostic quiz based on the predictive probability of success system

	Initial score: 60 points
1. Are you male or female? Male: Subtract 5 Female: No change	New score: _ points
2. How old are you? Under 30: Subtract 13 Age 30 or above: No change	New score: _ points
3. What level is this module? Level 1: Add 23 Level 2: Add 11 Other: No change	New score: _ points
4. What Faculty is this module? Arts: Add 16, Social Science: Add 8, Education: Add 7, Math: Add 6, Science: Subtract 3, Technology: Add 1,	New score: _ points
5. What is the credit point rating of this module? 15pts: Subtract 23 30pts: Subtract 9 60pts: No change	New score: _ points
6. What number of total modules are you taking this year? 1 module: Add 5 2 or more: No change	New score: _ points
7. Your current highest educational qualifications? Degree or equiv: Add 17 High school: Add 12 Middle school: No change None: Subtract 2 Other: No change	New score: _ points
8. How would you classify your occupation? Working: Add 10 Not working or other: No change	New score: _ points
	FINAL SCORE __ points

Having calculated their score the students were given a rough idea of their probability of success, as below:

Your Score

100 or above (70%+ chance of success): The outlook is very bright for you. You'll undoubtedly have your share of challenges but you should be able to get things off to a good start.

75 to 99 (50–60% chance of success): This will be a challenge you've taken on and it will be useful to see if you can increase your point score in some way. For example, do think about changing to a lower level module just for the first year—you can step up the pace later on. If you are taking more than one module, then again do think of switching to just one.

Under 75 (50% or lower chance of success): You'll still be able to succeed but if you can increase your score that would really improve your chances. You may not want to change sex(!), but you could change your course to one at a more introductory level, take fewer modules, increase your current educational qualifications by taking a short course of some kind—and so on.

The idea behind the quiz was not just to give students some idea of their probability of success, but also to give them the possibility of changing that probability by, for example, changing to a different and more suitable course.

I hesitated to evaluate the use of this questionnaire on ethical grounds, as I wasn't sure how it might affect students, but Pretorius, Prinsloo and Uys (2010) administered a similar questionnaire to students in a microeconomics course at the University of South Africa. They found that the respondents achieved a higher examination mark and pass rate compared to the class. This, of course, may be due to students who performed better being more inclined to respond to the request to complete the questionnaire. However, students felt that the questionnaire had built their confidence before the examination. Their scores indicated to them that they had the potential and capacity to pass. They felt "empowered."

Course-Specific Externally Assessed Materials

Where a potential student takes a test that is assessed by an adviser in the institution, such materials are relatively simple to apply, although for open learning institutions they may too closely resemble entrance exams for comfort. They may also be expensive. In trials in the U.K. Open University where they were voluntary, it quickly became clear that the potential students who submitted them were the students least needing to.

Course-Specific Self-Assessed Materials

These appear to be more suited to mass distance education. However, there are still difficult issues. It is relatively easy to design self-assessed diagnostic tests where the answers are clearly correct or incorrect, as in math, science and technology subjects, or where clear answers can be given, such as in language quizzes, where simple "cloze" tests (replacing blank spaces in sentences with appropriate words) can be used. It is more difficult where advanced courses with some background knowledge and skills are needed, such as courses in higher level arts or social science subjects.

It is also possible for diagnostic exercises to generate a "recruitment–retention" dichotomy. It may be hard for a diagnostic test writer to give "You shouldn't be taking this course" as a possible outcome when there is pressure to recruit students on to a course. There will be a temptation to argue that a diagnostic test result should be less directive and leave the door open to students by saying instead something along the lines of "You will find this course a challenge unless you prepare for it carefully." However, this may not be as helpful to a potential student. In one of the few evaluations of course-specific self-assessed materials I've been able to locate, Williams (1998) found that U.K. Open University science diagnostic quizzes that used such rubrics were not as effective as she hoped in persuading students to change their course choice. But that finding may well be specific to the quizzes concerned, as the messages to students completing the quizzes tended not to be directive.

Whatever the type of diagnostic material, there appears to have been little work published on their effectiveness in getting students on to the correct courses, or on any subsequent retention effect. And diagnostic materials may not be sufficient in themselves, because, although they may tell a student that he or she is at the right *level* for a course, they may not tell the student that the course has the right *content* for them.

Clearly, diagnostic materials are of less interest to conventional institutions that require entrance qualifications. However, they may still be of use where access students with uncommon or unorthodox entry qualifications are hoping to enter an institution and need further help in their choice.

Do Course Choice Materials Improve Student Success?

Finally, and obviously, is there evidence that the use of course choice materials of whatever kind actually improves student success? It has proved very difficult to devise evaluation methods for these materials, which can estimate their retention effect. It might be possible to compare the retention rates of students who have access to such materials to those who have not, but so far it has proved difficult to allow for the "self-selection" factor—that students who ask for such materials may be better organized, more motivated and more assertive in identifying their needs than students who do not request such resources.

Perhaps the best route to a satisfactory course-choice system is to borrow a concept from social science—that any reality can only be fairly represented by a set of "competing perspectives" and that a concept as complex as a course needs all the perspectives of descriptions, previews, comments and diagnostic materials in order to describe it completely.

Induction and Preparation for Distance Learning

After marketing, there are probably few areas of distance education support that attract more attention and effort than induction—the process of getting new students welcomed and initiated into the distance study method of learning, and preparation, and getting them up to speed with the skills they need in order to study. But, as so often in distance education, there is little in the way of research findings to give us clear evidence as to what is most effective in either process.

Induction

There are several aspects to induction but all are intimately related to the ways in which students gain access to the institution. Darkenwald and Merriam (1982) suggested that there are barriers that students need to overcome to participate in learning. These are:

- *informational*—getting adequate and accurate information about the institution, its courses and media used;
- *institutional*—an institution may have impenetrable procedures, unfriendly or complicated websites and so on;
- *situational*—a student's personal situation may present difficulties in accessing learning (in accessing face-to-face tuition or acquiring online facilities, for example);
- *psycho-social*—a student may hold beliefs about themselves that are likely to affect their retention (about their abilities, their knowledge and their confidence as a learner).

To some extent we have dealt with the informational aspects under course and module choice earlier in this chapter. The remaining barriers suggest that induction should address a number of factors:

- *The face of the institution* should be as friendly and accessible as possible, whether that face is a brochure or a website. Some of the most obvious barriers are the administrative procedures of the institution. All institutions have their own methods, jargon and codes of conduct that tend to act as the rites of a secret society and that exclude all but the initiated.
- *The variability of the student's situation* should be taken into account. All too often there is a one-size-fits-all approach—induction is largely through a website that students are expected to visit and which allows little interaction to suit individual students.
- *Psycho-social.* This is likely to be the most important aspect of induction—addressing the student's feelings about what they've taken on. In my personal experience of inductions, there is emphasis on the information transfer and too little attention paid to the affective nature of the experience.

Obviously there are essential administrative elements to this—assessing the institution's VLE for student-friendliness, the arrangements for tutorials whether face-to-face, phone or online, how to send in assignments and so on, all of which are probably unique to the institution. While these materials have to be covered at some stage, it is my gut feeling that too much material at the start is both off-putting to students who want to engage with the course materials, and possibly counterproductive—it will be largely unread or not understood free of its context.

One of the earliest reactions of new U.K .Open University students in the days when all materials were sent by correspondence was to comment on the amount of administrative "bumf" that came in the first mailing and the sense of being overwhelmed by it all. Indeed, a simple study found that on one Open University module, the first mailing weighed around 21 lb (9.5 kg), some 70% of which was such "bumf." It was not possible to link this to the early dropout phenomenon but it probably didn't help. New online students encountering their institution's website for the first time may well experience feelings of being overwhelmed and of easily getting lost in it.

Basics of induction

Thus it would seem the basic characteristics of an induction process should be:

(i) *Short*—it may be aiming too high to attempt the "social integration" of the students in an induction process, especially if that involves a lengthy pack or complicated website. The aim of induction should be not to stand in the student's path of getting on to tackling the module content. As we saw in Chapter 5, the concept of social integration may only be partially effective in getting students up and running.

(ii) Individual—the research quoted in Chapter 6 suggests that it is individual proactive support that is most effective in promoting student success. It seems likely that that applies as much to the induction process as support during a module. And, as also suggested in Chapter 6, there is good evidence that a simple 10-minute pre-course phone call can have a 5% retention effect at the end of a course nearly nine months later.

(iii) Just-in-time—rather than overload students with a great deal of material that may seem irrelevant at the front of a module, it seems best to remember Keller's ARCS Theory and only supply what is relevant at the point students have reached. So, for example, information about continuous assessment may be best supplied at the point when students are expecting to submit an assignment but not long before.

Content of Induction

However, it is the cognitive, and particularly the organizational and emotional aspects of distance learning, that are harder to explain.

(i) Cognitive induction. There is now general agreement amongst distance education practitioners that the cognitive skills needed for distance learning are best dealt with in the course material itself, as they become relevant, rather than separately in a preparation or induction website or pack. Thus essay writing skills should be taught within the context of an essay that students have to write for their course module, rather than in a separate activity.

(ii) Organizational induction. It is surprising to me how helpful very simple organizational advice can be to new students. Even advice as to where to file materials, how and where to start reading them, and what to do when, can be reassuring to novices. And, of course, simple ideas about time and space management can be helpful, with the caveat that it is important not to give the impression that there is only one way to organize study. Such advice may even be counterproductive. As Carey (2010) writes:

> psychologists have discovered that some of the most hallowed advice on study habits is flat wrong. For instance, many study skills courses insist that students find a specific place, a study room or a quiet corner of the library, to take their work. The research finds just the opposite. In one classic 1978 experiment, psychologists found that college students who studied a list of 40 vocabulary words in two rooms— one windowless and cluttered, the other modern, with a view on a courtyard—did far better on a test than students who studied the words twice, in the same room. Later studies have confirmed the finding, for a variety of topics.

(iii) Emotional induction. This is the most delicate induction. My unsubstantiated belief is that this is most likely to be achieved through using a motivational method such as Proactive Motivational Support (Chapter 6), but further research is needed on this point.

Preparation for Study

One of the most common explanations given by distance educators for the high level of dropout is that dropped-out students were insufficiently prepared for their courses. The solution, therefore, apparently lies in providing preparatory materials in an effort to bring students up to the right level, or "remediation" as it is often called. However, as Anderson (2006) notes, "Don't expect non-credit materials to do what credit courses have to accomplish." In rare cases where remediation efforts have been evaluated, the evidence suggests that this may be true—for example, in the report quoted in Chapter 5 that found that math remedial study was no help to economics postgraduate students.

Thus efforts to provide preparatory materials either on paper or online may be at least partly ineffective. It will be more effective to put the effort into getting students on to the right course in the first place.

Chapter 10

Retrieval

Ever tried. Ever failed. No matter. Try Again. Fail again. Fail better.

(Samuel Beckett)

At the opposite end of the support process from course choice and induction is *retrieval*—the process of getting a dropped-out student back into the institution. There are several reasons for seeing this as an important issue:

(i) Most, if not all, distance education institutions produce more dropout than graduates. I have argued previously that this has both financial and reputational consequences for institutions. It doesn't seem likely to do an institution much good if there are increasing numbers of ex-students in the population who have been let go with no apparent interest from the institution.

(ii) The evidence from dropout surveys and elsewhere is that much of this dropout is not for academic reasons as such. Generally these students are not intellectually doomed to fail. They drop out largely for non-academic reasons—being on the wrong course, overwhelming personal circumstances, not getting adequate support and, above all, losing the motivation to learn.

(iii) Institutions have invested heavily in these students in getting them as far as registration and sometimes further toward graduation. They are surely worth some small extra investment to get them back.

(iv) Finally there are ethical issues—if dropping out damages people (and admittedly the jury is still out on that in distance education), then it seems to me that institutions have an ethical obligation to minimize that damage.

Yet the evidence is that retrieval is not a high priority with institutions. Certainly there seems to be much less attention paid to it than would be paid by a commercial organization. For example, Clutterbuck (1995), in an article on managing customer defection in a commercial context, points out that an organization that allows its hard-won customers to fade away without some effort to retrieve them will be losing the considerable expense that was used in recruiting them in the first place. So many commercial companies have a customer retrieval strategy.

> In the mail recently I received a letter from the insurance company about a policy I'd cancelled:
>
> > Dear Mr Simpson
> >
> > Our aim at D_____ Insurance is to provide the highest standards of service and the best value for money products. We are therefore concerned that you have decided not to renew your home policy with us.
> >
> > We would like to know if there was some way in which our service or renewal offer fell short of your requirements. It would be of great help to us if you could find the time to complete the questionnaire below . . . Please be frank in your reply. We will be very receptive to your comments and this will help us improve our products for the future . . . We hope you will try us again in the future.
>
> I am fairly certain, were I to complete the questionnaire in a way that indicated that I was still purchasing insurance, that I shall receive another letter when the policy comes due again.

There is now some evidence that retrieval is being taken more seriously on a national scale. For example, in the U.K. there is now the "Back on Course" project (www.backoncourse.ac.uk), which seeks to contact students who have dropped out of full-time higher education and advise them on how and where to return. For various reasons it can be surprisingly difficult to ensure that similar effort is undertaken in a distance education context.

Spotting the Leaks

One of the reasons for the difficulty is that students do not slip out of the institution in an orderly manner. It can be quite difficult to spot all their exit routes. For example in the U.K. Open University I have suggested (see Chapter 7) that there are at least 12 different ways in which students can escape the organization:

1. Enquirers who do not follow up their original enquiry = 65%
2. Students who register but then withdraw before the course starts =10%
3. Students who withdraw sometime after the course start without submitting any work = 10%
4. Students who withdraw sometime after the course start but after submitting some work = 4%
5. Students who become inactive after the course start but do not formally withdraw = 4%
6. Students who submit assignments but do not take the final exam or submit a final project = 1%
7. Students who take the final exam but fail it and qualify for a resit = 0.4%
8. Students who take the exam and fail it outright = 1%
9. Students who take the exam but fail the continuous assessment part of the course 1%
10. Students who fail the subsequent resit 1%
11. Students who complete a course but then do not return for subsequent courses in the same program = 0.6%
12. Student who are eliminated by the institution—for example, for failing to pay fees, not following regulations or other reasons = 1%

These figures are very approximate and can sometimes only be estimated from other figures.

There is clearly a difficult choice to make here. If you are trying to be like the proverbial Dutch boy attempting to plug holes in the dike, then it is not just deciding the number of fingers that are needed, but a choice between blocking the torrent that represents the enquirers flooding out, or trying to close off the trickle of (say) students who are failing their exams.

One possible guideline might be to use the "level of integration or engagement" that a student or potential student has with the institution—how far they have become linked in to the institution and how far they see themselves as students of the institution. Then the more integrated they have been, the more effort should be made to retrieve them.

I suggest that it makes sense, therefore, to start from the position that *all dropouts should receive some kind of contact from the institution* but that contact might be graded according to a strategy that reflects the level of engagement of the dropout with the institution, the likelihood of retrieving them, the costs of doing so and so on. Thus enquirers might receive a mass email on an online course seeking to remind them to apply, whereas a pre-exam dropout might ideally receive an individual phone call that seeks to address his or her particular situation. Thus it is possible to establish a system of responses that at least has some logic to it.

I found the following response from a student in an end of module survey: "I stopped studying the module because my mother became ill. I didn't formally withdraw because I just didn't have the time. I was very disappointed that no-one seemed to notice—I had no contact from anyone. I'm not sure I'll try to carry on next year."

Retrieval Strategies at Different Stages

Taking the example of the different exit routes outlined above it is possible to draw up a strategy that addresses each "hole" in the dike.

Enquirers Who Do not Follow up Their Original Enquiry

This represents a very low level of integration so a simple letter or email reminder may be all that is worth doing.

Students Who Register but Withdraw before the Course Start

Although this is still a low level of integration, such students may have committed some payment to the institution depending on its policy. If they have withdrawn before receiving any services, then they may feel aggrieved if no attempt at contact is made. No institution can afford to have too many dissatisfied customers in the general population. But, more seriously, withdrawal at this stage suggests that attempts to integrate and induct the students have failed and it will be important to know why. Thus a mailing with a return questionnaire may be indicated if only to gather data.

Students who Withdraw Sometime after Course Start without Submitting Any Work

This is a category that needs breaking down into a finer structure. We can guess that some are students who find the first mailing or first assignment or activity of a course far more intimidating than they had expected. There is evidence of both—for example, see the evidence about reading levels in Chapter 12—but further work on the way such students respond to the initial demands of a course is needed.

For example, Lockwood (2000) pioneered a method in which students were invited to record their feelings straight into audiotape as they studied. He found that the "self-assessment questions" (SAQs) that are traditionally inserted into distance education texts at regular intervals did not necessarily enhance students' study. Students generally skipped such questions but felt guilty at doing so and tended to lose confidence in their learning skills. Since SAQs play such an important role in the design of both distance and online texts, this finding— if substantiated—could be very important. It is hard to see that it could have been established another way. Such a methodology might unpack the often very complex feelings that may lead a student to fail to start a course or submit work.

Students Who Withdraw Sometime after Course Start after Submitting Some Work

This, of course, is a large category covering those who have only done a little to those who have nearly completed the course. Withdrawal may occur after a disappointing result on an assignment, difficulties with the course or one of the life events that affect all students—birth and death and all that's in between. With such a range of possible causes, it's hard to devise a system that is sufficiently sensitive to respond appropriately. One obvious possibility is a questionnaire, but it can be difficult to decide whether such a questionnaire is an information-gathering exercise or a retrieval strategy.

In a study carried out by Gaskell, Gibbons and Simpson (1990), an attempt was made to reconcile these two aims. A short leaflet called "Bailing Out and Taking Off Again" was sent on a weekly basis to all students who had actively withdrawn. The text was illustrated with a graphic of a smiling person in a parachute and comprised a brief commentary on reasons for withdrawal in the hope that this might reassure students that withdrawal was the right choice for them and that they had no alternative—or did they? There was then a short open-ended questionnaire that was a compromise between the desire to accumulate data on dropout and to identify those students who might be retrievable.

This is an extract from the text (the full text can be found in the "StudyAid pack" at www.ormondsimpson.com):

BAILING OUT

We are sorry to hear that you have withdrawn from one or more of your courses. We hope that this is only a temporary setback and that you will be able to resume your studies soon. This leaflet is designed to help us find out more about why you withdrew and to see if we can find ways of helping you return.

● Did you have problems finding the time? Practically all our students tell us that finding the time is their biggest problem. If this was the case for you, then ask us for our leaflet "Finding the Time for Study" which has some ideas about how to keep up with your studies whilst dealing with all the other demands on your time.

● Did you have personal problems—illness, domestic difficulties and all the other things that can affect anybody? If so then we do sympathize. Sometimes the best thing to do is to "bail out" of study and then return when things are easier. You"ll be welcome back whenever you're ready.

● Did you have problems that were our fault? If so do please tell us. We're always very keen to improve our systems and maybe there's something we can do to help you better in future.

The leaflet then went on to cover the main causes of dropout as far as they were known. It ended:

● If anything in this leaflet has changed your mind about withdrawing then it may not be too late to restart your studies. Contact us straightaway to discuss how to catch up.

A questionnaire accompanied the leaflet. Because this was a retrieval exercise and not an information-gathering process, the questionnaire was different from a standard withdrawal questionnaire. It was much shorter, in the hope that that would encourage students to complete it, and it was open-ended in the hope that this would allow students to be clearer about their reason for withdrawal where this was a combination of factors that might have interacted in different ways.

Questionnaire

Please tell us why you withdrew and if you have any comments on any aspects of your studies:

A. I withdrew because of _____

B. I'd like to comment on the following aspects of the University's system:

    1. the course material _____

    2. the administration system _____

    3. the local support system—tutor, tutorials _____

    4. the assessment system—assignments and exams _____

    5. Other _____

There was a 35% return of the questionnaire and the reasons given were very similar to those given in Chapter 7. These are some of the collated responses:

A. I withdrew because:

"Lack of time"

"My work patterns were disrupted by my employer"

"I didn't manage to keep up with the assignments"

"Just before my second assignment was due I had a car crash and couldn't put it in by the due date"

B. Comments on the system:

    1. Comments on the course material *(there were very few comments on the course material, which may suggest that they were taken as given and not seen as a factor in withdrawal)*

"Units difficult to read (print type rather thin) and the author's preferences were too obvious—please keep gender and racist issues out of courses"

"They looked inviting but I never got around to reading them"

"Excessive amount of literature to wade through"

"I found the jumps between the preparatory materials and the course to be too great"

2. Comments on the administration system *(again there were few comments)*

"Quite complex—I needed a streamlined guide to the rules"

"Too bureaucratic—it took several phone calls to get the right person"

"Problems with meeting fees"

3. Comments on the local support system

"Excellent tutor—couldn't have been more helpful and supportive when my problems presented themselves"

"I found the initial tutorial very off-putting"

"Had to keep reminding him that I had a hearing difficulty"

"Boring"

"Excellent" (same tutor)

4. Comments on the assessment system

"There was a delay on the result of the first assignment which meant I did the second before getting feedback on the first"

"Questions asked did not correspond to the text"

5. Other comments *(this was easily the most comprehensively answered part of the questionnaire and it felt as though students needed to get something off their chests)*

"I originally applied in March—by the time the course had started the following February my enthusiasm had eroded"

"I was impressed by your 'Bailing Out' leaflet—thank you for asking. Sorry for any trouble I've caused"

"If I had had a longer and more flexible time to complete the modules I could have managed my time better"

"I felt badly treated about my withdrawal. I withdrew for personal reasons at home. Until I got your leaflet all I had was a standard letter of acknowledgement which told me that I was still liable for the fees. This made me feel that you didn't give a toss as long as you'd got my money. I needed a letter of the nature of your leaflet"

"After my shifts changed I couldn't face the tutorials after 12 hours at work. I was disappointed to bail out"

"Thank you for taking the time to write to me. I am sad I have had to quit and hope to start again next year"

Although systems did not exist to discover whether the leaflet had changed anyone's mind, it was possible to identify occasions where withdrawal had occurred through some misunderstanding of various procedures. For example, there were cases where students believed that missing one assignment ruled out the possibility of passing the course or misunderstood complex rules concerning attendance at residential schools. Such students were contacted and it proved possible to get some of them back on course—about 8% of those responding to the questionnaire were retrieved that way, an overall retrieval rate of about 2.8%. Given that active withdrawals were themselves about 60% of overall withdrawals (the rest being "passive" withdrawals) this meant that the exercise had an overall retrieval rate of about 1.6%.

It was clear that the success of retrieving such students was critically time-dependent; responses to possible retrieval cases had to be made in less than a week or the students had already become too detached from their studies and too far behind to catch up. In addition, as such responses were to individual students they were very labor-intensive and it is not clear how cost-effective such methods of retrieval are. Since these retrieval contacts were on an individual basis, the costs were quite high—possibly of the order of $48–64 (£30–40) per student retrieved. However, since each student retrieved, then generated, an income to the university of up to $2,400 (£1,500), this was an extremely cost-effective operation—see Chapter 11.

What also emerged from a proportion of the questionnaires is how apologetic some students were. They clearly tended to blame themselves for their "failure." This tendency must clearly be useful to the institution as it allows it to escape responsibility for retention activities or lack of them. But this institutional get-out clause may be decreasing in effect, as my personal impression is that students are becoming more assertive and are increasingly likely to assume that failure is not necessarily their fault. If this (entirely subjective) impression is true, it may have considerable impact on retention-unfriendly institutions.

The subsequent history of the project was interesting. After the report on the project was published, it was held to be a worthwhile exercise and control was passed to the University's quality assurance department. Here it became primarily a data collection system and the questionnaire became a much more substantial affair, with more than 30 questions. The replies then were processed in a central department before being passed on to sections where a response could be made to the individual students. By the time this happened any such responses were far too late, as students had fallen far too far behind to catch up.

Meanwhile the quality department issued annual reports giving detailed breakdowns of students' reasons for withdrawal, noting that these had changed little since the last report. This may be an example of how reducing autonomy in an area closest to students can have a deleterious effect on student retention.

Students Who Become Inactive After Course Start but Do not Formally Withdraw

These are the "passive withdrawers" and may present the most intractable retrieval problem of all. In a system with regular assignment submission dates, it may be possible to assume that missing one assignment is a sign of such withdrawal. But if the system allows some flexibility so that not all the assignments are required for the course, then it becomes more difficult. Similarly, not responding to a query from a tutor may be a sign of passive withdrawal but may also be the sign of an independent student who simply wishes to be left alone to work.

The river diagram of assignment submission in Figure 4.2 (in Chapter 4) suggests that in this particular system the non-submission of an assignment is a good indicator of passive withdrawal. Of the students missing the first assignment, only 2% submit the second and a negligible number submit the third. Thus progress–chasing a missing assignment on this course may be a good retrieval strategy, particularly at the beginning of a course. But again the delay in responding is a factor in whether retrieval is a real possibility; in a postal system with a set of submission dates where a tutor allows for a few days for mailing delays or just for human delay, it rapidly becomes too late for effective retrieval.

Stevens and Simpson (1988) carried out a study in a distributed system where tutors were responsible for monitoring assignment submission. They asked tutors to report on all the first assignments on their course that they hadn't received, on what efforts they'd made to follow up the students and what the results were.

The first (unexpected) finding was that more than 30% of the tutors did not make an effort to follow up the non-submission of assignments despite them being contractually required to do so. The principal reason some gave was that they had done so in the past only to discover that the data they had been given by the institution was out of date—for example, some, at least, of the students they were contacting had only provisionally registered on the course and had canceled their registration some weeks before. This data had not been communicated to the tutors in time. Of the remaining tutors who had tried to follow up non-submission some had found it a frustrating experience—it could take considerable time to find students at home when phoning and there was little response to letters or emails. Most had failed to retrieve any students, as the eventual delay was too long, so were not encouraged to try again the following year. However, all these reasons may be excuses for simple lack of motivation on the tutors' part.

> During this exercise a tutor wrote to me saying, "Frankly I don't bother chasing up these people. I know I'm going to lose about a third of them anyway so I concentrate my efforts on those who are left after the first few weeks." This may be a good illustration of the "Darwinista" approach.

It is possible that online modules may make it easier to identify passive withdrawers more quickly if there is a way of checking when students stop logging into the Virtual Learning Environment. Other more novel methods have been used—one conventional university in London monitors the use of the students' key cards used to enter the university's main building. Students who fail to enter the building within a given period are contacted to find why. I have been unable to find evidence as to whether either of these methods has resulted in the retrieval of passive dropout students.

Students Who Submit Assignments but Do not Take the Final Exam or Submit a Final Project

This is likely to be a small but significant group. It will be small, as not many students will persist to the end of a course, submitting assignments, but then fail to take the exam. On the other hand, these will be highly engaged students who have done considerable work towards their qualification—they represent a considerable investment by both themselves and the institution. The factors that cause them to give up at such a late stage are likely to repay investigation.

There may be several groups of such students:

(i)   Students who want the highest possible grade. There may be elements of perfectionism amongst those students who wish for the highest grade. In these cases "perfectionism may be the enemy of progress," particularly where the desired grades are unrealistic. Counterproductive perfectionism of this kind can be an extraordinarily persistent personal characteristic and I have very little idea how to counter it apart from encouraging students to lower their sights and to "skim, skip and scrape" where necessary—see Chapter 8 and the section on motivational emails.

(ii) Students who experience exam stress to a degree that ultimately deters them from taking the end of module exam. Surveys of students certainly suggest that such stress is very much a part of the student experience, but how far such stress actually stops students from taking exams does not seem to have been examined in depth. There is colloquial data.

Student A contacted me shortly before the exam. "I'm sorry," she said, "I cannot sit that exam. It's a pity because I've done quite well up to now but I know that when I go into that room I shall completely seize up. I'm going to cut my losses and get out now." We did a "guided fantasy" about how it would feel for her to go into the exam room, sit down at a desk and start writing and talked through the sources of her stress. We then devised some simple stress management techniques for her to use both before and during the exam, and in the event she sat the exam and passed. I can't take credit for this—it may be just the mere statement of her problem was a way of seeking reassurance to enable her to do something that she was going to do anyway—but I still counted her as a "probable."

Such one-to-one counseling is not an option in the majority of cases. But there are materials that can be made available to students either online or in hard copy—there is an example of a text called "Getting Through" designed for U.K. Open University students at http://www.ormondsimpson.com/page4.htm in the "StudyAid leaflets" that is freely available for adaption. See also the U.K. Open University "Skills for OU study" at http://www.open.ac.uk/skillsforstudy and "Revising exams and assessment" for an example. These materials deal with topics such as exam technique, simple stress management activities and ways of seeking further help. Some of the more sophisticated texts available elsewhere on the Web contain audio materials covering simple relaxation exercises. Such materials are cheap to produce and—particularly online—are very cheap to disseminate so that they are worth pursuing as a retrieval strategy even if more research on their effectiveness remains to be done.

(iii) Students who incorrectly believe they have no chance of passing or getting the grade they want. Students are not always the best analyzers of their own ability or the likely grade of any work they submit. In some cases the institution may not be offering clear feedback on individual assignments or on their overall progress through the module.

In an internal study, which she called "The Needless Fails" study, Blanchfield (2000) looked at a group of U.K. Open University students who had submitted some assignments on the course but had not sat the exam. She discovered that 28% of students who didn't sit their exam could have passed the course by just passing their exam. In part this may have been because the institution had a developed a complex strategy for conflating continuous assessment marks and exam marks to give the overall module grade, involving differentially weighted, threshold and substitutable assignments. This was very hard for students (and staff) to understand. Sadly institutional rules made it impossible to retrieve these students, as it was not possible to retake or resit an exam in these circumstances. But see Chapter 15 for a further look at this project as an example of institutional change.

Students Who Take the Final Exam but Fail it and Qualify for a Resit

Depending on the particular institution, there may be failed assessments that can be retaken in order to complete a course or program of studies. There may be certain conditions to qualify—passing continuous assessment or previous assignments and so on. But it's important to note that this single exit route actually disguises three possible "exit holes":

(i)   not accepting the offer of a retake;
(ii) accepting the offer but not taking it up when due;
(iii) taking up the offer but failing again.

The second of these is covered by the previous section to some extent and the third by the section below, but the first presents particular challenges.

Students who have just faced a failure may have had their sometimes fragile confidence shattered and be strongly disinclined to endure the experience again. They may need reassurance to re-register. Again there are materials that may be helpful. There is an example of a text designed for U.K. Open University students on http://www.ormondsimpson.com/page4.htm in the "StudyAid leaflets" called "Not the End of the World," which again is freely available for adaption. It covers topics such as how the student feels, the importance of not taking failure personally, that failure is a common event for students ("there's no such thing as failure—just feedback," as Neurolinguistic Programmers would say), and that the important thing to do is to understand it as far as possible and then to kiss it off as one of the natural hazards of being a student, and so on.

Given the high level of engagement of students at this stage, it may be possible to justify the option of individual proactive contacts face-to-face or via phone or email despite the much greater expense of such contact. However, there is currently not much evidence that such intensive contact is much more effective than a simple text. Informal unpublished studies in the U.K. Open University suggested that both text and proactive tutor contact increase the numbers taking retakes in the U.K. Open University by about 4%, with very little difference between them. Even with such a small retrieval, the activity is still probably cost-effective—see Chapter 11.

Students Who Take the Exam and Fail it Outright

In a well-designed continuous assessment system the numbers of students who fail the final assessment should be small. If a module has a high "getting to the exam" rate but then a high exam failure rate, then that is a cause for concern at senior management level—see Chapter 12. There may be special reasons in such cases, so some kind of questionnaire is indicated. With such small numbers of highly engaged students, this should not represent a large number to respond to individually. At least they should receive a version of the "Not the End of the World" leaflet referred to above. However, this also raises the question of how far to strive to keep students going at all costs and whether there are students who the institution does not wish to retain, either for the student's long-term welfare or for the institution's good—see below.

Students Who Take the Exam but Fail the Continuous Assessment Part of the Course

This again will depend on the institution's particular structures, but is likely to be very rare and should probably attract individual attention where possible.

Students Who Fail a Subsequent Final Assessment Retake

Some of these may be students who fall into the category of students the institution does not want—or at least does not want to encourage to persist if their failure is due to intellectual difficulties they are unlikely to overcome. See "Which Students not to Retrieve" below.

Students who Complete a Course but then Do not Return for Subsequent Courses in the Same Program

These students are an important section to retrieve having already been successful. They may of course have moved onto courses at other institutions, but if that is the case the institution that has lost them needs to know why.

Students Who are Eliminated by the Institution—for Example, for Failing to Pay Fees, not Following Regulations or Other Reasons

These cases are so individual that it is hard to make general recommendations. Some of these students may fall into the group of "Which Students not to Retrieve"—see later in this chapter.

Students who Have Completed a Final Qualification and Don't Return

This on first sight might seem a paradoxical heading. After all, students who have successfully completed a program of study are the institution's final product and don't need retrieving. However, every institution that spends any effort on developing an alumni association may in effect be reclaiming these students.

Some may be reclaimed to further study. Now that it is recognized that learning is a lifelong activity, it is likely that graduates at any level may return to update or raise their qualification or to change into another line of work entirely. Since these are by definition successful students with the institution previously, the likelihood of their success a second time around is very high indeed. So that they are just the kind of students the institution wishes to attract.

Some may be reclaimed to other roles—as mentors to new students (see Chapter 13), as informal publicity agents, working for the institution directly as tutors or providing support to the institution financially. This indeed might be one retrieval effort that directly pays for itself.

Students from Other Institutions You Could Try to Retrieve

One of the features of higher education now is the increasing level of competition between institutions. I note, for example, that the U.K. government now allows bodies other than chartered universities to apply for degree-awarding powers, as the United States has done for many years. A number of large companies such as BPP have set up their own education subsidiaries and are charging competitive fees. There will probably be competition between such providers to recruit students, but it seems unlikely that there will be active poaching of current students (although the vision of marketing people skulking virtually, if not physically, around other institution's campuses, making surreptitious offers to students they can't refuse, is not entirely unthinkable).

Other Exit Routes

In addition to the exit routes outlined above, some institutions may have their own unique ways of allowing students to escape. For example, courses may have compulsory elements in which students have to particulate to pass the course. Failure to participate might mean that the course cannot be successfully completed even if all the other elements have been passed. Some U.K. Open University courses have a residential school requirement halfway through the course, for example, and a student who doesn't show (5% to 10% of the total cohort due to attend) will automatically fail the course. Of course, non-attendance may often be a sign—possibly the first sign—of passive withdrawal at an earlier stage.

"Pro-active Critical Markers"

All the contacts outlined above rely on the institution being able to identify specific groups of students at particular times and then generate addresses, phone numbers or email addresses in order to send materials or contact them. The term "pro-active critical markers" has been suggested for systems that can identify such groups at various times. It will be important to develop such markers from an institution's IT databases through some kind of "data-mining" or version of "learning analytics."

Once such systems are in place, decisions have to be made as to what level of pro-active contact (if any) is appropriate and affordable.

The Effectiveness of Retrieval Strategies

There seems to have been little published work in the area of retrieval, although there appears to be increasing interest. In a report in the *Times Higher Education Supplement* (August 16, 2002), a researcher in a full-time university in Scotland reported that more than 10% of dropped-out students returned after being contacted by the university. The report suggested that a number of students dropped out because of difficulties unrelated to their course such as domestic and child-care responsibilities compounded by health problems in the family. In some cases they then assumed that they couldn't return. The survey suggested that there was little institutions can do to prevent students from withdrawing but that they can encourage them to re-enroll.

In distance education there also seems to have been little work on the cost-effectiveness of retrieval, which in any case will be very variable according to the institution, the types of dormant students that it is trying to reclaim, the timing of any contact and so on. Therefore, any figure for retrieval can only be the roughest possible guide. On checking the data for my own institution, the most recent exercise I could find was an ordinary mailing to roughly 1,000 recently (i.e., within a year) "dormant" students. This resulted in a retrieval rate of 5%, at a cost of £4.70 ($7.50) per student reclaimed. Compared with the costs of recruiting new students, this looks like a very cost-effective exercise. However, the study did not state how the students had become dormant, and without a control group of non-contacted dormant students it is impossible to know how many of these students would have re-registered in due course without the mailing.

Averkamp (1994) reported on a relatively small (15,000 students) private mixed-mode distance education institution in Germany that had mailed to all its students towards the end of their courses including dropouts. The letters were standard, but designed to be generally encouraging about re-enrolling, and contained a short reply coupon. Some 20% of dropouts re-enrolled as a result. The project was repeated the following year with letters which, although standard, were tailored to students' circumstances to some extent. The re-enrollment rate rose to 25%. Averkamp also calculated the costs and returns in terms of course fees for this exercise and found that there was an overall return on investment of 500%.

Which Students not to Retrieve

It may be appropriate to end this chapter by reminding ourselves that occasionally there are students who it may be better for all concerned not to retain or retrieve. There are various groups.

Students Who Try Hard but are Never Going to Progress

There are students who for whatever reasons are not going to ever progress their studies. They may have very challenging personal circumstances, or a change of circumstances such as increasing illness, disability, or the need to care for another person. Or they may simply not have the cognitive ability to study at the particular level of the module they've chosen. Some drop out quite early; others nevertheless continue to try, sometimes repeatedly. *They are still owed an ethical duty of care*. If there is always the possibility of failure in any kind of learning, then perhaps there should be an educational equivalent of the Hippocratic oath—i.e., if it is not possible to do good, then the educator should at least aim not to do harm. That will mean that any student who finally leaves and who is not retained or retrieved should, as far as possible, not be left with a permanent or personal sense of failure and that they should be helped to find other avenues to explore.

This is why most of the examples of materials for retention I have cited as examples in this book contain elements that attempt to address the feelings of failure students might experience. Such materials should tell students that dropping out is not a criticism of them personally, that it is something that has affected many people and that it is often a positive step towards new ways forward.

I had an elderly student who was taking the math course I was teaching. With help he passed the continuous assessment, but sadly he failed the end-of-module exam. He emailed me clearly quite hurt by what had happened. I emailed back saying,

Dear Fred

I was sorry to hear you'd failed the final exam. But that's not the important thing. The important thing is that not many people would have tackled this course at your stage of life—you gave it your best shot, came very close and I was proud of you. Well done!

I don't know if this helped him at all, but at least I'd tried to find what positives I could for him.

Students Who are More Trouble than They're Worth

There are—hopefully very occasionally—students you really would be glad not to retain or, if they withdraw, be really thankful not to have to try to retrieve. In a commercial environment, Clutterbuck (1995) noted that there are customers that any organization would prefer not to retain, such as persistent debtors or those who take up more resource from the company than they're worth. It sometimes feels as though distance education attracts such students in greater proportion than conventional education.

If such students exist, then this is not to say that you would actively take steps to make them withdraw (except for disciplinary reasons), but just that there are some students who absorb more resources than can be justified by their results. These are students who take up large amounts of time with emails and correspondence over trivial complaints, for example, or who harass their tutors, or who seek help and advice again and again about the same issue but without ever putting the advice into action.

This can be a very fine line to draw, as some students may have mental health problems and need to be treated with great care and caution. Neither should the problem be overestimated. In the area for which I am responsible, there are some 20,000 students. I keep a file of "students who make unreasonable demands," which contains only 20 names. My main problem is supporting the staff who have to deal with those students. They may feel frustrated and angry after yet another phone call about some unresolvable issue, and I sometimes need to make a difficult judgment about when to intervene and risk the student dropping out or leave a staff member badly demoralized.

Ms. Z. was a very demanding student. Every time an assignment was returned to her, she would bombard the hapless tutor with letters, which, while not actively insulting, were on the very brink of abusive, accusing her tutor of being biased against her. Her tutor at first tried to start a dialogue with her, but it merely generated more furious accusations. Letters were starting to arrive daily, along with audio- and videotapes, books, pamphlets, postcards and so on. When the tutor (after far too long) finally ran out of patience at this postal persecution, and brought the correspondence to me, it filled an archive box.

I found it difficult to know what to do. Behind the obvious aggression of the student, there was what appeared to be an educationally disadvantaged but lively mind, and I didn't want to lose her. But I had to protect the tutor. Finally I agreed with the tutor that she would simply send all further materials to me without opening them and I wrote to the student to say her tutor could no longer deal with this correspondence. As the student no longer received the reinforcement of replies, the torrent of material slowly dried up.

The student passed the course and went on. I warned the next tutor about what to expect, but in the event there was very little subsequent problem. The student continued to study and was ultimately successful.

However, I was reminded of this case study only last week when we received a letter from Ms. Z. about an unrelated problem. She had inadvertently enclosed a letter from the local authority to her about a complaint she had obviously been making. It ran:

> Dear Ms Z,
>
> Whilst you are welcome to write to us daily about this problem, you need not feel impelled to do so, as we are doing all we can to resolve the issue.
>
> Yours, etc.

For a moment we felt a kinship in the knowledge that there were other long-suffering bureaucrats out there who felt just the same as us . . .

This was a case with a happy ending, but sadly there are others:

M_____ was a student who had episodes of paranoid schizophrenia. In addition he was quite severely visually handicapped. It was suggested to him by a well-meaning psychiatrist that study might be a useful form of therapy, so he enrolled into a distance learning course that had a residential school. The member of institutional staff who was responsible for him had herself experienced problems of schizophrenia, leading to a tragic suicide in her own family. As a result of that experience, she had become a very firm advocate of the rights of victims of mental health problems. She was therefore particularly keen that M_____ should succeed and gave him great support.

All went well while he was studying at a distance with only phone contact with his tutor, although his progress was slow. However, his adviser was particularly keen that he should attend the residential school for the full educational experience. As soon as he arrived, problems began. He approached the advisers on the first day to say that he could hear voices plotting against him through the walls of his room, and the situation went downhill from there. He became suspicious of his tutorial group and sat just outside the circle without participating, apart from glaring sightlessly at them. Neither the tutor nor the students could deal with this and asked for him to be removed. The residential school director felt deeply sorry for M_____, but the student group was so disturbed that it was clearly affecting their enjoyment of the school, so he complied. M_____ went on to fail the course and not study again. The director [myself] still feels guilty.

Students Who are "Unbothered," Dream or Fight the Institution

Professor Frank Furedi (*Times Higher Education Supplement*, March 29, 2002) claimed to have identified another group of students. These were students who simply weren't bothered about whether they were making progress or not. Higher education was just one of a number of options that were open to them, and—as if they were in a supermarket—they were wandering around feeling the produce. If one course didn't work out for them, then (like any consumer) they'd try something different. "Many such students," Furedi writes, "regard their studies as a trial run: if it works out fine, and if it doesn't then dropping out and finding something else to do is no big deal . . . it's more akin to changing jobs than being forced to abandon a real commitment."

If such students exist, I haven't met them in large numbers. But if Furedi is right, then their rather instrumental approach to education strikes me as rather refreshing and healthy and perhaps higher education should respond to them as such.

I have certainly come across a few students who fall into a slightly different category that I think of as "dreamers" (see Chapter 6). They seem to be studying hopefully, rather than with real intention. They tend to resist attempts to help them or at least respond to suggestions as though they were playing the Transactional Analysis game of "Why don't you . . . ?"—"Yes, but . . . " with its typical exchanges, "Why don't you try studying this way?"—"Yes, but I can't do that because . . . " I have found such students very difficult to help and I suspect that deep-seated behavior patterns first identified by Charles Dickens' Mr. Micawber ("something will turn up") are to blame. More coherently, I sometimes wonder if these students are the "Entity theorists" of the psychologist Carole Dweck's definition, that is, people who believe that their level of intelligence is fixed and cannot be altered by effort. Thus they believe that they have either got what it takes to succeed or they haven't and that what happens is largely down to luck.

I also have come across students who appear to spend more time fighting the institution than studying with it.

I have just (I so hope) finished dealing with a business studies student who has been pursuing a complaint against the institution. He withdrew from a course on the grounds that he had been badly advised to take it. It seemed to me that the advice he had been given was fair in the context of what was known about his previous courses and that what had happened was that he had been unable to engage with the different nature of his new course.

He argued the case with me by phone, letter, email and face-to-face meeting. Slowly I began to realize that had he spent as much as a quarter of the time studying as he had spent fighting the institution, he could have passed the course with ease. It seemed to me that he was using his complaint to avoid real engagement with the course for whatever reasons and that the dialogue was getting us nowhere. I politely declined to continue the discussion and he withdrew.

Of course, students do often have legitimate complaints against their institution, which are a valuable source of feedback. It is only when those complaints seem to be taken to almost pathological limits that it may become necessary to set boundaries. What underlies this behavior pattern is hard to understand but it sometimes feels like another Transactional Analysis Game— "Blemish"—where a person seeks to find the blemish in another person in order to hide their own inability to perform adequately.

Students Who Will Succeed in Other Ways

Finally—and because it always crops up in discussion of retention issues—there are many students who will go on to succeed after dropping out. Indeed, in some cases, the experience of dropping out even seems to be a prerequisite of success. Famous examples abound:

- Bill Gates, who dropped out of his freshman year at Harvard but went on to become one of the world's richest men;
- Steve Jobs and Steve Wozniak—co-founders of Apple Computers—who also left college without graduating;
- Albert Einstein, who dropped out of high school and subsequently studied on his own;
- John D. Rockefeller, the billionaire businessman who dropped out of high school two months before graduation;
- Mark Twain, who was an elementary school dropout;
- Walt Disney, who finally received an honorary high school diploma when he was 58;
- Mick Jagger, the Rolling Stones' frontman, who dropped out of university to start a reasonably successful rock band.

The list could stretch on. And—although this may not be the safest example for my U.S. readers—President George W. Bush in a speech to Yale graduates said, "To those of you who received honors, awards, and distinctions, I say well done. And to the 'C' students I say, you too can become President of the United States."

Chapter 11

Cost Benefits of Student Support in Online and Distance Education

Follow the money.

(advice from "Deep Throat" in the Watergate saga)

One of the most potent arguments used in institutions for limiting the amount and quality of their student support is its cost. And indeed student support in online and distance education has often been seen as a pure institutional cost, a cost that needs to be carefully controlled and minimized as far as possible. Perhaps this perspective arises from the financial arrangements of the old correspondence colleges, which traditionally made their money from recruiting students who paid their fees and then swiftly dropped out, so requiring no further services from the college.

Yet this perspective can be quite wrong. Properly organized and aimed squarely at increasing student success, student support can make a profit for students, distance institutions and society as a whole.

Cost Benefits of Student Support for Students

There is clear evidence for the benefits of successful graduation for students in whatever form of education. Successful graduates from conventional full-time higher education are likely to have better chances of employment, earn more and have better health, both physically and mentally, than non-graduates. They also live longer—around nine years longer in the United States than those who do not graduate from high school (U.S. National Center for Health Statistics 2012). We have seen correspondingly from Chapter 1 that dropouts from higher education suffer in financial and health terms compared with their successful fellows.

Financial Benefits of Graduation for Distance Students

The financial benefits of graduation have often been quantified for full-time students. For example, in the UK a review of higher education funding in the UK (Browne 2010) found that the "graduate premium"—the average amount extra a graduate would then earn over a lifetime compared with a non-graduate—was estimated as being of the order of $160,000 (£100,000). This premium may now be a little lower, although graduates still show the advantages noted above.

There is less evidence for the financial benefits for distance education graduates. Woodley and Simpson (2001) found that U.K. Open University graduates had increased their earnings from 15% above the national average to 22% above. This equates very roughly to a graduate premium of $60,000 (£40,000) over a working lifetime, somewhat less than the $160,000 (£100,000) for full-time graduates. This is partly due to the older age at which distance students usually graduate and start to earn the premium. On the other hand, a distance degree usually costs its students considerably less, not only in fees but also as the cost of a full-time degree must also include the earnings largely foregone while studying full time—see Table 11.1.

There are other concepts that are helpful in understanding the financial analysis of distance education. These are: return on investment, risk, willingness to pay, "resale" value of qualifications and the Value Triangle.

Table 11.1 Costs of U.K. distance and conventional degrees compared

	U.K. Open University distance degree	Conventional full-time U.K. degree
Total fees for a degree	£15,000 ($24,000)	£27,000 ($43,000)
Loss of earnings while studying	£0	Up to £40,000 ($64,000)
Total cost	£15,000 ($24,000)	Up to £67,000 ($107,000)

Return on Investment (RoI)

The RoI of a degree is the increased income from that degree minus the cost of the degree all divided by the cost of that degree. Thus in the UK it is possible to compare full-time and distance degrees in these terms—see Table 11.2.

It can be seen that the RoI for a distance degree is considerably higher than for a conventional degree and may well be one of the continuing attractions of distance study, particularly as in many countries students are bearing an increasingly high proportion of the cost of their degree as government subsidies are withdrawn. However, there is one considerable caveat—risk.

Risk

As we now know very well from recent events in the world of finance, every investment carries a risk. In education that risk very roughly equates to the risk of a student losing their investment by dropping out. As we've seen in distance education, that is of the order of 80–90%, depending on the institution. That is a very high level of risk—for example, the risk of completely losing an investment in wildcat oil-well drilling is only around 10%. That risk of loss of investment may in turn affect another financial concept—willing to pay.

Willing to Pay (WtP)

WtP is a relatively new concept in economics that attempts to put a price on things that often might otherwise be difficult to value—such as clean air—by asking how much people would be willing to pay for it. It may be a useful concept in education in comparing the options open to a student. In this case, given the apparently high level of risk of investment loss in distance education, how far will potential students (or their parents) continue to be willing to invest in it? At the moment there seems little sign that potential students are deterred by high dropout rates, but that may change as competition in distance education continues to grow—see later. And, of course, the amount students will be willing to pay will depend on another factor—the "resale" value of a qualification.

Table 11.2 Return on investment for U.K. distance and conventional degrees

	U.K. Open University distance degree	*Conventional full-time U.K. degree*
Total cost of degree	£15,000 ($24,000)	Up to £67,000 ($108,000)
Graduate premium	£40,000 ($64,000)	£100,000 ($160,000)
Return on Investment	166%	50%

Resale Value of Qualifications

Clearly qualifications will have different "resale" values—the amount an employer is prepared to pay someone who has that qualification, compared with another candidate of equal personal qualities and qualification in the same subject but from another institution. A graduate with a degree from a prestigious institution such as Harvard or Cambridge is likely to be more employed and at a better salary than graduates from institutions with less prominent reputations. A student's prospects will also naturally depend on the subject they studied as well, with law, economics, business studies and numerate subjects more likely to lead to well-paid employment.

The resale value of qualifications can be a particular problem in distance education, as the growth in online distance education may make it difficult for students and potential employers to assess the value of qualifications from the many providers they might find on the web. Some of these possible providers may well be "degree mills"—simply offering a degree qualification ostensibly for an assessment of prior "life experience" and guaranteeing a degree certificate by return of post. Such institutions are amongst the fastest-growing "educational providers" on the web having risen from about 200 worldwide in 2000 to more than 800 in 2005 (Hansson and Johanssen 2005).

The "Value Triangle"

These considerations of Return on Investment, risk, willing to pay and resale value are important because they offer distance education institutions a perspective in which student support can be seen as a way of adding value to an institution's "brand" and increasing its income flow. A student who sees an institution that is prepared to invest in a better-quality product, including enhanced student support, which will lessen the student's chance of dropping out and thereby losing their investment, may be more willing to invest in that institution at a higher rate. That increased investment can be used to fund the extra student support in a "Value Triangle"—see Figure 11.1.

We shall see how this might work in practice in the next section on cost benefits of student support for institutions.

Cost Benefits of Student Support for Distance Education Institutions

The main student-related costs in a distance education institution are in course production and in student support. Course production is a primary cost but is amortized over the life of a course—possibly up to 10 years or more. Student support is a more flexible and recurrent cost, which is why perhaps it is

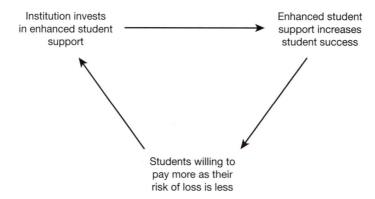

Figure 11.1 A "Value Triangle" for enhanced student support

sometimes seen as an optional add–on and easily targeted for cuts in times of financial stringency.

The benefits from increasing student success either by enhanced student support or by retention–focused course design can be threefold:

- increased student fee income;
- increased government grant income;
- savings on recruitment.

The actual cost benefits of investing in student support for institutions will depend on their funding models. There are probably as many different funding models as there are distance institutions, but the two main ones may be: (a) mainly government-funded, and (b) mainly student-tuition-fee-funded. Many institutions will be partly both. I will take two case studies to illustrate both models.

Case Study 1: Mainly Government-Funded—
The U.K. Open University before 2012

Before 2012 the U.K. Open University's income was largely in two streams: (a) student fees and (b) a government grant. (This is being replaced from 2012 by a system based far more on student fees funded through a government loan scheme. I have analyzed the pre-2012 system here as an example as it still applies to some other institutions.)

The government grant element was related to the number of students in "good standing" at the end of each year—that is the number of students who sat the end of module exam. In this case study the students' module fee was assumed to be $320 (£200), the government grant $1,760 (£1,100) per student in good standing, and the cost of recruitment around $800 (£500) per student.

So take a retention-focused student support activity costing $P per student that is applied to N students and increases student retention by n%. The total cost of the activity is:

$NP

and the added number of students retained is:

(nN)/100

The "cost per student retained" is then:

£[NP/(nN/100)] = £100P/n

Thus if a pre-module phone call costing £10 ($16) per call in staff time increases retention on the module by 5% (a real example taken from Chapter 7), the cost per student retained is:

£100 × 10/5 = £200 ($320)

The benefits of this activity are:

- increased student fee income the following year—$320 (£200) per student retained, assuming all the retained students carried on to the following module;
- Government grant—$1,760 (£1,100) per student retained.

In addition there will be some saving on recruitment costs, as the number of new students that need to be recruited to replace the dropped-out students to maintain steady student numbers will be reduced. The savings figure here is very arbitrary but I will assume that it is about 20% of the $800 (£500) needed to recruit a new student. So the final benefit will be:

- saving on recruitment costs—£100 per student retained.

So the overall saving per student retained will be:

£(200 + 1,100 + 100) = £1,400 ($2,240) per student retained

With a cost of £200 per student retained and a benefit of £1,400 per student retained, there is a "profit" on the activity of £1,200 per student retained and a Return on Investment of (1,200)/200 = 600%.

Thus, if this activity was applied to (say) 30,000 students (the annual new student entry into the U.K. Open University), then the increase in retention would be 5% of 30,000 = 1,500 students and the overall "profit" on the activity would be £(1,200 × 1,500) = £1,800,000 ($2.900,000), a sum that could be fed back into further enhanced student support.

Where an institution is mainly student-fee-funded, the analysis is more complex. Here an increase in retention will generate an increase in institutional income from an increased number of students taking the final exam and carrying on to a second module.

Case Study 2: Mainly Student-Fee-Funded— The University Of London International Programme

In the case of London University, the income from students consists of a registration fee = £F, and an exam fee that is paid by students completing a module = £E. The institutional expenditure on the module will consist of a fixed overhead = £V and an expenditure of £S per student enrolled.

So if N students start a module, the income at the start will be £NF, the institutional expenditure will be £(V + NS) and the surplus income if any will be:

$$£[NF - (V + NS)]$$

Then suppose a retention activity costing £P per student increases the number of students completing the module by n% then the increase in the number of students taking the exam will be Nn/100 and the total extra income in year 1 from the increase in exam fee minus the cost of the activity will be:

$$£([Nn/100)E - NP]$$

In addition, there will be an increase in income in year 2 from registration fees less the annual expenditure per student of:

$$£[(Nn/100)(F - S)]$$

as the increase in the number of students completing year 1 carries through to year 2.

Then suppose that for a particular module the number of students N = 1,000, the student expenditure S = £400 ($640), the student fee F = £800 ($1,300) and the exam fee E = £300 ($480), and that again a retention activity in year 1 costing P = £10 per student produces an increase in retention n = 5%. Then the extra income in year 1 will be:

$$£[(1,000 \times 5/100) \times 300 - 1,000 \times 10] = £5,000 (\$8,000)$$

The increase in income from the number of students registering in year 2 assuming they all carry on will be:

$$£[(1,000 \times 5/100)(800 - 400)] = £20,000 (\$32,000)$$

So the total increase in income will be £(5000 + 20,000) = £25,000 for an expenditure of £10 × 1,000 = £10,000, thus making a profit of £15,000 with a Return on Investment of

£(15,000 − 10,000)/10,000 = 50%.

It may be easier to see these calculations presented graphically. For a retention activity to make a profit, the individual profits need to be greater than the retention expenditure. That is,

(nN/100)E + (nN/100)(F − S) : NP

which simplifies to:

n : 100P/(E + F + S)

Putting in the values for E, F and S, this becomes

n : 0.14P

Figure 11.2 shows the graph of n = 0.14P.

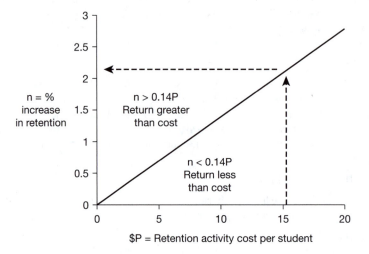

n = % increase in retention

n > 0.14P
Return greater than cost

n < 0.14P
Return less than cost

$P = Retention activity cost per student

Figure 11.2 Graph of n = 0.14P: example of retention activity cost versus % increase in retention

In this graph, retention activities that locate above the line will have a financial return to the institution greater than their cost. Activities below the line will cost more than they save. So, for example, following the dotted lines on the graph, a retention activity costing £15 ($24) per student will need to produce a retention increase of more than 2.1% in order to cover its cost and make a profit.

Cost Benefits of Student Support for Governments

Whatever the ways that a government supports distance education in its country, it is likely that it is a more economical way of producing graduates than conventional higher education. For example, in the U.K. before 2012, the cost of producing a graduate through distance education was about one-third that of conventional education, largely because of the lower overheads involved in distance education (Simpson 2011). Since distance students are also more economically active than conventional full-time students, contributing to Gross Domestic Product (GDP) and paying income tax, the advantages of distance education are even greater. It therefore makes sense to encourage government to invest even more in distance education, and particularly in student support, as it is that which is most likely to increase the efficiency of distance education. It may be that, where government funding is linked to outputs, there is another "Value Triangle" that can be exploited—see Figure 11.3.

It can certainly be argued that this is a very optimistic scenario at a time when governments worldwide are contending with the international recession. Yet there are examples to be had, such as the Science Foundation Project at the University of South Africa, where government funding is being directed toward the extra support of educationally underprivileged students on science and agricultural courses as an urgent investment in the country's human resources.

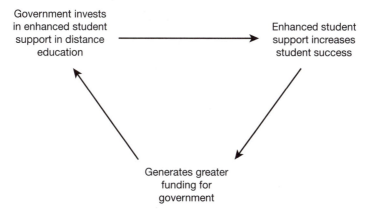

Figure 11.3 A "Value Triangle" for government investment in distance education

Funding Student Support versus other Funding Opportunities

This chapter will probably be at least as hard work for you to read as it was for me to write. The calculations I've made make a number of unsubstantiated assumptions as well as approximations, and very much need the attention of a proper accountant. So you may well ask why there should be such a chapter in a book on student support. The answer is that, if you wish to promote student support in any environment, one of the most useful things you can do—in the words of "Deep Throat" in the Watergate saga—is to "Follow the Money." You are far more likely to get backing for student support by showing that it has made sense financially than through any ethical arguments. This is not to be cynical about senior management in distance institutions; it is merely to reflect the fact that there will always be arguments in institutions as to where to direct funding, whether it is to higher quality print, more sophisticated e-learning objects or to more proactive student support. Showing that student support makes sense financially is an important part of winning that argument for better support.

Chapter 12

Course Design and Support for Success

Easy reading is damn hard writing.

(Nathaniel Hawthorne)

So far in the book I have passed over the distance course itself as a vehicle for student support for success. But it is impossible to write a text on student retention and success in distance education without considering the effect of the course material itself. In particular, it must be worth asking if it's possible to build motivational support into a course module, whether that module is presented in a print or online version. (Following distance education-habit I have used the terms "course" and "module" interchangeably, hoping it will be clear from the context which is appropriate.)

This is a particularly useful question to ask given the recent growth in "Open Educational Resources"—online modules freely available on the internet for anyone to use. While these resources are perhaps most useful for re-versioning by institutions who do not have the means to produce their own distance materials, there is increasing expectation that any student interested in a topic will use them. For example, the Gates Foundation has recently funded a remedial online math course "Succeed with Math," with which I was involved (http://labspace.open.ac.uk/course/view.php?id=7654), aimed at U.S. students who need introductory math. For such a course to succeed without tutor support, there will have to be some level of careful support built into the text itself. How that might be achieved, to some extent we shall see in this chapter. But first we need to ask how distance course modules stack up when it comes to retention.

Rating Courses for Retention

One question that immediately arises when discussing course and module retention rates is how we know what the retention on any particular course or module could—or should—be. Clearly even within an institution course modules can vary enormously in their pass rates. Figure 12.1 is a "scattergram" which shows the percentage of students getting to the final exam plotted against the percentage of students who pass the exam, for around 150 undergraduate modules in the U.K. Open University degree. Each point in the scattergram represents the values for one particular module.

The dotted crosshairs are at the average *getting to the exam* and *passing the exam* rates for all the modules, and divide the scattergram up into four quadrants. It can be seen that there are large variations in both the "getting to the exam" and the "passing the exam" rates, with the highest "getting to" and "passing" rates in the top righthand quadrant and the lowest in the bottom left.

The modules that concerned me most in this analysis were the ones in the lower right quadrant—modules where a large number of students got to the exam but then failed it. This seemed to me to be breaking the "contract" we have with students—that, if they put in the work and passed the continuous assessment part of the module, they would have a good chance of passing the exam.

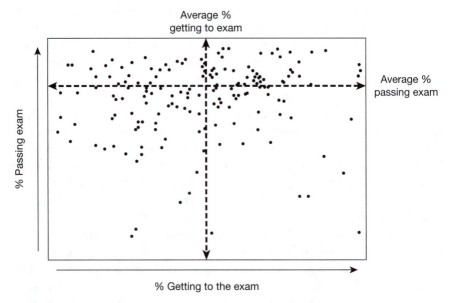

Figure 12.1 A scattergram of U.K. Open University modules "getting to exam" pass rates versus exam pass rates

It can also be seen, following on from the variations in getting and passing rates, that there are even larger variations in overall completion rates, since they are the product of getting and passing rates. The highest course module at the top righthand quadrant of the chart has an overall completion rate of more than 80%, compared with the lowest at the bottom left, which is in the region of 40%, despite, in this case, both modules being at the same level in the same faculty.

A colleague who helped me compile this scattergram—a man of more courage than me—approached the 40% completion rate course module authors saying, "We notice that the success rates on your module are rather low compared with others in the same faculty. Can we help in some way?"—to which the inevitable reply was, "No thanks; we know the rates are low, it's a difficult module." This struck me as a very "Darwinista" response (Chapter 6) and may be one of the barriers to writing courses for student success.

Benchmarking Modules

The "predicted probability of success" model described in Chapter 7 can be applied to course modules in order to predict what a module pass rate should be given the entry characteristics of its students. (If this model is applied to continuing students, then one of those characteristics can be their previous module performance, which is actually the highest predictive factor for subsequent success. This can make the prediction considerably more accurate than for new students with no previous record.)

Thus the U.K. Open University has been developing a "Course Pass Rates Model," where predicted pass rates can be compared with actual pass rates, using a statistical marker called a "z-score," which measures the significance of the difference. Modules can then be evaluated to see if they are doing something particularly well (a high positive z-score) or particularly badly (a high negative z-score). For example, there is a module that has a predicted pass rate of 59% and an actual pass rate of 53%, which gives a z-score of -2.95. This is highly negative in comparison with other modules and suggests that the module needs some evaluation to see why it should be doing particularly badly. Of course, what the course writers will do as a consequence of this feedback remains to be seen.

Course Design and Student Success

There may be four ways of designing courses to increase student retention—assessment (covered in Chapter 5), workload, structure, and writing.

Course Workload

Course workload would seem an obvious area in which retention would be affected. A high workload would lead to high dropout, given that students tell us again and again that the main reason they drop out is because of lack of time.

But studies in the U.K. Open University have not found a strong link between reported high workload and dropout (Crooks 2005). That seems not only counterintuitive but counter to some tutors' experience, such as my own.

A number of years ago I taught a course, "Technology of Music." It rapidly became clear it was very overloaded for its credit rating. It was a victim of what I think of as "Course Exuberance Syndrome'—the authors couldn't resist throwing in everything that interested them. "Course Exuberance Syndrome" may be a serious problem in distance education, especially for people writing online courses. It's very easy to add extra material to a course in the form of podcasts, additional websites to visit, video- and audioclips, social networking sites and so on. But, unless you're sure that such extras actually help students learn the material more effectively, then they may have the opposite effect and reduce retention.

Perhaps as my "Technology of Music" students used to tell me, it wasn't so much the quantity of material but the sheer number of new, different and often unrelated concepts that was the problem. Maybe it is easier to learn a large amount of material if it all relates together tightly. This would certainly be suggested by Cognitive Load Theory—see later in this chapter.

Course Structure

When it comes to how a course is structured, Crooks (2005) analyzed a module that had remarkably high retention and compared with similar modules with much lower retention. She came to the conclusion that *flexibility* was the key to retention—giving students a choice of how they navigate the module in terms of the material to be studied, variability in the time and pace of study, and some choice in assessment. Perhaps distance students need flexibility in order to be able to fit their studies into their everyday lives.

Course Writing

When it comes to course writing, there are two theories that might be helpful:

● Keller's "ARCS" Theory, which is essentially a motivational model; and
● "Cognitive Load Theory," which is a cognitive model.

The two theories may be helpful together, as they then address students holistically including their emotions, rather than as purely cognitive learning entities.

Keller's ARCS Theory

This theory has already been covered in outline in Chapter 6. The four elements as applied to course writing are:

A = ATTENTION

There are two aspects to attention—getting a student's attention and keeping it.

(a) *Getting attention.* There are a number of ways of getting attention, most importantly through:

- incongruity—humor may be the best example;
- displaying empathy—this is difficult in text, but telling stories and sharing the personal thoughts of the author can go some way;
- authority—displaying appropriate expertise.

Many distance texts seem to take an opposite line:

- they are serious—humor often seems to be out of place;
- they are sometimes written in impersonal terms and fail to acknowledge (for instance) that students may be feeling anxious about the material they're trying to learn;
- occasionally they are written anonymously or only the author's name is given without any qualifications.

However, I cannot claim clear evidence that course materials written using humor, empathy and authority produce better student success, although I can claim some historical backup for humor—the oldest reference to the use of humor in education is dated roughly AD 400 and is due to St. Augustine in *De Catchizandi Rudibus*—"Reawaken your students with remarks spiced with seemly good humor." And students report humour as amongst the nine most important characteristics of their teachers (Delaney et al. 2010). While this book contains no jokes, I hope I've allowed some lightness to creep in occasionally . . .

(b) *Keeping attention.* The second aspect of attention is keeping it, which may have two features—readability and typography:

(i) *Readability*. I suspect that keeping attention uses much the same qualities as getting attention, but adding in "readability"—matching text to students' reading skills. This may be particularly important at the start of a module for new students. Datta and Macdonald Ross (2002) used "cloze" tests (replacing blank spaces in text with appropriate words) on new students in the U.K. Open University and found that many would have significant difficulties understanding their course material. They judged that 42% new students had lower comprehension than needed for their modules.

They also found that that often students' previous reading was only tabloid newspapers and magazines. Subsequently, Moore (2004) used the "Flesch Reading Ease Scale" to rate the readability of various texts. This scale runs from a score of 0 "very difficult" to 100 "very easy" and is calculated from the sentence length and number of syllables in any given piece of writing (see Table 12.1).

Moore found that the first few pages of the U.K. Open University Arts Foundation module was 47.1 ("difficult"), compared with a widely read U.K. tabloid newspaper, the *Daily Mail*, which was 61.5 ("plain English"). The text in this chapter so far has a Flesch Reading Ease score of 53.1 ("fairly difficult"), so you're doing well.

Table 12.1 The Flesch Reading Ease Scale for readability

Readability score	Interpretations	Description	Examples
0–20	Very difficult	Best understood by university graduates	Harvard Law Review
20–50	Difficult		New York Times
50–60	Fairly difficult		This book
60–70	Plain English	Easily understood by 13–15 year-olds	Reader's Digest
70–80	Fairly easy		
80–90	Easy	Easily understood by 11 year-olds	
90–100	Very easy		

(ii) *Typography also affects readability.* For example, the text below is a short extract from the opening page of a distance text on communication:

> The field of communication studies runs wide. As a discipline, it borders on academic specialities such as linguistics, psychology, media studies, cultural studies, sociology, philosophy, marketing and business studies. Its diverse components include interpersonal communication, intercultural communication, workplace writing, organizational studies and mass communication. It can, at times, be difficult to limit the scope of communication studies—it seems to involve pretty much most things human beings do together. This is an indication of the obsession in modern times with communication. As Peters (1999) notes, communication has been viewed as the solution to humanity's diverse and profound troubles. How many times, for instance, during local or international conflicts, have you heard talk of communication breakdowns, or of the need to open channels of communication?

It has a Flesch Reading Ease score of 13.5 ("very difficult"). Merely by putting in some bullet points and an extra paragraph as below the score is raised through "difficult" to 39.5—"fairly difficult."

> The field of communication studies runs wide. As a discipline, it borders on academic specialities such as:
>
> - linguistics
> - psychology
> - media studies
> - cultural studies
> - sociology
> - marketing
> - business studies.
>
> Its diverse components include:
>
> - interpersonal communication
> - intercultural communication

- workplace writing
- organizational studies
- mass communication.

It can, at times, be difficult to limit the scope of communication studies: it seems to involve pretty much most things human beings do together.

This is an indication of the obsession in modern times with communication. As Peters (1999) notes, communication has been viewed as the solution to humanity's diverse and profound troubles. How many times, for instance, during local or international conflicts, have you heard talk of communication breakdowns, or of the need to open channels of communication?

Other changes, such as making the text justified "ragged right" instead of justified right and left, using more paragraphs and (in hard copy) changing the typeface to a serif on paper (for example, from **Arial** to Times), with perhaps doing the opposite for online text, can also help with readability. Of course, this may also mean using more paper in hard copy, but this may be a price worth paying to make the text more retention-friendly.

However, there is no clear evidence as yet that readability is connected with retention. Mouli and Ramakrishna (1991) looked at the link between readability of a number of courses in their institution and the average end-of-term exam scores and believed that they had found a positive correlation between readability scores and exam scores. However, their results were criticized by Patsula (2001), who concluded that the link was only very weakly supported by their data and that much more research was needed on a broad front before conclusions could be safely drawn.

R = RELEVANCE

All content in a course needs to be seen to be closely relevant to the learner's needs in order to maintain their attention and concentration. Thus it is necessary to avoid "course exuberance syndrome" and keep adding materials to a module on the grounds that they are "challenging" or of intrinsic interest without being clear that they are relevant to the student needs at that point.

> Only last week I phoned a student who had not submitted an assignment on the math course I teach. She told me that she had got stuck on a section on "Egyptian Fractions" (fractions of the form 1/x) and given up on the course. I had some difficulty explaining that this section had only been placed in the module for "enrichment," was not essential and could be skipped. Fortunately, I was able to overcome her perfectionist tendencies on this occasion and get her back on course. But I'm sure I've lost others that way.

Other Relevance issues are best explained under "Cognitive Load Theory" below.

C = CONFIDENCE

An activity needs to enhance students' confidence. I assume that at least one aspect of this is having confidence in the material they are studying, although I am less clear how this might be expressed in the course writing. It may relate to students' having confidence in the writers of the material as experts in the field. This is perhaps a reminder of the survey by Gaskell and Simpson (2001—see Chapter 3), who found that the two most important qualities students wanted from their tutors were "knowledge of the course" and "approachability," in that order.

Confidence in the material may also relate to how it is written. A surprising amount of distance material is written in the passive voice, avoiding use of "I" or "we." While this makes the material academically respectable, I wonder if it doesn't also make it distant and somewhat unapproachable and less likely to inspire confidence in its students. Perhaps it will be important to remember Holmberg's (1995) theory of "guided didactic conversation" in writing material.

S = SATISFACTION

Students need to feel a sense of satisfaction as a result of the activities. I interpret this as relating to Hattie's (2010) findings (previously mentioned in Chapter 4, in the section on assessment), in his meta-surveys of several thousand students, that the single most important factor in promoting student success is "self-reporting"—knowing how well they are doing. Clearly this presents problems in distance education. One strategy for tackling this issue has involved the introduction of "self-assessment questions" in the text, but as I suggested previously this is not an entirely satisfactory solution.

EVIDENCE FOR KELLER'S THEORY IN INCREASING STUDENT SUCCESS

As so often in distance education, clear evidence for the success of Keller's ARCS theory in promoting student success is somewhat lacking. There is some modest evidence of the use of Keller's theory in course content and presentation from Colakoglu and Akdemir (2010), whose results suggested that students on courses designed using Keller's ARCS theory were better motivated than controls.

Cognitive Load Theory

Cognitive Load Theory is due to Sweller (Paas, Renkel and Sweller, 2003), who suggests that learning is a two-stage process. The material to be learned is taken initially into the working or short-term memory (the memory that enables you to temporarily remember phone numbers or, in my case, what you went into the kitchen to get—sometimes). That then needs to be transferred into your long-term memory for learning to be complete—see Figure 12.2 (but only as an aide-memoire—it is not meant to be neurologically correct!).

Sweller says that there are three types of cognitive load:

1. *intrinsic*—the level of difficulty of the subject material;
2. *extraneous*—due to the way the information is presented—that is in the text in distance learning;
3. *germane*—how the information relates to previous knowledge.

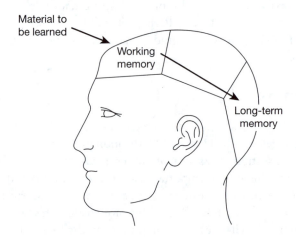

Figure 12.2 The two stages of learning in Cognitive Load Theory

Intrinsic load cannot be reduced as such. It just has to be managed—for example, segmenting it into smaller lumps of learning. *Extraneous load* should be minimized by ensuring that the material is relevant, avoids "split attention" and (as in the ARCS theory) not redundant. Split attention is where material is offered in two ways that are not both essential—perhaps like putting up a quote in PowerPoint and reading it out at the same time. *Germane load* needs to be maximized (slightly confusingly to me, in this theory) by ensuring that links are made between new knowledge and knowledge in the long-term memory.

The other thing you need to do in this theory is to help the working memory to be as efficient as possible. According to Sweller, this is achieved by:

1. using problem-solving methods that avoid approaches that impose a heavy working memory load—for instance, by using worked examples;
2. reducing working memory load due to having to mentally integrate several sources of information—for example, by actually integrating those sources;
3. reducing the working memory load by reducing redundancy;
4. increasing the working memory capacity by using auditory as well as visual information under conditions where both sources of information are essential (that is, non-redundant) to understanding.

There is some evidence from Impelluso (2009) to support this theory as enhancing distance student success. The author claimed to have rewritten his course using Cognitive Load Theory and that this had increased both learning and retention on the course. However, the article didn't really give sufficient detail to understand how he had done that, although in a wide literature search it was the only article I found that addressed writing course text for retention.

Course Evaluation for Retention

The question of how we can evaluate courses for their student retention capability is important. I have already mentioned the U.K. Open University's Course Pass Rates Model, which benchmarks courses for their actual retention against their predicted retention. Another way of evaluating courses for their capability is, of course, to ask the students.

Course Evaluation Questionnaires

Many distance institutions use student questionnaires of one kind or another to assess their courses. For example, the U.K. Open University uses an end-of-module questionnaire that is sent to students who are still registered at the end of the module. The questionnaire has five sections:

Q1. Organizing and Managing your Studies
Q2. Course Materials and Learning Activities
Q3. Assessment and Feedback
Q4. Study Support
Q5. Course Overall

and within each section there are a set of questions on a agree/disagree Likert scale. There are 10 questions in the Course Materials section, starting with:

1. "The printed course materials helped me learn effectively"
2. "The course materials delivered online helped me learn effectively"
3. "The Audio-Visual (AV) content for this course helped me learn effectively"

and so on.

Since the survey only goes to students who have completed the course, typically the results show a 95% satisfaction with the course and its elements. But I question just how helpful this is for improving the retention on the course. It might make more sense to undertake some "crash testing" with students who have withdrawn from the course, asking questions like:

Q1. "Please identify the particular point in the course (if you can) at which you decided to withdraw"
Q2. "If you can identify such a particular point, please try to say why that might have decided you to withdraw"
Q3. "If your decision to withdraw was caused by a particular assignment, then please state the assignment number"

and so on. Of course, it is notoriously difficult to get feedback from withdrawn students, so I cannot tell if such an approach would ever be successful.

Barriers to Course Design for Student Success

Finally, what are the barriers to writing support for success into distance courses? I believe that they are largely attitudinal, as suggested in Chapter 6. There I proposed that, when it came to supporting students for success, there were three classes of institutional staff—the "Darwinistas," "Fatalistas" and "Retentioneers." I suggest that these classifications also apply to course design and that they fall on a spectrum of attitudes to courses—see Figure 12.3.

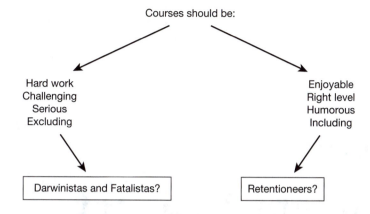

Figure 12.3 Institutional attitudes to course design

At one end of the spectrum, staff believe that courses should be hard work, challenging, rigorous and excluding some students—these, perhaps, are the Darwinistas and Fatalistas. At the other end, staff believe that courses should be designed as far as possible to be enjoyable, at the right level for students throughout, even humorous where possible, and including all students as far as possible—these are the Retentioneers. Where people fall on the spectrum may well be the determining factor in how far they write student support-friendly course modules.

Chapter 13

Student Support Outside the Institution

> It's important to involve families and friends as they can influence retention decisions.
> (Edward Anderson)

Why "Outside" Support?

This may seem a curious byway for this book—after all, student support from outside the institution can hardly be susceptible to management by the institution and so can only be of passing interest. Yet there are at least two good reasons why such support is important:

- there is evidence that many students rate some kinds of outside support more highly than internal institutional support;
- such support can be very economical for the institution—often free—and so possibly cost-effective in enhancing student success.

Therefore it is important to investigate ways in which such external support can be enhanced.

Sources of Support Outside the Distance Institution

There are a range of sources of distance student support outside the institution—work colleagues, staff in agencies such as libraries and advice centers, as well as more formal arrangements such as senior teachers mentoring students in teacher training schemes. Three of these sources seem particularly important:

● partners, families and friends of the student;
● other students of the institution;
● employers.

In a small-scale survey (Asbee and Simpson 1998), U.K. Open University students were asked to rate the relative importance of support from their partners, families, friends, tutors, other students (whether on their course or not) and from the rest of the institution (support from employers was not covered in this survey). Table 13.1 shows the proportions that gave particular modes as the most important source of support.

Support from family and friends was more highly rated than support from tutors and other students. Nearly twice as many students rated support from partners as most important than those who rated support from the institution as most important.

Support from Partners, Families and Friends

Thus, it appears that the most important single form of support for students is outside institutional control (and thus is possibly largely ignored by institutions). The report also raises two questions: "Who gives the support and what kinds are most valuable?" and "Can the institution enhance that support in any way?"

Table 13.1 Percentage of students giving source as most important

Source	Most important
From family and friends	32%
From tutors	29%
From other students	21%
From the institution	17%

Asbee wrote that:

> In the majority of cases the support was from a partner but not always so. There were cases such as a woman whose most important support was from her teenage son by working together on their studies, although the son noted ruefully a negative aspect—"lack of meals on assignment days."

The kind of support that is most valuable varies:

- Ideal partners help most by providing time and space for their students to study by taking on child care and chores, or more directly by proofreading assignments.
- Partners also provide emotional and moral support through encouragement, showing an interest in the course and keeping students in touch with their motivation—"He helped me to keep going even when I felt thoroughly fed up with it all." They can also help keep studies in proportion—helping students put a low assignment grade into perspective, for example.
- From time to time they will also put their own needs second, over such things as holiday dates.
- They will even support by simply leaving alone—"He allows me to get on. I don't get nagged about doing essays . . . I'm allowed to do what I need when I need."
- Above all, what came through in this part of the survey was the message that partner, family or friends' support is overwhelmingly important—"It has to be a joint commitment. Involve your partner if you want to succeed."

But partners can be resentful and even obstructive. Certainly study can upset the status quo: "He was happy with the stout floral-clad housewife he had before; he is not so keen on the woman who is not dependent on him for opinions or confidence." And, conversely, this study has again demonstrated the devastating effects of relationship breakdown on student progress: "Since starting studying I have separated from my husband of twenty-one years. I don't think my studies were the cause but it may have been a small contributory factor. Studying after the breakdown of my marriage has subsequently been very difficult."

Enhancing Support from Partners, Families and Friends

Enhancing family and friend support may not have been a priority with distance institutions in the past. Nor is it clear how to go about it, nor how effective it would be to try to do so. Nevertheless, there may be simple ways of acknowledging its importance. One finding that emerged from this report was the need for partners and families to know more about what "their" student had taken on, what was going to happen to them and how they as "student supporters" might help them better. The following extract is taken from a short leaflet that I wrote for partners to give to their students—"Helping your Student" (this leaflet has been copied in Australia, Germany and Botswana, which might suggest that the importance of family and friends support is non-culturally specific). The full text can be found in the "StudyAid" pack at **www.ormond.simpson.com**.

HELPING YOUR STUDENT

A Leaflet for Partners, Family or Friends of Intending Students

The leaflet begins:

To intending students: do please pass this leaflet on to your partner, family or friends. It's designed to help them help you in the most effective way and to tell them a little about what you will be doing as a student.

To the Partner, Family or Friends of an Intending Student

Thank you for taking a few minutes to read this little leaflet. Our research has shown that one of the most important factors in the success of our students is good support from their partners, families and friends. This leaflet is designed to tell you a little bit about what "your" student will be doing and to help and encourage you to support them.

The leaflet then covers topics like:

What will happen to "your" student and how can you help?—simple ideas about negotiating study time, understanding stress points, giving encouragement and motivational support.

The pay-off—graduation means increased intellectual satisfaction and perhaps better incomes plus thanks at the graduation ceremony.

Why not become a student yourself?

How far such a simple device can enhance external support remains to be seen, but generally such leaflets seem to be well received—these are a few comments that were received in an evaluation:

"Clear and attractive—something that can be read immediately, rather than put aside until time is available and consequently never read."

"I thought the style was about right: my husband thought it rather patronising."

"I liked the 'bite-sized' paragraphs."

" . . . my wife is now a little more understanding since reading your leaflet although she's still not happy at the neglect caused by my studying."

Support from Family and Friends Online

A recent survey of U.K. conventional universities revealed that many of them are taking family and especially parent support seriously, and have dedicated web pages with electronic newsletters for parents. There is one Scottish university where the parental website has a link to a local food store that will take orders over the web to deliver food direct to allegedly starving offspring.

The U.K. Open University now has a web page development for family and friends based on the text "Helping Your Student" quoted earlier—see Figure 13.1.

There was originally an intention to set up a link from the page to a chat facility where family and friends would be encouraged to exchange experiences, moderated by a family and friends coordinator. However, this has not happened yet.

Does Support from Families and Friends Increase Success?—The "Black Box" Experiment

It is clearly difficult both practically and ethically to test the hypothesis that support from families and friends increases student success. Nevertheless, a few years ago we set out to try to investigate the issue. The research model was taken from the aircraft crash investigation example. When an aircraft crashes, the investigators not only look at the wreckage on the ground (equivalent in retention studies to asking why students dropped out after the event), but they

Figure 13.1 The front page of the U.K. Open University friends and family site

also look at the "black box"—the events leading up to the crash. We therefore chose a group of new students we thought were very likely to drop out and interviewed them at weekly intervals to see if we could catch the "tipping point"—the point at which they made their withdrawal decision. We called this the "Black Box Study."

We should have foreseen the outcome; in practice, very few of the students we interviewed actually dropped out. As the principal investigator remarked, it was not possible to speak to the students without in effect offering them extra support simply by taking an interest in their studies. Nevertheless, it seemed that those students who did drop out were those who were perceived by the investigator not to have close family support (Temperton 2000). The study was not sufficiently clear to be publishable, but it serves as some kind of evidence that family and friends' support does enhance student success.

Support from Other Students

Support from other students can fall into three types:

1. Support from students on the same module or at the same level, moderated by a tutor—*tutor support*. These groups can occur face-to-face, phone and online and are covered in Chapters 4 and 8, on academic support and media for support.

2. Support from students on the same module or at the same level, not moderated by a tutor—sometimes called study groups or self-help-groups—*peer support*.
3. Support from students who have completed the module in question or are on the same module but have more experience—*mentoring*.

Peer and mentoring support vary in the ways they can be set up (peer support can be set up relatively simply; mentoring requires much more substantial input) and the activities they undertake (peer support can be informal; mentoring requires rather more structure).

Peer Support

Peer support in distance education has been around for many years and, as noted previously, is often highly rated by students—sometimes as highly as tutor support. Strictly speaking it is not external to the institution, which, although having little control over it, can do quite a lot to organize, encourage and enhance it. It is obviously especially important to particularly isolated students. Peer support groups can be of any size from two upwards.

There are several aspects to peer support—the initial setting-up process, the media of contact, how peer support groups operate, and the queries and problems that can arise.

Initial Setting Up

Peer support groups can be set up face-to-face, online or even by phone. An initial face-to-face contact is often a good way to get groups going, if that is possible. But, whatever media is used, it does not seem very effective to leave it up to students themselves—the institution needs to be proactive. For example, tutors might have the setting up of groups clearly in their role specification. Then the institution needs to support that role with appropriate resources—lists of students and permission for address, phone and email address release—and there needs to be staff development to help tutors acquire appropriate techniques for encouraging students into peer support groups. Such techniques would include a facilitative approach with students as described in Chapter 4.

Other ways of initiating groups tend to be less successful. Institutions with offline students can offer the opportunity in a general mailing to students, collating the responses and mailing out lists by course (although this can be labor-intensive). However, it is quite difficult for any student to take the initiative to "cold-call" someone else from a list by phone or email, and then even more difficult in security-conscious times to set up a face-to-face meeting with people who may be unknown.

Media for Peer Support Groups

Peer groups can meet by various media. Face-to-face groups can be popular but may be inaccessible because of difficulties in travel. Phone networks can work well—for example, using Skype, which allows three-way calling—but they tend to be difficult to set up and their value tends to be underestimated by students. For online students, computer conferencing is surely the most accessible peer group, but is not necessarily the most rewarding academically, as experience suggests that these can be more social in nature. Of course, such socializing may play an important part in overcoming isolation and eventual success for some students, although there appears to be no evidence for that either way.

What Happens in Peer Support Groups

What evidence there is about peer groups suggests that groups operate best if they interact relatively regularly, have a clear agenda and focus and take turns at various roles. Some sort of guidance from the institution may be helpful. I wrote a leaflet called "Getting Together—A Guide to Organizing Study Groups," which I sent to U.K. Open University students at the start of their course. It covered topics like

Why a Study Group?

1. Contacting other students
2. Organizing the first meeting
3. Running a face-to-face meeting
   a) breaking the ice
   b) discussing the next assignment
   c) just chatting?
4. Running an online group
5. Snares and pitfalls

A copy of the text can be found in the "StudyAid Pack" at http://www.ormondsimpso.com/page4.htm.

"Study Dating"

Not all students want to link into an online conference group any more than all students want to participate in face-to-face tutorials. For some it's a question of simply wanting to study on their own or, as mentioned previously, some experience social anxiety in such situations. Others simply find conferencing unrewarding for other reasons. As one student said to me, "Whenever I've joined an online conference it's usually full of people discussing the third assignment when I haven't even looked at the first. Or there's nothing happening at all."

For such people I wondered if some kind of internet "study dating" system would work. So I started to devise a "Find a Study Friend" website where students could register their name, course and whatever contact details they were happy to give. They could then look for a "study friend" with whom they could link one-to-one by email, phone or face-to-face—see Figure 13.2.

Unhappily, this idea never got past the project stage for reasons that are used as an example in Chapter 15.

Does Peer Support Increase Student Success?

Despite the amount of effort that has gone into peer support in distance education, there is not much firm evidence that it enhances student success. Clearly students who conference well are more likely to succeed, but since they are a self-selected group this is not necessarily good evidence that conferencing and success are linked in any specifically causal way. The research remains to be done.

Mentoring Support

Mentoring support—student support from students more senior in the system—has a long history reaching back to the Greeks. It was used in England

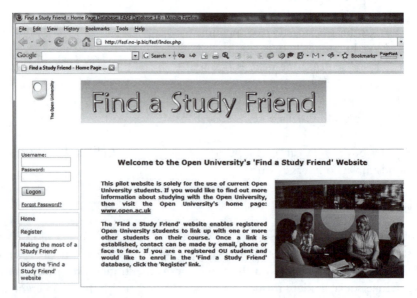

Figure 13.2 The front page of the proposed "study dating" website

in the nineteenth century but became discredited as merely a way of saving money on teachers. It was reintroduced in a full-time education context in North America, and Supplemental Instruction, as it is called, is now used in many U.S. higher education institutions. It has spread to the UK and elsewhere and involves student leaders, often second-year students, helping new undergraduates. Mentoring in full-time education is seen as informal, supportive, empowering and confidence-building, and a particular help to a teacher who may have forgotten what it was like to be a new and uncertain student.

Given the particular characteristics of distance learning—the isolation and lack of confidence, particularly of new students—the characteristics of mentoring might make it particularly applicable. However, while it is relatively easy to set up mentoring schemes in face-to-face education, it can be much harder in distance education.

Organizing a Mentoring Scheme

In a very small-scale pilot in 1998, Asbee, Simpson and Woodall (1999) set up a mentoring program in the U.K. Open University. The individual stages in such a scheme were:

1. finding volunteer mentees and mentors from new and existing students;
2. "vetting" volunteers for possible problems;
3. matching and linking them;
4. briefing them;
5. monitoring and evaluation.

There were issues at each stage: Will enough mentors and mentees come forward? What kind of briefing would be appropriate? How can you "vet" mentors and mentees in distance education when all you know of them is an application form? For example, just on the last issue, to interview every volunteer would be a mammoth task and not necessarily reliable. On the other hand, the very isolation of students makes the vetting processes less critical, as it is possible to release only phone numbers or email addresses for safety reasons. And the position and possibilities for any kind of harassment are no worse than in any other student–student contact.

Briefing Mentors and Mentees

It is also very important that mentors and mentees know what to expect of one another, particularly the boundaries of the roles. This is an excerpt from a short briefing document that we sent to both mentors and mentees after they had volunteered and been matched. The full text can be found at www.ormondsimpson.com.

After an introduction on various ways of linking up, the leaflet goes on:

What kind of Advice can Mentors Expect to Give?

The most valuable asset that mentors have is their experience of a course. That means they are very well placed to give the student's perspective on:

- Finding your way around the course materials
- Getting started on the course: what works best?
- Time—how much do you need to spend
- Going to the first tutorial: what happens?
- Tackling the first assignment and getting it back
- Falling behind and catching up
- Preparing for the exam (if there is one)
- Surviving the exam

The leaflet then goes on to cover what issues should be outside the relationship, where to refer such issues and how to end the relationship on either side.

Mentoring Outcomes

In the event, in this project there were considerably more volunteer mentors than mentees, and the linking and briefing processes were carried out simultaneously by phone by the pilot project worker. Such a labor-intensive approach would not easily work if the project was scaled up. Yet the results were very positive. Mentees reported that in some cases support from their mentor made all the difference between withdrawal and keeping going: "I got a very low grade on my first assignment and I was on the brink of withdrawing. I just didn't feel I could contact the tutor and if I hadn't spoken to my mentor I would certainly have withdrawn," and "My mentor had only just completed the course so it was very fresh in his mind and he could really relate to my difficulties. I don't know if my tutor ever studied this course but it must have been a long time ago!"

It was not too difficult to see what mentees got out of the scheme, but interestingly mentors valued it very highly. It valued and broadened their experience and there was the possibility of a qualification outcome for some students: "It was an extraordinarily rewarding experience," wrote one mentor; "the improvement in her scores and general level of confidence during the year was really dramatic!"

Does Mentoring Enhance Student Success?

There is some evidence from some later projects that student mentoring can have a retention effect. In an international study involving the U.K. Open University, the Korean National Open University (KNOU) and the Open Polytechnic of New Zealand, Boyle et al. (2010) found an increase in retention in a small-scale study at the U.K. Open University, as shown in Table 13.2.

This is too small a sample to draw conclusions from. However the Korean sample was much larger, with a student enrollment each year of approximately 7,000. It showed similar results, with increase in retention of an average of 8.45% at various stages—see Table 13.3.

Table 13.2 Comparison of pass rates of mentored and non-mentored students in U.K. Open University

Mentees' passes	Control group passes
17/19	14/21
89%	**67%**

Table 13.3 The KNOU Mentoring Program—increase in retention rates 2007 and 2008

	Increase in retention of mentored students at each stage				
	First semester		Second semester		
	Midterm exam pass rate	End-of-term exam pass rate	Re-enrollment rate	Midterm exam pass rate	End-of-term exam pass rate
2007	+7.1%	+9.3%	+7.9%	+4.6%	+5.8%
2008	+9.8%	+12.9%	+14.6%	+5.8%	+6.7%

The Open Polytechnic of New Zealand study did not examine retention data, but did conclude that mentoring substantially increased the confidence of disadvantaged Maori students.

Costs of Mentoring

Student-student mentoring is not a zero cost to the institution. The estimate in this pilot is that the cost of setting up each mentoring pair in the U.K. Open University will have been high—about \$55 (£35) largely in staff time. However, some of this cost was fixed in initial development time, so that the cost of a project involving larger groups of students would be less—perhaps of the order of \$32 (£20) per pair.

A formula (see Chapter 11) enables researchers to identify the cost to the institution per student retained by any specific retention activity, which is

$$= 100P/n$$

where P is the cost per student of the activity and n% is the retention increase due to that specific activity. Applying the retention increase suggested by the figures in Table 13.2, the cost per student retained for this mentoring project is

$$= £(100 \text{x} 35/22) = £160 \ (\$240)$$

This figure seems large but it compares favorably with the approximately \$300 (£200) cost per student retained by the Proactive Student Support (PaSS) Project in the U.K. Open University (a pre-course personal motivational phone call—see Chapter 6).

Importantly, both figures were cost-effective for the U.K. Open University. Prior to 2012, I estimated the "benefit per student retained" to the University to be of the order of \$2,200 (£1,400) in 2002. Thus the return on investment of investing in a mentoring scheme could be

$$1,300/160 = 800\%$$

that is, for every \$1.6 (£1) invested in the scheme there will be a return to the OU of around \$13 (£8).

Such estimates are, of course, very approximate indeed, given the tiny sample involved. However, they suggest that investment into student mentoring schemes may be worthwhile on a larger scale. Other institutions will have different funding arrangements, but it is still likely that improving retention in a cost-effective manner will reward the institution in both funding and reputational ways.

Support from Employers

Student support from employers is usually of a fairly straightforward organizational kind—payment of fees for particular courses, sometimes conditionally on passing, time off for study and exams, and promotion possibilities. I do not know of any research that has assessed the affective or cognitive support from employers, but it would be reasonable to assume that there are workplaces where such support exists either formally or—more likely—informally. With distance learning now so widespread, it is very likely that there will be management and co-workers who have had some experience of it and act as mentors, if not peer supporters.

While institutions may approach employers for financial help for their students, I am not aware of any that ask employers for other kinds of support for their students of the kind outlined in the "Helping Your Student" leaflet or the "Friends and Family" website. This is part of an early draft of a leaflet for employers of U.K. Open University students, which an employer who had experience of distance education wrote at my request (although it was never published). The full text can be found at www.ormondsimpson.com.

Helping your Open University Student—A Leaflet for Employers

"What can I do as employer to help my student?"
"Thanks for offering; there are a number of possible options (not all financial)."

The leaflet then covers the following topics:

● encouragement and interest;
● leave for exams and residential schools;
● set books;
● IT support;
● IT equipment loans;
● paying for your student's course;
● the pay-off for an employer.

There is some evidence for the latter point in a study from New Zealand. Zajkowski (1997) found that there seemed to be a retention effect where students' fees were paid by employers—particularly where these were paid after the course was passed. See Table 13.4.

Table 13.4 Module pass rates and employers paying students' fees

Fee payment	Pass rate
Fees paid by students themselves	40%
Fees paid by employer	57%
Fees paid by employer if student passes course	64%

Other Support Outside the Institution— Referral Agencies

It is important to remember that there are many possible support organizations outside the institution to which students can be referred when circumstances dictate. There needs to be no formal referral mechanism and probably should not be a recommendation—simply the suggestion, "You could try . . ."

For example, students who suffer severe exam stress may be surprised to have it suggested they should see their doctor, but there are certainly doctors who are sympathetic to stress problems and able to offer useful help. I have had occasional success by suggesting students could try hypnotherapy for similar problems.

At any rate a referral list is like a lifejacket under your plane seat: you hope you will never use it but it is nice to have it there. It is also a help when setting boundaries to your support. My current "suggestions" list contains the following (these are U.K. terms, but similar organizations exist worldwide):

- the student's doctor;
- Citizens' Advice Bureaux—useful as a starting point;
- law surgeries;
- Relate (a relationship counselling organization);
- disability resource centers;
- Samaritans;
- volunteer centers;
- careers guidance offices;
- housing advice centers;
- Age Concern.

Above all, remember as a student adviser or tutor, that there are other resources for students to turn to that may be effective, sometimes more than the institutions itself.

Chapter 14

Student Support for Different Students

> You've got to accept the fact that you are basically not teaching a subject, you are teaching people.
>
> (Madeline L'Engle)

One of the most obvious (and attractive) features of online and distance learning is that it often brings in students from a wider range of backgrounds than conventional education. Students may be from educationally disadvantaged backgrounds, have physical or mental disabilities, be in prisons, traveling or working abroad, from a different culture, have English as a second language or simply be elderly. Whoever they are, their support needs may be somewhat different from "average" students.

Support for Educationally Disadvantaged Students

Educational disadvantage can arise in a number of ways through both previous educational experience and current circumstances.

1. *Previous educational experience.* Students' previous educational experience may have been disrupted through illness, family breakdown or in other ways. They may have had a poor educational experience at school or become part of a peer group that did not value education. Whatever their experience, they may be characterized by extreme lack of self-confidence, motivational concerns, low reading skills (see Datta and Macdonald Ross 2002) and a considerable fear of further failure.

Certainly as I noted previously, previous educational qualification is the principal predictor of progress in the U.K. Open University—there is a clear decline in retention rates from 80% for students with existing degree level qualifications to less than 50% for students with no previous educational qualifications.

2. *Current circumstances.* Circumstances that appear to disadvantage students educationally are being a shift worker, unemployed, isolated in some way, being a man and studying math, science and technology-based courses (McGivney, 1996). Unfortunately, it is difficult to disentangle all of these characteristics—is shift workers' higher tendency to withdraw a reflection of their socio-economic class, probable sex (male) and educational level? The same applies to the unemployed, and more men than women tend to study math, science and technology courses, which have higher dropout rates.

Clearly more sophisticated research is needed in this complex area—I had always been fascinated, for example, by the number of low-qualified students who succeed. What is the difference between them and their failing co-students? I now believe that it is quite a lot to do with their "Self Theory," as described in Chapter 6—whether, as Dweck says, they can be persuaded that their intelligence is malleable, rather than fixed.

Targeting Support for Educationally Disadvantaged Students

There are clearly issues about targeting support on students who are educationally disadvantaged.

What Medium of Support Will be Appropriate?

It seems possible that the most suitable support will be on a one-to-one basis. Bringing together a group of educationally disadvantaged students, whether face-to-face or online, may not be a positive way forward—being identified as being at risk in such a way might well be more demoralizing and all too reminiscent of being "picked on" at school. Offering specific support to such students, or even offering general support to all students, in the hope of reaching them may not work either, as they may well be less likely to respond to such offers, perhaps because of lack of confidence.

There is one exception to the problem of using groups. Where a group already exists, the group itself can be a powerful support medium. Young mothers on a housing development who have come together as a child-care group who go on to study together; a group of workmates following a particular interest; a pair of friends who decide to learn together—all have been successful against the odds in the past. Building on the work of such informal and more formal access groups can be the most effective way of overcoming educational disadvantage. But finding or setting up such groups is certainly not easy.

What Kind of Support Will be Appropriate?

I suggest that motivational support is the most important, rather than remedial support, which as Anderson (2006) suggested is not very effective.

How Effective and Ethical is Targeting?

To illustrate some of the issues in targeting educationally disadvantaged students I will take the example of the PaSS project already mentioned in Chapter 6 and analyze it in more detail.

The PaSS Project (Simpson 2004b)

As so often with student support activities, it is hard to assess how effective targeting support on at-risk students is. In the Proactive Student Support (PaSS) Project in the U.K. Open University, we used the predictive probability of success model to place some 3,000 new students in order of their predicted success. We then divided the list into two by taking alternate students from the list and allocating them to an experimental and control group respectively, thus setting up two groups of the same average predicted probability of success—see Table 14.1.

The experimental group were then proactively contacted by phone, starting with the lowest predicted probability of success. There was just one phone call to each student lasting up to 10 minutes. This process continued until the funding ran out, some 800 students having been contacted by then. The result was a 5% increase in retention of the experimental group at the end of the course over the control group. There were three points to note:

1. Starting at the bottom of the probabilities meant that the study was largely aimed at the "most at risk" students.
2. This also meant that men were disproportionally present in the group that were phoned.
3. The prediction was not shared with students.

These last two points raise ethical issues, examined in detail in Simpson (2008). Point 2 suggests that focusing on one characteristic introduces gender biases—in this case, it means extra support for male students. Personally, I am fairly relaxed about this bias as it is now increasingly recognized that, in

Table 14.1 New students listed by predicted probability of success

Number on list	Student	Predicted probability of success %	Group
1	Male	9.1	Experimental
2	Male	9.6	Control
3	Male	10.2	Experimental
4	Male	10.6	Control
5	Male	11.2	Experimental
6	Male	11.5	Control
7	Male	11.9	Experimental
8	Male	12.0	Control
9	Male	12.1	Experimental
10	Male	12.3	Control
↓	↓	↓	↓
3123	Female	83.1	Experimental
3124	Female	83.2	Control

Western society, men—especially young men—are failing in higher education in higher proportions than young women.

More serious is the ethical question raised about the confidentiality of the results. The decision not to share the result with students was taken on the grounds that telling someone that they had (say) only a 10% chance of success would possibly demoralize them to the point where they would drop out straightaway. A counterargument to this was that, in not telling someone that their chances were small, we were allowing them to waste their time and money on a very risky investment with all the consequences that might flow from that. As we know from Chapter 1, this might be not just in terms of their time and money but also in terms of their consequent depression and other effects (in fact, because the information was stored on a computer database, under U.K. law students would have had the right to request it).

This seems a typical conflict between the ethics of justice (telling the "10%" student on the grounds that they are entitled to the information) and the ethics of compassion (withholding the information on the grounds that it would do them harm). Such conflicts lie at the heart of much educational debate (Pratt 1998).

The self-assessment questionnaire mentioned in Chapter 7 was one way forward on this knotty ethical issue, but, as I noted there, I never piloted it. However, as I also noted, subsequent work at the University of South Africa (Pretorius, Prinsloo and Uys 2010) suggested that, not only were there no negative effects, but there were positive motivational outcomes.

A similar ethical issue arose in the "At Risk" Project described in Chapter 7 where tutors were allowed to give extra support to students with low previous educational qualifications. However, as the researcher Professor M. Thorpe (1978) noted, "This had had the result of quite a lot of tutors opposing the approach . . . Some tutors saw it as stigmatising—it felt as if they were highlighting somebody's inadequacies."

Support for Students with Disabilities

Students with disabilities, both physical and mental, are often particularly drawn to distance learning. For many, it may well be the only form of education open to them, their disabilities making it impossible for them to study in full-time or face-to-face settings. There are an increasing number of technical aids to assist such students, but the most important source of support will be the awareness and sensitivity of the institution's staff. Such staff will need well-developed disability awareness and equal opportunities skills.

Disability Awareness

It may be easiest to illustrate the issues around disability awareness through a couple of personal case histories.

Case Study 1

I held a face-to-face session with a group of new students. I noticed that one student didn't seem to be paying much attention and wasn't responding to the questions that I was putting on the board. I got the impression that she was bored and got mildly irritated. However, I made a point of talking to her afterwards and she explained that she was visually handicapped but didn't declare it beforehand. She couldn't actually see the board clearly. I arranged for her to receive enlarged material and ensured that I wrote in larger figures on the board in future.

Case Study 2

I arranged a workshop for new students in a local college. The main rooms had wheelchair access, but as numbers increased at the last minute I had to book a temporary classroom as well. I knew that a wheelchair user was coming but I failed to check the room out. Sure enough, when he turned up (a little late due to parking difficulties), he had been allocated that room, which turned out to have steps. He refused the indignity of being carried up the steps or have the groups switched round to accommodate him. He left in an unhappy frame of mind. I had to write a letter of profuse apologies the next day.

These studies illustrate how being aware of the possibility of disability can allow simple but effective action, but also how it must be a factor in everyday planning.

They also illustrate that students with disabilities can be both very non-assertive and not want to cause any bother, like the visually handicapped student, or, alternatively, can be frustrated when their needs are not met and can react strongly, like the student with impaired mobility. Above all, students with disabilities generally want to be as independent as possible but have their needs met how and when they want.

Diagnosing Disability Needs

Students' needs can vary very widely, even with the same disability, and the simplest method of diagnosis is to ask students what they believe their disability is and what help might best compensate. They may need to be reassured of the flexibility of the institution in meeting their needs, since their previous experience may not have been particularly good in that respect. Help can be offered mainly in two ways: technical and organizational.

Meeting Specific Disability Needs

It is impossible to list the full range of disabilities or the corresponding help that can be provided. This is a very brief list:

1. *Visual handicap.* Technical aids can be enlarged print or Braille materials, magnifiers including CCTV scanning systems, audiotapes, text–voice

converters or simply readers. Obviously computers can be a great help in enlarging or reading online materials. Help in face-to-face settings will include setting up a well-lit, quiet environment (some visually handicapped students rely particularly on their hearing) and allowing extra time to complete assignments and exams.

2. *Hearing impairment.* Technical aids can be using hearing loops, text phones, transcripts and (in some cases) interpreters or lip-speakers. Organizational help will particularly involve briefing tutors on the practical considerations and best environment for lip reading using handouts.

3. *Mobility impairment.* Mobility impairment can affect either people's ability to move around or their ability to hold and move objects such as books or pens. Technical aids can include specially adapted typewriters or computers and comb-bound materials. Organizational help could include the availability of parking or transport arrangements and wheelchair access and special arrangements for assignments and exams.

4. *Learning difficulties.* The most common learning difficulty is dyslexia. Some students with dyslexia seem particularly drawn to distance education, perhaps because of previous unsatisfactory educational experience and consequent comparative lack of educational qualifications. Their dyslexia may well not have been formally recognized and one organizational help is to brief tutors and advisers to be aware of symptoms of dyslexia, such as poor spelling, expression and organization of work, especially when oral work suggests evident abilities. It may then be possible to suggest assessment by a trained specialist or educational psychologist. This usually precedes a needs assessment, which provides useful technological support such as read-back and spell-check facilities on a computer, as well as individual specialist tutoring. Although this assessment is costly, it may be possible to claim some of the costs back through grants in some countries. It can be very helpful to students both in terms of their confidence and in suggesting different learning strategies. Technical help can include computers and possibly using tape recorders to record notes and tutorials. There is now a great deal of useful information available on the internet.

Support for Students with Mental Health Difficulties

It sometimes seems that students with mental health difficulties can be particularly drawn to open and distance learning. There are indeed students for whom learning can be therapeutic and can help them manage their disability. But students with mental health difficulties can be significant not only because of their support needs, but the occasionally difficult demands they can make on institutional staff.

Mental Health Awareness

These demands arise because such students seldom identify themselves (although with the destigmatization of mental health difficulties it is thankfully becoming easier for them to do so). Thus, the first evidence that there may be a problem can come as a surprise to staff and not be easy to understand or handle. Staff therefore need to be aware of the symptoms of illnesses like schizophrenia, depression, anxiety and autism. They should also be aware of the boundaries of their roles and what support is possible and what is not. They must be prepared to take action where necessary to protect the interests of other students who may become involved.

Case Study 1

Recently I was contacted by a tutor who was concerned about a student's strange behavior in a face-to-face tutorial—the student was attempting to dominate the discussion with personal references and introducing irrelevancies. The behavior was not in itself unusual, but (and this is typical) it was the degree and persistence that worried the tutor: his efforts to modify the student's behavior proved unfruitful and some of the other students approached him with concerns.

On checking our records, I discovered that the student had identified herself to us several years previously as having a "psychotic condition" following a mental breakdown. In a not unparalleled administrative breakdown, this information had not been passed on to the tutor. It was also apparent from the records that sadly the student had not made any progress in her studies since her breakdown.

The tutor found this news very reassuring: after some discussion, he decided to persist with his efforts to modify the student's behavior in the tutorial. On my part, I agreed that if he found he was unsuccessful and the student became unreasonably disruptive, we would take steps to exclude her from the tutorial and offer some phone support instead. In the event he was able to contain the situation.

Such a case is typical of the way that staff can blame themselves for not being able to contain a situation, and are subsequently relieved to find that it is not their fault. It is also typical of the way that the institution may need to step in to protect the interests of its staff and students as a last resort, whilst remembering equal opportunities requirements.

Support for Specific Mental Health Difficulties

Again it is impossible to describe the full range of possible mental health difficulties that staff may come across. Four conditions crop up more frequently than others.

1. Anxiety or phobia. There can be many kinds of phobia, but the most commonly encountered in distance education is probably agoraphobia—excessive fear in ordinary situations, such as being in a crowd or even in a public place. People suffering agoraphobia can be particularly drawn to distance learning and in fact can do quite well: a small-scale study of self-declared phobics suggested that they made better than average progress in their studies (Palmer 1984).

Case Study 2

Jenny is a relatively mildly agoraphobic student. She can drive and can even attend face-to-face tutorials, as long as the groups are less than five or she can sit near the door (her "escape route," as she puts it). The only specific support she needs is to be allowed to sit her exam at home, since the combination of exam stress and agoraphobia is intolerable for her. Of course, she welcomes studying online as this is much less threatening.

---

2. Depression. This is characterized by feelings of deep sadness that do not seem to arise out of the person's situation. Depression sometimes alternates with short periods of overexcitement and inflated self-esteem—bipolar disorder (previously called "manic depression"). Depressed students can sometimes be recognized by their irregular production of assignments and their inability to respond to contact, and great reluctance to express any optimism or sense of self-worth about their studies.

Depressives are not as successful as agoraphobic students, but some can make progress, particularly in periods when the depression is under control. They can be helped by giving encouragement and maximum flexibility in their studies. They do not usually present problems to staff or students, although depressive students can be difficult to support and do not have a very good track record of progress. Manic states can very occasionally cause problems and recently I have been trying to support a tutor who received a threatening phone call from a student in a manic state. However, this is only the third time in 20 years that I have had to deal with such a difficult situation.

> ## Case Study 3
>
> Alan suffers from depression. At first his tutor didn't realize that there was a problem, but on trying to contact him she realized that he was often not responding. She got worried about this and tried offering more and more support, to which again he didn't respond. She began to feel rejected and inadequate. Finally realizing the problem, she set herself realistic boundaries, giving him praise and encouragement when she could and not hassling him about assignments. Alan has made erratic progress but has had some success.

3. *Schizophrenia.* This term is used to cover a variety of symptoms, but generally they relate to people's inability to distinguish between their own and other people's realities. Paranoid schizophrenics will have experiences of imagined plots against themselves.

Schizophrenics are very seldom able to study effectively, as it is hard for them to keep to a rational train of thought and concentration. They are easily distracted and will introduce irrelevancies, and a tutor may have difficulty controlling them in a tutorial.

Support can be very difficult and must be within agreed boundaries. These boundaries will need to be carefully defined once schizophrenia is a possible diagnosis.

> ## Case Study 4
>
> His tutor noticed that David behaved very oddly in face-to-face tutorials. He would sit out of the circle of students and would refuse to participate, although continuing to attend. The other students found this disturbing and eventually asked that he be excluded. This was done to the distress of the tutor, who felt that she had failed him in some way. Eventually it was discovered that David was a paranoid schizophrenic and the tutor was reassured by this. She continued to offer him one-to-one support over the phone and by email and he made some progress.

4. *Autism and high-functioning Asperger's syndrome.* People diagnosed with autism tend to have difficulties developing social relationships and are unable to understand emotional expressions such as voice tone and body language. They appear uncommunicative and obsessive. Sadly they may be unlikely to study effectively in any way.

Case Study 5

Bill is autistic. He is quite disruptive in tutorials, interrupting, being irrelevant and wandering around the room. His tutor found him threatening and came close to resignation. Eventually he was excluded from tutorials. He subsequently dropped out.

High-functioning Asperger's syndrome is a much milder form of autism and such students have been successful in distance education, particularly in science, technology and music courses.

Some years ago one of my students wrote a short note for me on her experiences of being a distance student with Asperger's syndrome. She wrote:

When you hear the word "Autistic" what do think of? Maybe you imagine Dustin Hoffman's character in *Rain Man*, or possibly of a person who avoids contact with people or collects strange objects, or who is academically gifted in some way. But you probably don't think of someone like me.

Someone said to me that my greatest disability is my ability. I seem fairly average; I'm a teacher, play in a band, have friends, and when not studying I have a social life. I just find it harder than the average person to keep up with this average life; I'm good at hiding that I'm struggling.

"Neurotypicals" ("NTs"—non-autistic people) are complex creatures and it's taken me years to understand their social rules. The fact that the correct response to "Do I look fat in this?" is "No!" regardless of the evidence seems nonsensical to me. However, I've learned that to fit in you have to follow these rules. I'm not good at figuring out correct responses in social situations and find them exhausting and confusing. Nevertheless, as I've observed more NT behavior, I've acquired quantities of data on it which are stored in my "social behavior database"—my brain. I can now handle small social groups, but occasionally still misread situations and respond inappropriately. I've come a long way from the little girl who refused to speak for fear at being laughed at, but I still feel stuck in a bubble that insulates me from understanding the intricacies and pleasures of relationships.

Asperger's affects me less obviously too. I'm incredibly literal, and although I realize that the phrase "I'll only be a minute" doesn't mean "I'll be 60 seconds," I still struggle with ambiguities and lack imagination to extemporize when instructions aren't precise. (I once spent an hour wandering outside a college because the name on the sign wasn't exactly the same as the one I'd been told and I wasn't sure what to do.) I'm also distracted by everyday phenomena and have synesthesia, occasionally "hearing" colors and "seeing" sounds.

But I do have an amazing memory. Not just for useful information like dates, but also for completely inconsequential information, such as the registration numbers of all the cars every member of my family has ever owned. That might seem great in exams but actually it's of little use, because by the time I've become accustomed to the glare of the fluorescent lights, the multicolored frieze on the wall (which sounds like saucepan lids being struck together), the feeling of the fabric of the chair through my clothes and the rustling of another student's chocolate wrapper (sounds like gunfire), I've lost an hour. Then it takes me hours to construct a paragraph, as I think in pictures, not words, and describing these takes time. The result is that my exam scores are much lower than my assignment scores.

So maybe I'm not so unusual after all.

She also reminded me that we are all on a spectrum and that I exhibited several Aspergic tendencies myself . . .

Implications of Support for Students with Mental Health Difficulties

These case studies suggest that there are two particular implications of trying to support students with mental health difficulties.

1. *Protecting staff.* Unanticipated contact with such students can be very upsetting for staff, who may become too involved not realizing what the underlying problems are. The institution will need to have clear policies about setting boundaries for staff, supporting them and taking action to protect them when necessary.
2. *Not prejudging issues.* It is important to remember that many students with mental health difficulties will be able to progress their studies with sensitive and appropriate support. Staff may well need help in deciding what is appropriate and in overcoming their own prejudices.

Support for Students in Institutions

This is likely to be a minority interest but there has been a growth in recent years in the number of institutionalized students—students in prisons, secure mental health units or long-term nursing care—for whom distance education is one of the few possibilities. The comments below apply particularly to the prison situation.

Issues for Students in Prison

Many of the problems that students in prison encounter are similar to those encountered outside, but greatly magnified.

1. *Isolation.* Students in prison may not be allowed the use of the phone, email or the internet. There may not be other students in the prison and there may be a culture of opposition to education. As a prisoner said to me, "There's an anti-intellectual environment here. People can harass someone who's trying to study because they resent it!" Visits from tutors will be very restricted and contact with other students almost zero (although at some lower security prisons I've succeeded in getting small groups of outside students to go in with the tutor for a tutorial with an inmate. The outside students emerge saying that it had been an important experience for them).

2. *Disruption.* Students' prison lives are very fragmented. They can be moved to other prisons at very short notice and security alerts can put them in cells for days without their course materials. The physical environment is very unhelpful: constant noise and interruption from other prisoners, TV and radio is fatiguing and badly affects concentration. "Prison is rarely quiet. It's hard to concentrate with the noise—particularly as the television always seems to be on" (prison student).

3. *Time.* Contrary to received opinion, prisoners do not usually have much free time. They may have to work and may have very little effective free space and privacy in which to study.

4. *Stress.* Prisons are very stressful places. To add the stress of study can be overwhelming: "At times the thought of studying starts me into a real panic—I just feel that I've made a big mistake taking this on" (prison student). That stress can ultimately be overwhelming. Only a few days before writing this, I took a call from a high-security prison. One of our students had just transferred in from another prison, which had failed to pass on his course materials. In such a position of total disempowerment he had slit his wrists. How serious his suicide attempt was I can't say, but it was enough for the prison to put him on a 15-minute "suicide watch." We were able to find a tutor willing to go into the prison and talk to him and I'm hoping for the best.

Issues for Tutorial Staff Working in Prison

If being in prison is a stressful experience for students, then going into prison can also be very stressful for tutors:

1. *Security*. Particularly at a high-security prison, the procedures to get in are formidable. There are security checks beforehand, and at the prison, "rub-down" searches and the emptying of pockets and bags for x-ray. Then being led through the prison through endless locked doors, hearing keys jangling and dogs barking can reduce even the calmest of people to a state of dependent anxiety.

2. *One-to-one support*. In normal circumstances, one-to-one support can require considerable concentration and be very draining. In the prison environment the stress of such support is increased: "You do sit here occasionally wondering what the man on the other side of the table did to get a 15-year sentence" (tutor at a high security prison).

Yet, despite these difficulties for tutors and students, there are very special rewards: "I really didn't know what to expect but my student was very pleasant and intelligent. I enjoyed tutoring him" (another prison tutor). And students can study in prison successfully and achieve quite extraordinary results.

Last year I was in a high security prison at a "graduation ceremony" for a student nearing the end of a 15-year sentence. We held it in the prison chapel and a number of his fellow inmates were present, as well as some prison warders. The student had previously been a lorry driver but had ended up successfully studying high-level math and could now discourse on Advanced Vector Algebra and Fourier Transforms. His elderly parents had come in for the ceremony and at the end the student stood up and said that this was the first time in his life that he felt he'd been a credit to them. He then burst into tears—and he wasn't the only one.

While writing this section I had a request for an academic reference from a young man who had been given a long sentence for murder. He had completed his degree in prison, had finally been released and the reference was to allow him to undertake a master's degree at the University of Oxford. I had remembered his case because I had been visiting the prison when he had been taking his exam. He had been supervised by a prison warder with a dog and there was a shift change halfway through his exam, so another warder with another dog came in to take over. The dogs immediately began to fight, warders shouted, alarm bells went off and general chaos ensued. Our student just kept on writing: "I wasn't going to miss my chance," he said to me later.

Support for Older Students

Clearly older students (aged 50 and up) can find distance education very much suited to their needs. The flexibility of distance learning, the way the study can be introduced into a routine without the complete upheaval involved in full-time study, and the wide range of courses available, can make it attractive to such learners. Since the older age groups are growing in the population at large and more people are retiring early, the numbers are likely to increase substantially in the next few years.

That being the case, do we need to offer them special support? Do they have particular difficulties because of their age and experience? The answers appear very largely to be "No" on both counts. What research there is suggests that older students differ relatively little in their needs from younger ones (Clennell 1987). It may take them a little longer to adapt to learning, but they often bring a wealth of previous experience to their studies. We should nevertheless be sensitive to needs that, while not unique to older students, are perhaps particularly pronounced amongst them. They may, for example, suffer more frequently from fatigue or mobility problems. They may feel inhibited amongst younger people in a face-to-face environment and need more encouragement to contribute without being obviously singled out. They may be less familiar with the internet and the exigencies of e-learning.

Support for Students Abroad

Competitive pressures have meant that many distance education institutions now actively recruit outside their country's borders. In addition, of course, one of the great advantages of distance education—its portability—means that students who are posted abroad can take their studies with them. And the internet means that issues of delivery and isolation are much more easily overcome than hitherto—assuming that students are in countries with reasonably good access to the internet so they can use emails, a VoIP phone such as Skype and their institution's Virtual Learning Environment. There are still places where such access is a challenge, however, especially for the poor.

But despite the growth in communication possibilities, there are still issues when working with students overseas.

Second Language Students

If students are recruited abroad, then there will be some for whom the language of instruction is their second language. The issue of support to such students in terms of diagnosing their skills and providing appropriate help is too big for this book. However, anyone providing support should be aware that such students might well be more at risk in situations where their language skills are under stress.

I recently met a German student studying at the U.K. Open University, where the language of instruction is only English. I complimented him on his excellent English. "I still have a problem," he told me. "When I have time to write I do very well. But when I am under pressure my language skills tend to desert me. So I never do very well in exams." Thus support to such a student may well need quite sensitive and empathic understanding of how his language skills may be affected by the different stresses of learning.

Support for Students from Different Cultures

In the long term, overseas students may have unexpected effects on distance institutions. As such institutions grow to become global providers, they will attract substantial numbers of students who may not share the common cultural background of the institution. Their demands may well affect what the institution does in terms of both its course and its student support. Even if a distance institution does not recruit students from overseas, it will certainly have many students from various ethnic and cultural backgrounds in its home population. Such students may have different educational and social values, which may make supporting them a more subtly different process. Again support staff will need to have an acute awareness of equal opportunity issues. For example in some cultures the influence and authority of the family may well be more than others. This can be both positive (the high value placed on education by many Asian families is thought to be a factor in the relative success of their children) and negative.

Case Study I

A student of Vietnamese extraction talked with me about family support for his studies. His problem curiously was too much support—his mother took a highly developed interest in his studies and put him under tremendous pressure. I hope that talking to me was a little help at least in managing the stress of the situation.

Case Study 2

A female student from a very strict religion wished to study with us. However, her family and husband held very firm views as to what was allowed to a woman in their culture and refused to let her enroll. She was quite determined, however, and used a neighbor's address for post and studied while her husband was out at work. We arranged for a tutor to visit her occasionally at her neighbor's to support her. This in itself raised some ethical issues. How far were we encouraging her in what could possibly be a dangerous course of action for her?

At any rate, she passed her courses with ease and graduated.

Other examples of cross-cultural issues can arise from, for example, the use of cultural references that may be unfamiliar. In the first edition of this book I received comments from readers about references that I should have recognized would not be understood outside a British context. I have tried my best to eliminate such references in this edition.

There are also subtler cross-cultural issues of style and approach. I have had the privilege of having some of my materials adapted to other cultures. In front of me, as I write, I have a version of a leaflet I wrote on how families can support their student that has been redrafted by a distance institution in Botswana. I note that the writer has produced a much firmer and less tentative document, which I imagine may be more appropriate for his students than my original.

Support for Ethnic Minority Students

Related to the issue of culture is that of minority ethnic students, although what those minorities are will depend on where this book is being read. Much of the minority-directed effort in distance education appears to have gone into recruitment under the heading of "Equal Opportunities," with mixed success in the U.K. at least. In U.K. distance education Asian students are well represented, but black students much less well. However, there is a considerable discrepancy on outcomes for all minority ethnic students in terms of their final grades which tend to be markedly lower than for white students (Richardson 2010). It is not clear why this should be so—perhaps the methods described by Cohen et al. (2006, and in Chapter 6) for reinforcing values should be applied to ethnic minority distance students.

Support for the Different Sexes

Finally, it seems clear that support is received and used differently by the different sexes. Research (Kirkup and Von Prümmer 1990) conducted in the

U.K. and Germany suggests that men and women make different demands on student support services. Women tend to be more regular attenders at face-to-face sessions and appear to value interaction with other students more than men.

It is certainly a matter of frequent observation in student support that women appear to seek advice and help more often than men in face-to-face situations. It's possible that men may make more use of more "neutral" media, such as email. Thus, the gender balance in an institution may be a factor in deciding on the design of a student support service. It is certainly again an issue for an equal opportunities analysis.

Chapter 15

Evaluation, Research, Innovation, and Change in Student Support

If everything you do works, you're not trying hard enough.

(author unknown)

Any distance institution will want to be continuously improving itself through evaluation, research and innovation. But, as I suggested in Chapter 3, actually changing an institution following that evaluation, research and innovation can be a challenge.

Evaluation

It's difficult to make a clear distinction between evaluation and research, but I will define *evaluation* to mean the processes of getting and using feedback to improve systems, and *research* to mean the processes of developing new systems and approaches. Evaluation will be essential for the processes of quality assurance in an institution.

One of the difficulties of evaluating student support is that distance institutions are complex organizations and support can take a number of different forms, use different media and come from a number of different sources. For example, academic support could be through teaching and assessment of assignments, delivered face-to-face, by phone or online and come from (say) a local part-time tutor or a distance full-time team or some other combination of sources. Evaluating all these activities, routes and sources can be a complex and time-consuming job.

Of course, such complexities could in theory be short-circuited by simply asking the recipients of those services—the students. But as I've argued previously there are problems in doing that; for example, getting feedback from students who have succeeded may be less useful than getting feed-back from dropped-out students. And getting feedback from dropped-out students appears to be very difficult, both in terms of the proportion responding (which tends to be very low) and accuracy of those responses, since such students often seem to give "acceptable" answers rather than realistic ones.

Student Surveys

Nevertheless, surveying students for their views is an essential part of any quality assessment process in any institution. I've already briefly described the U.K. Open University's dropout surveys and end-of-course surveys in previous chapters. Another example is the way student surveys are used to evaluate the support to students from its tutors.

The U.K. Open University has a system called Developing Associate Lecturers through Student feedback (DALS). An email is sent to all the tutors' current students at the end of a module inviting them to link to a webpage that contains the questionnaire. The questionnaire contains around 18 questions under various headings and tutors can add extra questions if they wish. Students can add general comments to their response.

The results are sent to tutors and are also available to their line manager, who can comment. The University collects data on response rates—in 2007, the average response rate was 43%—and also feeds back to the tutor the average, university-wide, on each question.

Typical questions are:

"Overall I was very satisfied with the tutor"
"The tutor made a very positive impact on my progress"
"I would very much welcome having this tutor for another course"
"The tutor met my expectations"

and so on.

The results are fed back to the tutor via their line manager in the form of basic data. For example, see Table 15.1 for a tutor who had 15 students who were emailed, of which 14 started the course, 12 finished and 8 replied—a response rate of 53%.

Table 15.1 Example of DALS feedback to tutors

	Strongly Agree	Agree	Neither	Disagree	Strongly Disagree
Percentage of students	88%	12%	0%	0%	0%
Number of students	7	1	0	0	0

There is also a chart showing the result compared with the averages for the university (Figure 15.1).

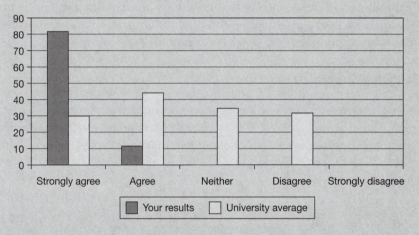

Figure 15.1 Chart of DALS feedback to tutors

In this example, there are five students' comments:

1. "X has been a great tutor, who also has a sense of humor about a very dry subject. I did most of my contact via email and he was excellent in responding to me every time."
2. "An approachable tutor, who was keen for his students to get the most benefit from the course as possible."

and so on.

The feedback to tutors comes with suggestions about how to use the results to improve their teaching.

Given the limitations of this kind of feedback mentioned before, less direct ways of evaluation may have to be used for different aspects of support.

Evaluating Non-Academic Support

If non-academic support is offered from one central point in an organization, then it may not be too difficult to monitor it. Whether the support is given by phone or email (I assume that it will be relatively rare to offer it face-to-face), records can be kept and recordings can be made. However, I've not seen any reports of such activity—possibly because they are likely to be held confidentially by the institutions concerned. Neither have I seen any criteria used, apart from simple "customer relationship management" software records of time taken to pick up a phone call, delays in replying to emails, and so on. The problem with using such data as targets for quality assurance can be that "what gets measured gets done"—the implication being that other qualities such as the content of the responses are ignored.

Evaluating Support from Tutors

If non-academic support is offered by a cohort of part-time tutors or adjunct faculty, then the evaluation becomes more difficult, since it is hardly possible to monitor a tutor's phone calls or even their emails. It is possible to monitor a tutor's work in an online forum, as in the example below.

This an example of a feedback email I sent to a tutor recently:

Tutor: Steve Tutor   Course: TXXX
Number of tutor messages in all conferences: 15
Average speed of reading students messages: 2–3 days
No. of students thought to be active: 8

Dear Steve,

As you know I've spent an enjoyable few hours looking through some of your forums recently—I like the way you introduced me to your group ("He's not there to judge you or your work, so you can safely ignore him")!

   Clearly I haven't read everything, but on the evidence of what I've seen I think you're handling the conferences very well. I noticed particularly:

(i) The general tone of your comments, which is friendly and supportive. You clearly have an excellent rapport with the group; for instance Jeff felt happy to respond jokingly about your friendly comments on holidaying while they write their assignments (April 19). The exchanges between students suggest that they are very supportive of each other. You seem to have succeeded very well in setting the tone of the forum.

(ii) I thought you also handled individual concerns very well. June's anxious points about almost everything on March 22 received a very prompt and supportive reply from you on 23 March, which invited further contact if necessary.

(iii) I like the way you are encouraging students to indicate any concerns and set the agenda. For instance, you checked that students had understood technical terms and encouraged input in the sub-forum.

Generally then, I think you are handling the conferences and encouraging student input and interaction very well. You manage to prompt student input on appropriate occasions as well as allowing students to discuss subjects among themselves such as the "Accidental Empires" discussion.

Well done and keep it up!

Ormond Simpson

Obviously this level of feedback is very time-consuming, but my personal opinion is that tutor line managers need to make it a high priority. The key to the quality of tutor support to students is the support they receive in turn from their line managers. As Charles Handy (1985) says, "individual attention" is perhaps one of the most rewarding things any person can get in an organization. That must be particularly true of staff working in the isolation of distance or online learning, where a pat on the back today is far more motivating than an appraisal at the end of the year.

Tutor Reports

Another way of monitoring non-academic support given by a tutor is to ask them for occasional reports on their students.

Some years ago I supervised a group of some 70 or so part-time tutors (adjunct faculty). I attempted to set up a schedule by asking them for occasional reports on their students' progress. I rapidly found that some tutors—about one-third of the group—very seldom sent in any reports on their students and when I asked for any specific information, they seldom knew what had happened to their students. It seemed to me that it was those tutors who consistently got the lowest level of feedback from their students.

Evaluating Academic Support

Teaching

Evaluating online teaching can be carried out by online observation as above. Face-to-face teaching can be evaluated by visiting and sitting in on a session, but that is very time-consuming for the line manager. I have seen evaluation conducted at a distance by getting the tutor to record their session using a video camera and either uploading it to the web or posting it on a memory stick to the line manager.

Assignment Marking

The re-marking of a sample of tutor-marked assignments can be used to both check on the standard of marking for comparison and the feedback that students are receiving from a tutor. This process is often known as "monitoring" and the results are fed back to the tutor. This is an example of some feedback I received myself recently:

To tutor Ormond Simpson

From monitor Y

Your grading—Acceptable—I feel that this is accurate marking. I particularly like your comments—clear and concise.

We agree closely on the marking of this script. I have made a number of comments on the photocopied script, which I hope you will look at. You will see that, in some cases, we have awarded/deducted marks for slightly different things—but this is inevitable!

I marked down 1(a) more than you did. Did you try and break this kind of question down and see whether the student has addressed each point in the question? Would it be advantageous to indicate even more?—e.g., by subdividing each mark where the student has lost marks?

Generally: Sound marking and good teaching comments. Well done.

It's notable that the monitor has used the same marking technique, "feedback sandwiching," placing slightly critical comments in between more positive ones—as the tutor is expected to use with students.

Other Methods of Evaluation

There are other methods of evaluating distance learning, such as focus groups, data analysis, self-evaluation and complaints.

Focus Groups

Focus groups have had some popularity as an evaluation tool. Such groups usually consist of 10–15 people, with a facilitator and an observer who also videos or tapes the process. It is supposed that a skilled leader and observer team can draw out and illuminate issues in ways that would escape a questionnaire, and the recording allows conclusions to be drawn at leisure afterward.

Focus groups can be useful for getting at the feelings behind an opinion. Here, for example, is a finding from a report of a focus group in my own institution, where students explored their responses to support from their Student Support Centre and tutor.

Focus Group Report

Contacts with the Centre lacked a personal feel. Students felt isolated in their studies and wanted information about contact people and resources—an Open Day, staff photos in brochures, pictures on the Web site were all suggested.

The problem with focus groups is that, inevitably, sample sizes are very small and are often drawn from successful students. Ideally, any focus group finding should be checked out through a questionnaire to a wider group.

Data Analysis

Most distance institutions collect large amounts of data, which can be a valuable source of information if analyzed carefully. For example, collecting data on tutor group pass rates can reveal trends as long as they are treated statistically, as random variations over the short term can be misleading—see, for instance, the example in Chapter 4 comparing two tutors' pass rates. Data can also be used in the developing field of learning analytics (see Chapter 7).

Self-Evaluation

I have made efforts over the years to encourage tutors I've supervised to undertake their own evaluations by, for example, providing them with questionnaires to use with their students. However, it was my experience that the tutors who did so were generally the ones that didn't need to do so.

Complaints

Finally, students find they are paying more for their courses and competition between providers increases; it may be that students will complain more vociferously about the services they receive. In any case it will be necessary for any institution to have a complaints procedure that not only answers complaints but records them in way that allows useful information to be drawn from them where possible.

Research

I previously criticized distance education research in Chapter 7 as not being focused on student retention and success. I would go further and suggest that the methodology of much research is often rather inadequate. What I mean is that I often see a report of some initiative—usually some novel e-learning software—which is then evaluated by a student questionnaire that finds that students thought the initiative was helpful. The report then concludes that it "enhanced the student learning experience." Very seldom is there any acknowledgment that the questionnaire only went to the survivors of the initiative or hard evidence of increased retention. In fact, student success, dropout and retention are barely mentioned in the literature. Much of the academic discourse in distance education feels peripheral—it's as if car manufacturers spent all their time arguing over the shape of their cars' interior mirrors while ignoring the fact that 80% of their production is unsafe at any speed.

I know that educational research is not easy. But there needs to be a way to emulate the medical research model, with its randomized controlled studies comparing experimental and control groups. That is difficult, but not wholly impossible; there are some good examples and I think we need to demand more of researchers and reports. Research in the future also needs to focus on institutional attitudes to retention—what the psychosocial and attitudinal barriers are to increasing retention, not just amongst students but amongst distance education staff. We also need to try to learn from the new developments in research outside distance education—for example, from learning psychology—and in particular what motivates students to learn and what keeps them motivated.

Institutional Innovation and Change—"Agitation"

I suggested in Chapter 3 that "agitation"—contributing to innovation and change—in distance education was an important role for anyone working in student support. As a student supporter, you are probably closer to students' needs than anyone else in the institution and experience tells us, that whatever the propaganda, large bureaucratic institutions (as distance institutions inevitably tend to be) can very easily lose touch with their customer base. And their very size means that change can be slow—one vice chancellor of a large distance institution I worked in once suggested that it was like a large oil tanker that needed much hard work in the wheelhouse to change course. Some of his staff felt that this was not quite the right simile and that his institution more resembled a large flotilla of smaller craft, not all of whom were heading in the same direction . . .

What, then, are the challenges to someone who wishes to change something within their institution? In Chapter 3, I mentioned Cornford's (somewhat tongue-in-cheek but not inaccurate) suggestion that it was necessary to consider prejudice and politics. He also suggested that there were several arguments against change, such as:

- The change would set a dangerous precedent.
- It would block the way for more sweeping change.
- The machinery for affecting the proposed change already exists.
- There is an alternative proposal (as soon as three or more alternatives are in the field there is pretty sure to be a majority against any one of them).
- "I was in favor of the proposal until I heard Mr. X's arguments in favor." (A few bad reasons for not doing something neutralize all the good reasons for doing it.)
- "Exactly the same proposal was rejected 10 years ago."
- "Comma hunting"—a few small mistakes undermine a case.

and so on. Some, at least, of these suggestions may have a familiar ring.

I also mentioned Pinchot's suggestion that to instigate successful change in an institution, it was helpful to become an "intrapreneur"—someone who could agitate within an institution. He outlined "Ten Commandments for Intrapreneurs" (Pinchot 1990):

I.   Build your team; intrapreneuring is not a solo activity.
II.   Share credit widely.
III.   Ask for advice before you ask for resources.
IV.   Under-promise and over-deliver—publicity triggers the corporate immune system.
V.   Do any job needed to make your dream work, regardless of your job description.
VI.   Remember it is easier to ask for forgiveness than for permission.
VII.   Keep the best interests of the company and its customers in mind, especially when you have to bend the rules or circumvent the bureaucracy.
VIII.   Come to work each day willing to be fired.
IX.   Be true to your goals, but be realistic about how to achieve them.
X.   Honor and educate your sponsors.

For student supporters in distance education, I would suggest a modification of these principles (particularly VIII), some of which I can illustrate from my own (frequently unsuccessful) career in attempting to change institutions in which I have worked.

1. Do your research—at least check to see if there's anyone out there who's tried something similar to your idea.
2. Get the technology right—if you're using a new piece of equipment or software, make sure you've thoroughly tested it before launching your project.
3. Find allies for your proposal—this may not be easy, as many people prefer not to poke their heads over the parapet for a new idea, but it's well worth looking. Sometimes allies can emerge from unusual places.
4. "Follow the Money"—very importantly, work out the financial implications of your proposed change. Is there any chance you can show it will make a profit?
5. Be prepared to go to the top—don't be afraid to network upward. This may be unrewarding in some cases—in one institution where I worked, there was a senior manager who notoriously ignored all contacts from junior staff. Of course, if you do get a response it may be to forbid you to go ahead. In which case, consider Principle 6.

6. Hold your ground publicly, if certain. But subversion may be better. As I noted previously, Pinchot says, "It is easier to ask for permission than forgiveness."
7. Don't dismiss ideas from unlikely sources—you shouldn't act as a censor of ideas yourself.
8. Don't give up too soon—projects take stamina. See Principle 9.
9. Be prepared to wait. Change always takes longer than you hope.
10. Remember that "If everything you do works, you're not trying hard enough."

Case Studies in Innovation

My case studies are not necessarily of important innovations but I hope they illustrate some of the principles above.

Audiotext Service

The phone has a continuing role to play in distance education and I developed a simple phone support system using an ordinary answerphone called "Adviceline."

Students could dial the Adviceline number any time day or night and hear a tape-recorded message that offered them the choice between a number of longer messages on topics of interest that they could listen to. The average length of the messages was three to four minutes and they covered topics such as what to do if they were getting behind with study, thinking of dropping out, losing motivation, together with a recruitment message recorded by a celebrity Member of Parliament.

The most popular message was Examline, which offered some basic exam advice followed by a relaxation exercise. I had this vision of students sitting on the floor next to their phone listening to me saying, "Now sit back, let your arms dangle by your side and feel the tension run out of your fingertips."

I don't know if that ever happened, but we were getting 400 calls a week at one point. The advantage of the system was that it only required a phone. This disadvantage was that the equipment I had wasn't sufficiently robust and broke down after a couple of years. I hadn't got the persistence to replace it—Principles 2 and 8. But, once set up, it was so cheap to run that I've often thought about doing it again. Especially with the advent of mobile phones, an Adviceline service could be really accessible on the move. For example, I gather that in Africa, audiotext systems (as they're called) are being widely consulted, by farmers, for instance, so they can see what local market prices are before taking their produce to town.

Voicemail Support

Another phone system I tried was "Voicemail Support." I'd tried telephone conferencing, but it was a problem—trying to get people together at the same time and then having them speaking at the same time and so on. It seemed to me that what you needed was an asynchronous phone conferencing system. So we used a "Voicemail Attendant System" and set it up so that tutors and students could leave messages for each other and the whole tutor group—in effect, it was an audio analogue of computer conferencing without the need for a computer.

A tutor could dial the system and leave a message for his or her group, which they could hear at any time. Students could then phone the system at any time, listen to the tutor's message and leave one of their own, which the tutor and all the other students could listen to. Ideally it would work like this:

1. Student Steve enters the system and hears a message from his tutor, Mike.
2. He can then hear a message from another student, Jenny.
3. He can leave a message of his own asking (say) for some explanation of the messages.
4. This can be picked up by the tutor, who can leave a message to reply to everyone at once.

I tried this out on around about a dozen different tutor groups and it worked well, especially for language course students who could chat away in French or Spanish. It worked well, in fact, until the machine broke down in the middle of the year, and by the time I got it fixed, students had lost confidence in it and I never really got it going again—Principles 2, 8 and 10.

"Marx"

I mentioned a retrieval activity in Chapter 10 called the "needless fails." This retrieval activity was based on an interesting example of the use of the web and ambivalent institutional attitudes. Calculating what each student in the study had to do to pass would have been labor-intensive, so Blanchfield (2000) used a piece of grade analysis software. This software had been independently developed by a student, who whimsically called it "Marx." (I had ignored this idea when it was first put to me. Fortunately I remembered Principle 7 in time.) A student inputting his or her current grades to the program would be able to see exactly what they had to get in their remaining assignments and exam to obtain any particular grade of pass.

Interestingly, the institutional exams office took very great exception to this and tried to dismiss the program for reasons I outlined in Chapter 3 under "Informing."

In the event, I was ordered to remove the offending software, which I didn't do—Principle 6. And ultimately the efforts of the exams office to prohibit the Marx program were unavailing: once on the internet, it is impossible to prohibit such information from being publicly available, and after several years the exams office was finally forced to provide its own version—Principle 9.

Find a Study Friend

This attempt to set up a "study dating service" for students was described in Chapter 13. It failed to take off, because I left the institution before I could put enough effort into it—Principles 8 and 9.

Students' Reviews of Courses

This project of putting students' comments on courses on the web was outlined in Chapters 3 and 9, and was originally undertaken somewhat surreptitiously— Principle 6. It became mainstream when it was unexpectedly taken up by the University's Director of Communications, to whom the idea had appealed (Principle 3).

Support from Friends and Family Website

This project, to help families and friends of students to help their students more effectively, was described in Chapter 13. I had been suggesting this idea for a website through the university's various committees for some time, with no success, until at a degree ceremony I heard the Deputy Vice Chancellor give a speech thanking the families and friends of students who had come. I was always very poor at approaching my seniors, but emboldened by a good lunch I suggested the idea to her and a website was set up within a couple of months—Principle 5.

Proactive Support (PaSS) Project

This project of making early proactive phone contact with new students was described in Chapter 6. I ran it on a relatively small scale to start with, and there was little interest in the rest of the University until I was able to show that it made a profit on its investment (Chapter 11). Then it was mainstreamed around the whole university—Principle 4.

Conclusion

I don't claim that any of these projects were particularly groundbreaking or breakthroughs in student support for success. But perhaps they indicate some of the obstacles in the way of innovation in student support within distance education—and perhaps also some of the sheer enjoyment that's to be had, as well.

Chapter 16

Staff Development and Institutional Structures for Student Success in Distance Education

> Those who are expected to promote retention should have the same personal support they are expected to give to students.
>
> (Edward Anderson)

When writing about student support in distance education, it seems to me that there are two topics in which it is impossible to be prescriptive, because they depend so much on the institutions concerned. These topics are:

(i) staff development for student support—how staff in the area can be trained;
(ii) institutional structures for student support—how institutions organize themselves internally to deliver student support.

Nevertheless, there may be common fundamental ideas that are applicable in both topics.

Staff Development for Student Success

Whatever the roles of staff in an institution, the success of any student support system will depend critically on them and their development and support. Student support staff will bring existing perceptions and attitudes to their work in distance education. Some of these will be appropriate and some not so appropriate, for example, a particular tutor's "Darwinista" tendency. Changing what may possibly be deep-seated patterns of behavior may be difficult.

Kolb (1984) suggested a model that has been used extensively in distance education partly for that reason. This suggests that learning takes place through a cyclical process (see Figure 16.1).

A person:

1. experiences some concrete activity or event;
2. reflects on that experience;
3. conceptualizes the experience to develop new perspectives;
4. experiments from those perspectives, leading to future changes and developments.

The theory has been extended by Boud, Keogh and Walker (1996). Here the emotional and possibly difficult nature of the reflection process is very important; looking back on a teaching experience that went wrong can clearly be painful. Thus those feelings must be addressed, "by being expressed openly in a sustaining environment, for example on a one-to-on basis or within some kind of support group, so that an emotional obstacle can be removed." (Boud et al. op. cit. p. 30).

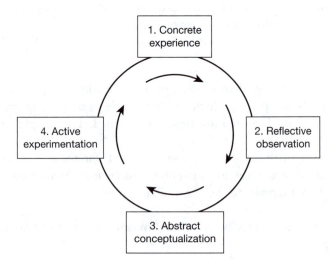

Figure 16.1 Kolb's learning cycle

Kolb's theory seems to have attained almost iconic status in distance education, despite claims by Ileri (2007) that it ignores the social dimensions of learning. Nevertheless, Kolb's theory may still be a good basis for designing staff development programs in distance education.

Designing Staff Development

In practice, Kolb's approach means that the methods used in a staff development session should mirror the methods that we would expect those staff to use with students—that is, the methods used should be experiential, reflective and supportive. Staff should have a chance to experience an activity, reflect on that experience in a safe and supportive atmosphere, and then practice the results of any changes in their perceptions as a result.

One of my colleagues recently ran a face-to-face workshop for new tutors on supporting their students. Her plan for the session was as follows (my comments are in italics):

Session 1—A "snowball" activity

1. Ask individual participants to take a few minutes on their own to think about good and bad learning experiences from their own history. They should try to identify what factors made a particular experience good or bad.
2. Join with one other participant to see if they can identify common factors in their experiences.
3. Share their findings in groups of four, depending on the size of the workshop.
4. Each group to report back to a plenary to draw up a list of what makes a good or bad learning experience *(this short "snowballing" exercise serves the purpose of getting participants to reflect on their experience and construct the supportive and facilitative ambience to enable them to do so. Part of the aim of the exercise is also to put tutors into the frame of what it might be like to be a student again).*

Session 2—A short presentation from a tutor on his or her teaching experiences *(using a colleague to encourage the feeling of a joint supportive endeavor)*

Session 3—Thinking like a student
   In groups of three or four, make a list of the problems you think you might encounter as a new student studying in isolation from other students, such as:

● not having anyone to talk to when you encounter some difficulty with the course;

- thinking that you are the only one having difficulty with the course and, therefore, feeling worried and inadequate;
- feeling the strain of having to juggle the conflicting demands of family, work and study;
- worrying that your work is not up to standard and having no means of checking this;
- having no one with whom to share ideas, enthusiasms and enjoyment (*the aim is to give tutors a better "feel" for what it might be like to be a new student, thereby hopefully developing their "approachability" skills*).

Session 4—Plenary discussion (*this allows for further reflection and reinforcement*)

Session 5—Farewell (*it is useful to have a "consequent action" activity at the end of any session where the participants are bound together in an informal contract to continue to experiment with new and different methods*)

Media for Staff Development

Just as for students, the media for staff development can be varied:

(i)   *Face-to-face sessions*—expensive but probably worth it on one-off special occasions such as the start of a new program.
(ii) *Correspondence texts*—very useful as easy access and backup to other forms. For example, the U.K. Open University has a series of booklets for its "associate lecturers" (part-time tutors or adjunct faculty); the first is called "An Introduction to Your Role with the Open University" and covers topics like developing learning motivation, proactive support, e-learning, assessment, setting boundaries and so on. There are other specialized materials available on specific topics such as disability.
(iii) *Online*—materials such as the videos on student support mentioned in Chapter 8 and podcasts—examples of various topics can be found at www.ormondsimpson.com, but also computer forums to enable staff to support each other.

Topics for Staff Development

The main topics for development might be academic and non-academic support skills, including motivational skills, support values and attitudes, communication skills (face-to-face, phone, online), boundary-setting skills—referring on, interpersonal skills and so on.

Methods for Staff Development

I have used a range of methods over the years:

(i) *Activities*—many things can be used to generate discussion in small groups, perhaps using the "snowballing" method described above (it's not usually sufficient for a discussion just to give a topic to the whole group and hope for the best). The "Values" exercise described in Chapter 3 has worked well for me, and even the simple "Dweck questions" in Chapter 6 can generate lively debate.

(ii) *Role plays*—can be particularly useful, especially if recorded for playback and analysis. But role-playing can be quite exposing and intimidating and needs a great deal of support.

A number of years ago I was using role-play exercises with a group of my colleagues. I gave one particular pair a demanding exercise, where a tutor was phoning his line manager because one of his students had just committed suicide. The manager was unable to answer with a simple human response, but retreated into bureaucratic mode: "We must complete the appropriate form . . . " The tutor became more and more desperate for support and the role play became a very good example of non-communication and unmet needs. But in retrospect I did not give appropriate support to the players afterward, leaving them feeling alienated from the process and devalued by the experience.

(iii) *Simulations or games*—can be an excellent way of tackling issues and less threatening than role plays. For example, in my own staff development program, for new tutors I use a game called "On Course," where players work in groups of four or five. There is a game board representing progress through the year and each player has a counter, which they move forward on the throw of a dice. If they land on a particular square, they pick up a card that contains a typical student query by various media—face-to-face, phone, letter, email—which can affect the response. The player says how they would respond to that particular issue; the other players comment on how useful and complete they found the response and what they might have done themselves, and move the player's counter on a suitable number of squares. A facilitator ensures that the discussion is apposite and supportive—the game framework means that the approach is light-hearted and informal and that the queries arise in random and unpredictable ways.

Here are a few examples of student issues—other examples can be found scattered throughout this book:

By phone: "Sorry Jane, I'm going to be late with my assignment. Can you give me another couple of weeks?"

By letter: "Dear Jim, sorry I've dropped out—I just can't manage with the children and everything."

By email: "Jen—I'm being sent abroad by my firm next week. What can I do?"

(iv) *Boundary-setting*—the game format can also be used to explore an important activity in staff development: setting limits to what staff can reasonably achieve and what they should refer on and not try to tackle themselves. Boundaries are set by various factors, such as staff time, availability, skills, knowledge and priorities. Members of staff exceeding their boundaries may become stressed and give inappropriate help, while staff not working up to their boundaries may be ineffective and feel disempowered.

It is important, therefore, to include some boundary issues in a simulation and explore how comfortable people are in accepting the limits to student support. Ultimately, boundaries are personal. This is an example of an activity I have used with student support staff to try to define their personal boundaries.

In small groups, discuss how far they would be prepared to deal with, or respond to, any of the statements below. If they felt anything was outside their personal boundary, what would they do?

"My tutor's given me a D for this essay. I think it's at least a B. Would you have a look at it for me?"

"This course has been an absolute shambles from start to finish—you'd better get me my money back or I'll sue!"

"Well, you see, my husband really doesn't think I should be doing this course." (Starts to cry quietly)

"Of course, you're an intelligent woman, you know your whole organization's riddled with Marxists . . . "

"You've been ever so helpful—I'm really grateful. Would you come out for a drink with me?"

> "Of course I cheat on assignments—doesn't everybody?"
>
> "I don't suppose you can help me—no one else has . . . "
>
> "I'm in here [prison] for a sex offence."
>
> "What's a pretty woman like you doing working for an organization like this?"

   Obviously there needs to be a clear system for staff to refer issues beyond their boundaries.

(v)   *Computer conferencing skills.* For an online support skills exercise, there'll be no substitute for an exercise that puts staff into a conferencing situation. That doesn't have to be online itself; one of the most successful computer conferencing activities I remember was a face-to-face simulation using yellow sticky pads stuck to a wall substituting for emails. The advantage was that the process was much faster than the online activity could be and allowed for speedy discussion.

Ongoing Staff Development

Of course, staff development is not a one-off activity for new staff. There are various ways of ensuring that it is an important continuing activity.

Mentoring

This can be a very appropriate medium for staff development when used to promote reflection. It works well because it sidesteps the authority of the line manager and allows a new member of support staff to experiment and reflect with the facilitative help of a colleague who is not in any supervisory role. Moreover, mentoring can be conducted at a distance by regular phone calls and emails.

Supervising Staff

An important staff development activity is to supervise staff, particularly in two respects—communication and validation.

(i)   *Communication.* If an institution uses a localized system with local part-time staff, then (like their students) one of the characteristics of their work will be isolation. They may be isolated both from their students and from the institution itself, so anyone responsible for management of such staff needs to look at their communication routes very carefully. Do staff have easy and reliable access to their manager? If that manager goes off to an important meeting, are the staff's communications dealt with in his or her absence? Are staff enabled to have good links to other staff with the same role? Do they feel part of the team that produces the courses?

(ii) *Validation*. If good communication systems are set up, what should be the content of the communications? My experience from being both the sender and recipient of such communication is that the line manager should be using his or her communication to encourage reflection on the part of staff and to validate that reflection. Validation is not just praise: it is acknowledging the rightness of the efforts made and the conditions under which they are made, and encouraging further reflection and experimentation and activity.

Where members of staff are not working as well as they might, then it will be necessary to examine the reasons for their poor performance. A program of extra monitoring and support may need to be set up. By "sandwiching" their deficiencies between validations, what they are doing well will still be a sound foundation for their improvement.

> A tutor emailed me recently: "This student is terrified of exams and is convinced she will fail. I've spent a little time talking with her on the phone and telling her she'll be fine and she seems a little calmer now." I replied, "Thanks very much, Sheila—that sounds like a most helpful conversation. Would you have time to talk to her again nearer the exam if you think it appropriate? Perhaps you could talk about some 'stress management' techniques—I'll send you some material on that. Thanks again for your helpful work."

Thus, validation is rather more than just saying "Well done"—which, alas, is rare enough in the educational environment that all too often seems more committed to criticism and blame. But, in addition in this example, there is a very gentle suggestion for something else the tutor could have done sandwiched in between the praise.

Ultimately there is always one single simple question that will apply to everyone supporting support staff: "Am I supporting this person in the way I expect them to support students?"

Institutional Structures for Student Success

In writing this book I have assumed that the reader is likely to be working in one or two of a few basic types of institution (after Rumble 1992).

(i) *Campus-Based Universities (CBUs)*—distance education schemes are sometimes based on existing educational institutions where some students come to the institution. Academic and non-academic support is largely carried out on the institution's premises even if the students study at home using distance education materials. Some students may be full-time in an "on-campus" situation. Staff are often from the full-time face-to-face side of the institution and seconded to the distance education section. Such institutions enjoy flexibility but may lack the focus and skills of specialized institutions.

(ii) *Distance Teaching Universities (DTUs)*—these are generally specialized distance learning institutions where students study largely at a distance but may meet at local "Study Centers." Academic and non-academic support may be offered by local, sometimes part-time, staff at study centers, but also direct from the institution, or in some cases its regional centers, or over the internet.

Such institutions offer national approaches and economies of scale, but can find it hard to maintain as high a profile locally as CBUs. They may also have to have a high administrative input into supporting and monitoring of local staff and liaising with Study Centers.

(iii) *Hybrid institutions*—there are many hybrid possibilities, of course: departments within institutions that have considerable autonomy and their own staff, such as the University of Wisconsin Extension; departments that have their own administrative staff but rely on their parent institution for subject specialist teaching, such as Murdoch University; and cooperative structures, where materials may be developed in one institution but are used by another institution that offers support, such as "flexistudy"-type schemes in the UK. The growth of e-learning has also meant the development of Open Educational Resource (OER)-based courses, where institutions use freely available materials developed on the web by other institutions.

Student Support Structures

Within institutions, student support structures can also be very different.

Centralized and Localized Models

Support can be centralized or localized:

- *Centralized models*—all course production, student support and assessment is carried on from one location from which all the staff work. Many CBUs conform to such a model, but not all.
- *Localized models*—typically, course production and administration is centralized but student support is localized. Generally, an attempt may be made to provide support locally (in the nearest large town) for both advice and tuition. Such localization is only possible where an institution covers a specific area or has very large enrollment. The U.K. Open University is an example of the latter, where attempts are made to provide students with part-time tutors, who offer support from bases at home and face-to-face in local educational institutions, as well as by phone and online.

Again, where the internet is available these models are changing—for example, the U.K. Open University is moving away from face-to-face models toward more online modes of support, possibly mostly on grounds of cost, as face-to-face provision is expensive.

Individual and Team Models

Another way of categorizing support can be in terms of who gives it. In some institutions, such as the Open Polytechnic of New Zealand, support can be from a member of full-time staff who gives both academic and non-academic support, possibly assisted by part-time staff undertaking specialized tasks on an ad hoc basis, such as assignment marking.

Hitherto, as noted previously, in the U.K. Open University support mainly came from locally based part-time tutors for each course module. Since students might take as many as a dozen modules toward their degree, this meant that students might have as many as a dozen different tutors during their studies. Accordingly, whilst progress within a module ("microprogress") was usually adequately monitored, progress over a degree program from module to module ("macroprogress") was no one's responsibility. Once it was recognized that consequently dropout between modules was a real issue, it was decided to move both academic and non-academic support to "Curriculum Support Teams." These comprise a team of faculty and central student services staff working together with associate lecturers, and will be curriculum-based rather than locally based and be focused on macroprogress as well as microprogress. The process will be brought in during the course of 2013.

Structures for Student Success

Given this wide variety of institutional structures, are there common organizational factors that encourage student success most effectively? So complex is this issue that I suggest that it can only be answered by posing series of questions about any particular or proposed support structure. I suggest a set of questions below. Not all of them will be appropriate to every institution, but most will be. And they won't have straightforward "yes/no" answers but a lot of "maybes" or "not very oftens," as answers may suggest areas that need looking at. And they will suggest many other questions that could be put.

Twenty-One Questions about Student Support

A. Support Activities

1. Are there systems for dealing with contacts from students by all communication media?
2. Does that system provide accurate and speedy responses by appropriate media without delay or a lot of referral elsewhere?
3. Is there a proactive system of support that reaches out, particularly to disadvantaged students using appropriate media?
4. Is there a reasonable choice of media for support so that all students can participate easily by one method or another?
5. Is there an equal opportunities policy that makes study accessible to all students regardless of physical or mental need?
6. Is the support system timely? Does it offer support at the right time—for example, particularly before and at the beginning of a course?

B. Support Staffing

7. Are the criteria and procedures used for selecting staff appropriate and clear?
8. Is there a staff development program for all staff involved in student support (even if only distantly) that meets their needs?
9. Do staff have a chance to interact and reflect on that program and feed back and influence it?
10. Is there good ongoing support for staff—clear line management links, good communication and feedback and clear commitment to supporting staff as they support students?
11. Are there robust procedures for dealing with staffing problems, poor work and absences, which are supportive rather than punitive?
12. Are staff continually helped to be aware and empathic towards the problems of students—especially those with special requirements?

C. Advisory Materials—Both Correspondence and Online

13. Are there advisory materials to cover most of the possible student problems and issues that arise?
14. Is the advice empathic, acknowledging the student's feelings, written in a friendly, approachable but unpatronizing style without gravitas? Has a readability check been done on them?

D. Supporting Students in Practice
For this set of questions, I shall put myself in the position of a new student—call her Jo—and ask, "What does the institution look like to her?"

15. Does it look daunting and inaccessible or friendly and approachable?
16. Are the enrollments procedures complex and hard to understand?
17. What happens after enrollment? Will she begin to feel a part of the institution straightaway?
18. What happens when the courses start: will her sense of isolation be overcome immediately or enhanced?
19. If Jo starts, but starts to lose motivation, will that be picked up and will there be appropriate support for her?
20. If Jo fails or withdraws, is there appropriate support to get her back?
21. Are there "macroprogress" (progress across entire programs) monitoring systems in place, as well as "microprogress" (progress within individual modules) monitoring systems?

And finally an extra catch-all question.

Looking back in time at all the students who have been in the institution, have they always had the support they needed, when they needed it, within resource constraints? If not, where did the system let them down and how might it be reinforced?

Chapter 17

A Last Word

What goes with the flow? Dead fish.

(Roy Keane, soccer player)

There were many topics I would have liked to have explored in much greater depth in this book. But, as Eastwood (1973) remarks, "A man's gotta know his limitations"—or at least his publisher's . . .

In addition, the subject of student support in distance education is a fast-moving one and, even while I was writing this book, I was coming across new and interesting innovations that may—or may not—be important. Many of these innovations are to do with the developments in technology, but the key to any innovation will always be to ask "What is the *evidence* that this new development improves not just student learning amongst some of the students, but retention and success for all of them?" Ultimately, it seems to me that the key to that kind of student success will not be primarily in technology, but because there will be people in a distance institution who care that students succeed the best they can and can use technology where appropriate to express that concern in practical terms.

So, although I hope that much of what appears in this book can be applied to any online open and distance learning institution, I would have to say—like Charles Handy in *Understanding Organisations* (1985)—that "at this point I'd suggest you burn this book and start to write your own—it's the only way to own the concepts." Ultimately, the "retentioneer" in an institution will require those qualities that a student needs to survive the online open and distance learning experience—that is, the questioning, the commitment, self-efficacy, resilience and, above all, the motivation to keep going. If you've persevered to the end of this book, then you've probably demonstrated most of those qualities. Good luck in your efforts!

References

Adams, C., Rand, V. and Simpson, O. (1989) But what's it really like? The taster pack idea. *Open Learning*, 4(30).

Anderson, E. (2006) Retention for Rookies. Presentation at the National Conference on Student Retention, San Diego.

Anderson, E. and Clifton, C. (2001) *StrengthsQuest: Helping Students, Staff and Faculty Achieve Academic, Career, and Personal Success.* www.strengthsquest. com, accessed October 18, 2006.

Asbee, S. and Simpson, O. (1998) Partners, families and friends: student support of the closest kind. *Open Learning*, 13(3), p. 56.

Asbee, S., Simpson, O. and Woodall, S. (1999) Student-student mentoring in distance education. *British Journal of Access and Credit Studies*, 2(2).

Averkamp, M. (1994) How to reactivate dropouts. *Epistolodidaktika*, 2, pp. 63–66.

Baath, J. (1979) *Correspondence Education in the Light of a Number of Contemporary Teaching Methods.* Malmo: Liber Hermods.

Bajtelsmit, B. (1998) Predicting distance learning dropouts: testing a conceptual model of attrition in distance education. *Report to the International Council for Distance Education Research Committee.*

Balaban-Sali, J. (2008) Designing motivational learning systems in distance education. *Turkish Online Journal of Distance Education, 9*(3). Retrieved from https://tojde.anadolu.edu.tr/tojde31/pdf/article_13.pdf

Berne, E. (1964) *Games People Play.* Harmondsworth: Penguin.

Black, P. and Wiliam, D. (1998). Assessment and classroom learning. *Assessment in Education, 5*(1), pp. 7–74.

Blanchfield, L. (2000, unpublished) The needless fails. *Internal Report to the Open University East of England Region.*

Bloom, J. and Martin, N. A. (2002). Incorporating appreciative inquiry into academic advising. *The Mentor: An Academic Advising Journal, 4*(3).

Bogdan Eaton, S. and Bean, J. P. (1995) An approach/avoidance behavioral model of college student attrition. *Research in Higher Education, 36*(6), pp. 617–645.

Boniwell, I. (2003) Student retention and positive psychology. Presentation at the U.K. Open University.

Boniwell, I. (2005) Positive psychology in a nutshell. Retrieved from http://www.practicalpsychology.org/books/books.html

Bonk, C. (2012) The TEC-VARIETY Model. Retrieved from http://www.trainingshare.com/pdfs/TEC-VARIETY_Blackboard.pdf

Boud, D., Keogh, R. and Walker, D. (1996) Promoting reflection in learning—a model. In *Boundaries of Adult Learning*, ed. R. Edwards, A. Hanson and P. Raggatt. London: Routledge, p. 32.

Boyle, F., Kwon, J., Ross, C. and Simpson, O. (2010) Student-student mentoring for retention and engagement in distance education. *Open Learning, 25*(2).

Browne, J. (2010) Securing a sustainable future for higher education. Retrieved from http://www.bis.gov.uk/assets/biscore/corporate/docs/s/10-1208-securing-sustainable-higher-education-browne-report.pdf

Burt, G. (2007, unpublished) Educational design options: what do students think? Milton Keynes: UKOU Institute of Educational Technology.

Bynner, J. (2001) HEFCE Report 01/46—The wider benefits of higher education. http://www.hefce.ac.uk/pubs/hefce/2001/01_46.htm

Carey, B. (2010) New studying advice a surprise. The Tech online edition. MIT. Retrieved from http://tech.mit.edu/V130/N34/studyhabits.html

Case, P. and Elliot, B. (1997) Attrition and retention in distance learning programs, problems strategies, problems and solutions. *Open Praxis, 1,* pp. 30–33.

Chyung, S. Y. (2001) Systematic and systemic approaches to reducing attrition rates in online higher education. *American Journal of Distance Education,* 15(3), pp. 36-49.

Clayton, P. and McGill, P. (2000) Access issues in adult vocational guidance and counselling for people at risk of social exclusion. *Journal of Access and Credit Studies, 2*(1), pp. 4–17.

Clennell, S (1987) Older students in adult education reviewed. *Open Learning, 4*(1).

Clutterbuck, D. (1995) Managing customer defection. *Customer Service Management, 7.*

Cohen, G., Garcia, G., Apfel, N. and Master, A. (2006) Reducing the racial achievement gap: a social psychological intervention. *Science 313*(1307).

Colakoglu O. and Akdemir, O. (2010) Motivational measure of the instruction compared: instruction based on the ARCS motivation theory vs. traditional instruction in blended courses. *Turkish Online Journal of Distance Education,* *11*(2).

Community College Research Center (CCRC) (2012) Columbia University. Retrieved from http://ccrc.tc.columbia.edu/Publication.asp?uid=1049

Copeland, L. et al. (2011) Recommendations for using computer-assisted career guidance systems (CACGS) in career counseling practice. *Journal of Psychological Issues in Organizational Culture, 2*(3), pp. 86–94. Retrieved from http://onlinelibrary.wiley.com/doi/10.1002/jpoc.20070/abstract

Cornford, F. (1908) *Microcosmogaphica Academica.* Cambridge: Bowes and Bowes.

Crooks, B. (2005) *Students' Perceptions of Interactions between Course Design, Workload and Retention.* Open University Knowledge Network. Retrieved from http://kn.open.ac.uk/document.cfm?documentid=6719

Daniel, J. (2011) International Keynote, 4th Annual Australian Higher Education Congress, 2011. Retrieved from http://www.col.org/Site CollectionDocuments/Daniel_110308AustraliaHE.pdf

Darkenwald, G. G. and Merriam, S. B. (1982) *Adult Education: Foundations of Practice.* New York: Harper & Row.

Datta, S. and Macdonald Ross, M. (2002) Reading skills and reading habits: a study of new Open University undergraduate reserves. *Open Learning 17*(1), pp. 69–88.

de Board, R. (1983) *Counselling People at Work.* London: Gower Press.

Delaney, R Johnson, A. Johnson, T. and Tresland, D. (2010) Students' perceptions of effective teaching in higher education. University of Wisconsin 26th Annual Conference on Distance Teaching and Learning. Retrieved from http://www.uwex.edu/disted/conference/Resource_ library/handouts/28251_10H.pdf

DeSantis, N. (2012) E-textbooks saved many students only $1. Retrieved from http://chronicle.com/blogs/wiredcampus/new-study-shows-e-textbooks-saved-many-students-only-1/34793

DeTure, M. (2004) Cognitive style and self-efficacy: predicting student success in online distance education. *American Journal of Distance Education 18*(1), pp. 21–38.

Dweck, C. S. (1999) *Self-theories: Their Role in Motivation, Personality, and Development.* Philadelphia: Taylor & Francis.

Dweck, C., Blackwell, L. and Trzesiewski, K. (2007) Implicit theories of intelligence predict achievement across an adolescent transition: a longitudinal study and an intervention. *Child Development, 78*(1).

Eastwood, C. (1973) Quote from the movie *Magnum Force.* Burbank, CA: Warner Brothers, 124 minutes.

Egan, G. (1975) *The Skilled Helper: A Model for Systematic Helping and Interpersonal Relating.* Monterey, CA: Thomson-Brooks/Cole.

Ellis, A. (1962) *Reason and Emotion in Psychotherapy.* New York: Citadel Press.

Fuchs, T. and Woessmann, L. (2004) *Computers and Student Learning: Bivariate and Multivariate Evidence on the Availability and Use of Computers at Home and at School.* Centre for Economic Studies Ifo Group, Munich Working Paper No. 1321. Retrieved from https://www.cesifo-group.de/portal/pls/portal/docs/1/1188938.PDF

Furedi, F. (2002) 'You can't count on the carefree.' *Times Higher Education* (29th March 2002).

Garland, K. (2012) Cited in M. Szalavitz. Do e-books make it harder to remember what you just read? *TIME Healthland.* Retrieved from http://healthland.time.com/2012/03/14/do-e-books-impair-memory/?iid=hl-main-lede

Gaskell, A. and Simpson, O. (2001) Tutors supporting students. *Proceedings of the European Distance and E-learning Network Conference "Research and Innovation in Open and Distance Learning."* Prague.

Gaskell, A. Gibbons, S. and Simpson, O. (1990) Taking off and bailing out. *Open Learning, 3*(2), p. 49.

Gibbs, G. (1981) *Teaching Students to Learn.* Milton Keynes: Open University Press.

Gibbs, G. (2010) Does assessment in open learning support students? *Open Learning, 5*(2), pp. 163–166.

Gibson, K. and Walters, J. (2002) Access and guidance in tutor-student relationships. *Journal of Access and Credit Studies, 4*(1), pp. 20–31.

Goodwin, V. (2012) Private communication.

Haigh, M. (2007). Divided by a common degree program? Profiling online and face-to-face information science students. *Education for Information, 25,* pp. 93–110.

Handy, C. (1985) *Understanding Organisations.* London: Penguin.

Hansson, H. and Johanssen, E. (2005). Fake online universities and fake degrees—international and Swedish trends. *Proceedings of the Annual Conference of the European Distance and E-learning Network—Lifelong E-learning, 2005.* Helsinki.

Hattie, J. (2009) *Visible Learning: A Synthesis of over 800 Meta-analyses Relating to Achievement.* Abingdon: Routledge.

Hattie, J. (2010) Visible Learning Laboratory, University of Auckland. Retrieved from http://www.visiblelearning.biz/uploadedfiles/asttle/VisibleLearning10v4.pdf

Hattie, J. and Timperley, H. (2007) The power of feedback. *Review of Educational Research, 77*(1), pp. 81–112.

Higher Education Funding Council for England (HEFCE) (2009) Part-time first degree study: entry and completion. Retrieved from http://www.hefce.ac.uk/pubs/hefce/2009/09_18

Holmberg, B. (1995) *Theory and practice of distance education*. London: Routledge.

Honey, P. and Mumford, A. (1986) *The manual of learning styles*. Maidenhead: Honey.

Hoppe, C. and Stojanovic, J. (2008) High aptitude minds. *Scientific American Mind, 19*(4).

Huelsmann, T. (2000). *Costs of open learning: a handbook*. Oldenburg, Denmark: Verlag, Bibliotheks und Informations system der Carl von Ossietsky Universitat.

Huett, J., Kalinowski, K., Moller, L. and Huett, K. (2008) Improving the motivation and retention of online students through the use of ARCS-based e-mails. *American Journal of Distance Education, 22*, pp. 159–176.

Hughes, G. (2012) Aiming for personal best: a case for introducing ipsative assessment in higher education. *Studies in Higher Education, 36*(3), pp. 353–367.

Huppert, F. (2004) A population approach to positive psychology. In *Positive Psychology in Practice*, ed. P. Alex Linley and Stephen Joseph. New Jersey: Wiley.

Ice, P., Curtis, R., Phillips, P. and Wells, J. (2007) Using asynchronous audio feedback to enhance teaching presence and students' sense of community. *Journal of Asynchronous Learning Networks, 11*(2), pp. 3–25.

Ileri, K. (2007) *How we learn*. New York: Routledge.

Impelluso, T. (2009) Assessing cognitive load theory to improve student learning for Mechanical Engineers. *American Journal of Distance Education, 23*(4).

Johnson, M. (2000, unpublished) Course choice advice. *Internal report*, Open University, London.

Johnston, V. (1998) Presentation at the University of Lancaster Retention Conference, Preston.

Johnston, V. (2001) By accident or design? *Exchange, 1*, pp. 9–11. Milton Keynes: Open University Press.

Johnston, V. and Simpson, O. (2006) Retentioneering higher education in the UK: attitudinal barriers to addressing student retention in universities. *Widening Participation and Lifelong Learning, 8*(3).

Joint Information Services Committee UK (JISC) (2010) In their own words. Retrieved from http://www.jisc.ac.uk/media/documents/programmes/elearningpedagogy/iowfinal.pdf

Kasser, T. and Ryan, R. M. (2001) Be careful what you wish for: optimal functioning and the relative attainment of intrinsic and extrinsic goals. In *Life goals and well-being,* ed. P. Schmuck and K. Sheldon. Gottingen: Hogrefe.

Keller, J. (1998) Development and use of the ARCS model of instructional design. *Journal of Instructional Development, 2*(3), pp. 2–10.

Kember, D. (1995) *Open learning courses for adults: a model of student progress.* Englewood Cliffs, NJ: Educational Technology Publications.

Kim, C. and Keller, J. (2008) Effects of motivational and volitional email messages (MVEM) with personal messages on undergraduate students' motivation, study habits and achievement. *British Journal of Educational Technology, 39(1),* pp. 36–51.

Kirkup, G. and Von Prümmer, C. (1990) Support and connectedness: the needs of women distance education students. *Journal of Distance Education, 5*(2), p. 29.

Kluger, A. and De Nisi, A. (1996) The effects of feedback intervention on performance: a historical review, a meta-analysis and a preliminary feedback intervention theory. *Psychological Bulletin, 119*, pp. 254–284.

Kolb, D. (1984) *Experiential Learning: Experience as the Source of Learning and Development.* Englewood Cliffs, NJ: Prentice Hall.

Layard, Richard, Clark, David, Knapp, Martin and Mayraz, Guy (2007) Cost-benefit Analysis of Psychological Therapy. London: Centre for Economic Performance, London School of Economics and Political Science. Retrieved from http://eprints.lse.ac.uk/19673

Lewin, K. (1951) *Field Theory in Social Science: Selected Theoretical Papers*, ed. D. Cartwright. New York: Harper & Row.

Lockwood, F. (2000, unpublished) Private communication.

McGivney, V. (1996) *Staying or Leaving the Course: Non-completion and Retention of Mature Students in Further and Higher Education.* Leicester: National Institute of Adult Continuing Education.

Mager, J. (2003) Personalisation and Customisation—Your Keys to Recruitment and Success. Presentation at the National Student Retention Conference. San Diego. Retrieved from www.noellevitz.com

Mansell, A. Greene, B. and DeBacker, T. (2004) Searching for Meaning: Epistemological Beliefs and Their Relationships with Motivation to Learn. Paper presented at the 9th International Conference on Motivation "Cognition, Motivation and Effect." Lisbon.

Marton, F. and Säljö (1976) On qualitative differences in learning—1: Outcome and process. *British Journal of Educational Psychology, 46*, pp. 4–11.

Marx, K. (1845) 'Theses on Feuerbach.' Retrieved from http://www.marxists.org/archive/marx/works/1845/theses/theses.htm.

McNichol, T. (2006) 'AC/DC—the savage tale of the first standards war: Jossey-Bass.

Moore, G. (2004) Readability Project. Internal project, U.K. Open University in the East of England Region.

Moore, M. (1985). Some observations on current research in distance education. *Epistolodidaktika, 1*, 35–62.

Moore, M. (1990) Recent contributions to the theory of distance education. *Open Learning, 5*(3) pp. 10–15.

Morgan, A., Taylor, E. and Gibbs, G. (1982) Variations in student approaches to studying. *British Journal of Educational Technology, 13*(2), pp. 107–113.

Morgan, C. and Tam, M. (1999) Unravelling the complexities of distance education student attrition. *Distance Education, 20*(1), pp. 96–108.

Mouli, C. R. and Ramakrishna, C. P. (1991) Readability of distance education course material. *Research in Distance Education, 3*(4), pp. 11–13.

Noble, D. (1998) Digital diploma mills: the automation of higher education. *First Monday, 3*(1), pp. 1–5.

O'Hara, K. and Sellen, A. (1997) A comparison of reading paper and on-line documents. CHI97 electronic publications. Retrieved from http://www.sigchi.org/chi97/proceedings/paper/koh.htm

Open University Institute of Educational Technology Student Statistics Team (2002) *Annual Courses Survey.*

Open University Institute of Educational Technology Student Statistics Team (2005, unpublished) What did the students say about using the technology—did it affect retention? Presentation at the Tracking Technology for Academic Advantage Workshop, April 13–14, Walton Hall, Milton Keynes.

Paas, F., Renkel, A. and Sweller, J. (2003) Cognitive Load Theory and instructional design: recent developments. *Educational Psychologist, 38*(1).

Pajares, F. (2004) Self-efficacy theory: implications and applications for classroom practice. Paper presented at the Ninth International Conference on Motivation "Cognition, Motivation and Effect." Lisbon.

Palmer, F. (1984) Seriously stressed students. *Teaching at a Distance, 22*, p. 77.

Patsula, P. J. (2001) Readability of distance education materials. *Usable Word Monitor.* Retrieved from http://patsula.com/usefo/usableword/report 20008201_readability.shtml

Pei-Luen, P., Gao, Q. and Wu, L. (2008) Using mobile communication technology in high school education: motivation, pressure, and learning performance. *Computers and Education, 50*, pp. 1–22.

Perraton, H. (1987) Theories, generalisations and practice in distance education. *Open Learning, 2*(3), pp. 3–12.

Perraton, H. (2000) Rethinking the research agenda. *International Review of Research in Open and Distance Learning, 1*(1).

Peters, O. (1989) The iceberg has not melted: further reflections on the concept of industrialisation and distance teaching. *Open Learning, 4*(3), p. 3.

Pinchot, G. (1990) The intrapreneur's Ten Commandments. Retrieved from http://www.pinchot.com/MainPages/BooksArticles/InnovationIntraprenuring/TenCommandments.html

Powell, R. (2009) Openness and dropout: a study of four open distance education Universities. Retrieved from http://www.ou.nl/Docs/Campagnes/ICDE2009/Papers/Final_paper_262powell.pdf

Pratt, D. (1998) Ethical reasoning in teaching adults. In *Adult learning methods: a guide for effective instruction*, ed. M. Galbraith. Malabar: Krieger.

Pretorius, A., Prinsloo, P., and Uys, T. (2010) Exploring the impact of raising students' risk awareness in introductory microeconomics at an African open and distance learning institution. *Progressio, 32*(1), pp. 131–154.

Price, L. and Richardson, J. T. E. (2003). Meeting the challenge of diversity: a cautionary tale about learning styles. In *Proceedings of the 2002 10th International Symposium of Improving Student Learning, Improving Student Learning Theory and Practice—10 years on*, ed. C. Rust. Oxford, UK.

Rachman, S (1997) The evolution of cognitive behaviour therapy. In *Science and Practice of Cognitive Behaviour Therapy,* eds. D. Clark, C. G. Fairburn and M. G. Gelder. Oxford: Oxford University Press. pp. 1–26.

Ramsden, P. (2003) *Learning to Teach in Higher Education*, 2nd edn. London: Routledge.

Rekkedal, T. (1982) The drop out problem and what to do about it. In *Learning at a distance—a world perspective*, eds. J. Daniel, M. Stroud and J. Thompson. Edmonton: Athabasca University: International Council for Correspondence Education.

Richardson, J. T. E. (2010). Widening participation without widening attainment: the case of ethnic minority students. *Psychology Teaching Review, 16*(1), pp. 37–45.

Rickwood, P. (1998). From many, one: a research paper on components of study. Internal paper, Open University West Midlands Region.

Riener, C. and Willingham, D. (2010). The myth of learning styles. *Change,* (September/October), pp. 32–35.

Rogers, C (1961) *On Becoming a Person*. Boston: Constable.

Roy, R., Potter, S. and Yarrow, K. (2007) Designing low carbon higher education systems: environmental impacts of campus and distance learning systems. *International Journal of Sustainability in Higher Education, 9*(2), pp. 116–130.

Rumble, G. (1989) "Open learning," "distance learning," and the misuse of language. *Open Learning, 4*(2), pp. 28–36.

Rumble, G. (1992) The competitive vulnerability of distance teaching universities. *Open Learning, 7*(2), pp. 31–45.

Rumble, G. (2004) E-education—whose benefits, whose costs? In *Papers and debates on the Economics and Costs of Distance and Online Learning.* No. 7 of the series Studien und Berichte der Arbeitsstelle Fernstudium Forschung der Carl von Ossietzky Universität, Oldenburg, Germany. Retrieved from http://www.mde.uni-oldenburg.de/download/asfvolume7_ebook.pdf

Russell, G. C. (2008). Social anxiety: the elephant in your classroom? *Education and Health. 26*(3), pp. 50–53.

Ryan, R. and Deci, E. (2000) Self-determination theory and the facilitation of intrinsic motivation social development and well-being. *American Psychologist, 55*(1), pp. 68–78.

Sadler, D. R. (1989) Formative assessment and the design of instructional systems. *Instructional Science, 18*, pp. 119–144.

Schwartz, B. (2004) *The Paradox of Choice*. New York: HarperCollins.

Seidman, A. (2006) A retention formula for student success. *Finally*, putting the pieces of the retention puzzle together. Center for the Study of College Student Retention. Retrieved from http://www.cscsr.org/docs/Retention FormulaUpdateForWeb2006.pdf

Seligman, M. E. P. (1998). *Learned optimism*. New York: Pocket Books/Simon and Schuster.

Shin, N. (2003) Transactional presence as a critical predictor of success in distance learning. *Distance Education, 24*(1), pp. 70–86.

Siemens, G. (ed.) (2011) Connectivism: design and delivery of social networked learning. *International Review of Research in Open and Distance Learning, 12*(3).

Siemens, G. (2012) Learning and knowledge analytics. Retrieved from http://www.learninganalytics.net/

Simpson, O. (1977) Post foundation counselling. *Teaching At A Distance, 9*, pp. 60–67.

Simpson, O. (2003) *Student retention in online, open and distance learning*. London: Falmer Press/Routledge.

Simpson, O. (2004a) Student retention and the course choice process. *Journal of Access Policy and Practice, 2*(1).

Simpson, O. (2004b) The impact on retention of interventions to support distance learning students', *Open Learning, 19*(1).

Simpson, O. (2006) Predicting student success. *Open Learning, 21*(2), pp. 125–138.

Simpson, O. (2008) Open to people—open with people: ethical issues in open learning. In *Ethical Practices and Implications in Distance Learning*, ed. U. Demiray and Ramesh C. Sharma. Anadolu University/Indira Gandhi National Open University: IGI Global.

Simpson, O. (2011) Issues in e-learning marketing. In *Marketing online programmes: frameworks for promotion and communication*, ed. U. Demiray and Ramesh C. Sharma. Anadolu University/Indira Gandhi National Open University: IGI Global.

Skaalvik, E. (2004) Achievement goal theory: classroom applications. Paper presented at the Ninth International Conference on Motivation "Cognition, motivation and effect." Lisbon.

Stevens, V. and Simpson, O. (1988) Promoting student progress by monitoring assignments submission. *Open Learning, 3*(2), pp. 56–58.

Temperton, J. (2000, unpublished) The black box of student withdrawal. Report to the Open University in the East of England.

Thorpe, M. (1978) The student special support scheme, *Teaching at a Distance 15*, pp. 1–14.

Thorpe, M. (1988) *Evaluating open and distance learning*. Harlow: Longman.

Times Higher Education (2006) Maths support at the LSE. Report. April 14.

Tinto, V. (1993) *Leaving college: rethinking the causes and cures of student attrition*, 2nd edition. Chicago: University of Chicago Press.

Tinto, V. (2008) Untitled keynote presentation at the International Conference on Student Retention, Bogotá, Colombia.

Trow, M. (2000) *Some consequences of the new information and communication technologies for higher education*. University of California Center for Studies in Higher Education, Research and Occasional Paper Series No. 5.00. Berkeley: Center for Studies in Higher Education, University of California.

Tudor Hart, J. (1971) The inverse care law. *The Lancet, 297*, pp. 405–412.

Twyford, K. (2007) *Student Retention in Distance Education using On-line Communication*. University of Technology Sydney, Australia. Retrieved from http://books.google.co.uk/books/about/Student_retention_in_distance_edu cation.html?id=k9gaNAAACAAJ&redir_esc=y

U.S. National Center for Health Statistics (2012) Reported in *USA Today*. Retrieved from http://www.usatoday.com/news/health/story/2012-05-16/health-of-USA-nation/54984404/1

Vansteenkiste, M. (2004) Self-determination Theory: Further Insights in Autonomy-supportive and Controlling Teaching Styles' Learn. Paper presented at the Ninth International Conference on Motivation "Cognition, Motivation and Effect." Lisbon.

Venkaiah, V. and Salawu, I. (2009) Student attrition in Dr. B. R. Ambedkar Open University. *Indian Journal of Open Learning, 18*(1), pp. 139–148.

Visser, L. (1998) The development of motivational communication in distance education support. Doctoral dissertation, University of Twente, Enschede, The Netherlands.

Weimer, M. (2012) Challenging the notion of learning styles. *Faculty Focus*. Retrieved from http://www.facultyfocus.com/articles/learning-styles/challenging-the-notion-of-learning-styles

Wigfield, A. and Eccles, J. S. (2002). The development of competence beliefs, expectancies for success, and achievement values from childhood through adolescence. In *Development of Achievement Motivation,* eds. A. Wigfield and J. S. Eccles, pp. 92–120. San Diego: Academic Press.

Williams, R. (1998, unpublished) The science diagnostic quizzes. *Report to the UKOU Science Faculty*.

Woodley, A. (1987) Understanding adult student dropout. In *Open learning for adults*, eds. M. Thorpe and D. Grugeon, pp. 110–124. Harlow: Longman Open Learning.

Woodley, A. and Parlett, M. (1983) Student drop-out. *Teaching At A Distance, 24*, pp. 2–23.

Woodley, A. and Simpson, C. (2001) Learning and earning: measuring rates of return among mature graduates from part-time distance courses. *Higher Education Quarterly, 55*(1).

Woodley, A., De Lange, P. and Tanewski, G. (2001) Student progress in distance education: Kember's model revisited. *Open Learning, 16*(2), pp. 113–131.

Woodman, R. (1999) Investigation of factors that influence student retention and success rate on Open University courses in the East Anglia region. Dissertation submitted to Sheffield Hallam University for the degree of M.Sc. in Applied Statistics.

Wright, A. (1987) Putting independent learning into its place. *Open Learning, 2*(1).

Wright, N. and Tanner, M. S. (2002) Medical student compliance with simple administrative tasks and success in final exams—a retrospective cohort study. *British Medical Journal, 7353*, June 29, 2002, pp. 1554–1555.

Yorke, M. (1999) *Leaving early*. London: Falmer Press.

Yorke, M. and Longden, B. (2004) *Retention and student success in higher education*. Berkshire: McGraw-Hill.

Zajacova, A., Lynch, S. and Espenshade, T. (2005) Self-efficacy, stress and academic success in college. *Research in Higher Education, 46*(6).

Zajkowski, M. (1997) Price and persistence in distance education, *Open Learning, 12*(1), pp. 12–23.

Zawacki-Richter, O. Bäcker, E. and Vogt, S. (2009) Review of *Distance education research (2000 to 2008): analysis of research areas, methods, and authorship patterns. International Review of Research in Open and Distance Learning, 10*(6). Retrieved from http://www.irrodl.org/index.php/irrodl/rt/printer Friendly/741/1433

Select Bibliography

This is a very short selected list of the resources for a reader wanting to undertake further studies.

Books

Anderson, T. and Zawacki-Richter, O. (2012) *Online Distance Education— Toward a Research Agenda*. Edmonton: Athabasca University Press.

Bramble, W. J. and Panda, S. (eds.) *Economics of Distance and Online Learning*. London: Routledge.

Demiray, Ugur and Sharma, Ramesh C. (eds.) *Ethical Practices and Implications in Distance Learning*. Hershey, PA and London: IGI Global.

Macdonald, J. (2006) *Blended Learning and Online Tutoring: Planning Learner Support and Activity Design*. Aldershot: Gower Publishing.

McGivney, V. (1996) *Staying or Leaving the Course: Non-completion and Retention of Mature Students in Further and Higher Education*. Leicester: National Institute of Adult Continuing Education.

Moxley, D., Najor-Durack, A. and Dumbrigue, C. (2001) *Keeping Students in Higher Education—Successful Practices and Strategies for Retention*. London: Kogan Page.

Pintrich, Paul R. and Schunk, Dale H. (2002) *Motivation in Education: Theory, Research, and Applications*. Princeton, NC: Merrill.

Szücs, András,Tait, Alan, Vidal, Martine and Bernath, Ulrich (eds.) (2009) *Distance and E-learning in Transition—Learning Innovation, Technology and Social challenges*. Hoboken, NJ: Wiley/ISTE.

Tinto, V. (1997) *Leaving College: Rethinking the Causes and Cures of Student Attrition,* 2nd edition. Chicago: University of Chicago Press.

Visser, Lya (1998) The development of motivational communication in distance education support. Doctoral dissertation, University of Twente, Enschede, The Netherlands.

Yorke, M. (1999) *Leaving Early*. London: Falmer Press.

Yorke, M. and Longden, B. (2003) *Retention and Student Success in Higher Education*. Buckingham: Open University Press.

Internet Forum

Center for the Study of College Student Retention http://www.cscsr.org/retention_listserv.htm

Distance Education Journals

American Journal of Distance Education http://www.ajde.com

Asian Journal of Distance Education http://www.asianjde.org

Distance Education Association of New Zealand (DEANZ) Journal http://www.deanz.org.nz/journal

Distance Education (Australia) http://www.tandf.co.uk/journals/titles/01587919.asp

European Journal of Open Distance And E-Learning http://www.eurodl.org/

Indian Journal of Open Learning http://journal.ignouonline.ac.in/iojp/index.php/index/index

International Review of Research In Distance Learning (Canada) http://www.irrodl.org/index.php/irrodl

Journal Of College Student Retention http://www.cscsr.org

Open Learning http://www.tandfonline.com/loi/copl20

Turkish Online Journal of Distance Education http://tojde.anadolu.edu.tr

Public Database Resources

The O.U. Knowledge Network—a U.K. Open University database on teaching and learning http://kn.open.ac.uk/public

Open Research Online—a U.K. Open University open database of research findings http://oro.open.ac.uk

Index